FOUNDATIONAL PRINCIPLES OF TASK-BASED LANGUAGE TEACHING

This book introduces readers to the concept of task-based language teaching (TBLT), a learner-centred and experiential approach to language teaching and learning. Based on the premise that language learners can enhance their second language acquisition (SLA) through engagement in communicative tasks that compel them to use language for themselves, TBLT stands in contrast to more traditional approaches. Accessible and comprehensive, this book provides a foundational overview of the principles and practice of TBLT and demystifies what TBLT looks like in the classroom.

Complete with questions for reflection, pedagogical extensions for application in real classrooms and further reading suggestions in every chapter, this valuable and informative text is vital for anyone interested in TBLT, whether as students, researchers or teachers.

Martin East is Professor of Language Education in the School of Cultures, Languages and Linguistics at the University of Auckland, New Zealand.

ESL & APPLIED LINGUISTICS PROFESSIONAL SERIES

For more information about this series, please visit: www.routledge.com/ESL-Applied-Linguistics-Professional-Series/book-series/LEAESLALP

FOUNDATIONAL PRINCIPLES OF TASK-BASED LANGUAGE TEACHING

Martin East

Routledge
Taylor & Francis Group
NEW YORK AND LONDON

First published 2021
by Routledge
605 Third Avenue, New York, NY 10158

and by Routledge
2 Park Square, Milton Park, Abingdon, Oxon OX14 4RN

Routledge is an imprint of the Taylor & Francis Group, an informa business

Library of Congress Cataloging-in-Publication Data
Names: East, Martin, author.
Title: Foundational principles of task-based language teaching / Martin East.
Description: New York, NY : Routledge, 2021. |
Series: ESL & applied linguistics professional series |
Includes bibliographical references and index. |
Identifiers: LCCN 2020058074 (print) | LCCN 2020058075 (ebook) |
ISBN 9780367484002 (hardback) | ISBN 9780367479060 (paperback) |
ISBN 9781003039709 (ebook)
Subjects: LCSH: Language and languages--Study and
teaching--Methodology. | Task analysis in education.
Classification: LCC P53.82 .E37 2021 (print) | LCC P53.82 (ebook) |
DDC 418.0071--dc23
LC record available at https://lccn.loc.gov/2020058074
LC ebook record available at https://lccn.loc.gov/2020058075

ISBN: 978-0-367-48400-2 (hbk)
ISBN: 978-0-367-47906-0 (pbk)
ISBN: 978-1-003-03970-9 (ebk)

Typeset in Bembo
by Taylor & Francis Books

CONTENTS

ACKNOWLEDGEMENTS

This book about task-based language teaching (TBLT) marks a very significant point in a journey I have been undertaking over a number of years, and I would like to take this opportunity to thank just a few people who have helped to see it come to fruition.

Among those on the editorial team at Routledge whose support and guidance I greatly appreciated, I would like to thank in particular Karen Adler, Senior Editor at Routledge New York, for getting in touch with me in the first place. I valued Karen's personal invitation for me to consider writing a book about TBLT (something I wasn't contemplating at the time), alongside her enthusiasm as we explored what Routledge might be looking for and how my own background and experiences might contribute. It was great to also find out that Karen and I share the same birthday … something about which we could connect at a more personal level.

I am also very grateful to Eli Hinkel, Editor of the Routledge ESL & Applied Linguistics Professional Series in which this book appears. After Karen had made contact with me, and quite by coincidence, Eli and I attended the same conference in Germany, at a time when going to an international conference was as easy as getting on a plane! Bearing in mind our current locations, meeting up in person was not something we would have anticipated. It was a pleasure to talk with Eli face-to-face over a leisurely breakfast one morning at our hotel, and I appreciated Eli's positive interest, feedback and comments as I talked through with her the ideas I had begun to share with Karen.

I am very grateful, too, for all my colleagues on the Executive Board of the International Association for Task-Based Language Teaching (IATBLT), an organisation for which I began a term as President in 2017. It has been an inspiration to serve the international community of TBLT scholars alongside researchers of such high calibre who demonstrate keen support and evident passion for the TBLT project. In particular, I would like to acknowledge Andrea Révész (Professor of Second

Language Acquisition, University College London Institute of Education) and Laura Gurzynski-Weiss (Associate Professor, Spanish and Portuguese, Indiana University), both of whom kindly provided invaluable feedback on an earlier draft of the manuscript. Thank you, both, for your time and perspectives.

Last of all, I would like to thank and acknowledge the many students with whom I have worked over the years in different contexts as we have explored task-based ideas together. In a very real sense, my students are the inspiration for this book – I have always found our conversations around TBLT to be informative and enlightening, particularly when my students have shared with me both what has worked and what hasn't worked as they have tried out TBLT ideas with real language learners. These conversations have helped shape my understanding of what matters when it comes to TBLT in practice, and consequently what a book about the foundational principles of TBLT needs to be about.

Addendum

Whilst this book was in production, the TBLT community learned of the untimely passing of one of its most significant contributors – Professor Michael Long (1945 – 2021). Mike can truly be described as among the foremost influential and foundational figures in the development of TBLT. His substantial and prolific contributions to the field were recognised by the IATBLT in the awarding of the Association's Distinguished Achievement Award in 2017 (one of two presented in that inaugural year). I would like to think that Mike would approve of my presentation and interpretation of his ideas in this book, as well as my attempts to make his (and others') thinking accessible to a wide audience.

AUTHOR BIOGRAPHY

Martin East is Professor of Language Education in the School of Cultures, Languages and Linguistics, the University of Auckland, New Zealand. He is an experienced teacher and teacher educator in the languages field, and his research interests include innovative practices in language pedagogy and challenges for additional language learning in English-dominant contexts.

PREFACE

The TBLT Project

Over the last several decades, task-based language teaching (TBLT) has been a growing phenomenon of interest among different stakeholders in the language teaching and learning endeavour. These stakeholders have included researchers who have investigated, through a range of empirical studies and in varied ways, how language learning tasks can be used to enhance second language acquisition. A parallel strand of research has looked at the impact of TBLT from the perspective of teachers and learners working in a variety of contexts across the world. Teachers have also progressively shown great interest in the phenomenon of TBLT, whether motivated by what they hear about TBLT in different contexts or responding to task-based initiatives in their own contexts. Postgraduate students in applied linguistics and allied fields such as language teaching and education have increasingly had opportunities to explore TBLT and to add a TBLT-oriented course to their study programmes.

Additionally, we have seen the emergence of professional associations that promote the TBLT project, underscoring the growing interest in TBLT among academics and practitioners around the world. For example, the Association with which I am closely affiliated – the International Association for Task-Based Language Teaching (IATBLT) – was established in 2015 as an international and worldwide organisation of scholars interested in and active contributors to the field of TBLT. Its former iteration, the International Consortium for TBLT, arose from the very first international conference on TBLT, held in Leuven, Belgium, in 2005. Conferences subsequently take place in various locations every two years. These conferences bring together researchers and teachers from all over the globe who share a common interest in TBLT. A book series dedicated to TBLT (*TBLT: Issues, Research and Practice*) has attracted a range of authored and edited volumes since its first publication in 2009. *TASK*, an international journal wholly dedicated to TBLT, has recently been launched.

The wide interest in TBLT across the spectrum of those who have a stake in effective language teaching and learning might suggest that TBLT is now firmly established as a mainstream pedagogical approach. Furthermore, the task-related literature is expanding exponentially (*TASK* and the book series are two examples), taking our knowledge and understanding of TBLT forward in many ways. Many people may be forgiven for believing that TBLT in theory has been so well explained and its different facets both researched and tested over the years that there is little more to add to the literature on TBLT. Indeed, in the broad range of literature that exists on the subject, it would seem that there is something for everyone, and that, in one way or another, virtually all questions about TBLT have already been answered – theoretically, empirically and practically.

Nevertheless, uncertainty still persists about what TBLT actually is, leading to the reality that, although TBLT may be endorsed by research findings, it has not yet been fully embraced by teachers and other stakeholders as an approach to language teaching in its own right – a problem identified, for example, by Littlewood earlier this century (Littlewood, 2004) and still apparent in recent times (Bygate, 2020). Thus, empirical studies may demonstrate the efficacy of tasks to promote language acquisition, but if teachers and others cannot understand how to implement TBLT effectively in classrooms, these research findings are really not taking us very far. As Van den Branden (2016) put it, "the role of the teacher in TBLT is crucial. Teachers bring TBLT to life" (p. 179). In turn, Bygate (2020) reminded us that researchers need to engage with the problems confronting teachers as they explore TBLT ideas, rather than by their own academic priorities. Without an appreciation of the priorities and needs of classroom practitioners, their endeavours, Bygate suggested, will be "doomed to failure" (p. 275).

What Is this Book About?

What, then, is the purpose of this book? Among the wide range of books that have appeared over recent years, this book aims to fill a distinct position. With a view to demystifying the phenomenon of TBLT, the book goes back to basics by addressing some of the fundamental questions that stakeholders have: what exactly is TBLT? Where did TBLT come from? What is, and what is not, a task? Where do tasks fit into teaching sequences? What are the roles of teachers and learners in the TBLT endeavour? What makes TBLT different from other language teaching approaches? Through exploration of the theoretical and practical *foundational principles* of TBLT, the book aims to help those with an interest in TBLT (among them, postgraduate students, teacher educators, researchers and teachers) to develop a foundational understanding of some of these key issues that confront us in the field.

The contents of this book arise from my own background of many years as a language teacher educator and researcher. In this book, I aim to present, in a succinct and reader-friendly way, the dimensions of TBLT that I have come to regard as important as I have worked with students in different contexts. These contexts have included work with pre-service and in-service teachers of a range of languages in various teacher education courses, as well as postgraduate students in a dedicated Master of TESOL degree.

In particular, this book is shaped by my own reflections on TBLT as I have imparted knowledge to students, as students have taken that knowledge and tried out ideas with language learners in different contexts, and as they have shared with me and their peers the joys and struggles emerging from what they have experienced. It is also born out of my own specific contribution to TBLT research, with its particular focus on how teachers themselves have grappled with, implemented and evaluated task-based ideas.

Both my teaching and my research have been illuminating and informative, shaping my understanding of the core principles of TBLT that merit exploration. Feedback I have received from students, both formally through summative evaluations and informally through emails, indicates that students have found course content and the principles I have explored to be valuable in enhancing their knowledge and understanding of TBLT. Recent comments include:

- "Task based teaching helped me to see another method of teaching language other than what I was already familiar with. It made me question how I was teaching and how I could make changes."
- The course enabled "a new view of teaching and learning."
- This "totally different approach for language learning stimulated my motivation."
- The course "expanded both my knowledge and my perceptions of education."

How Is this Book Structured?

The principles I present in the book follow, to a large extent, the structure of the input I explore with my own students. The book contains three parts, each with three chapters.

The focus of Part I is on the *theory* that informs TBLT. Chapter 1 explores several fundamental principles that have informed classroom-based language teaching and learning, and maps these theoretical perspectives onto contrasting approaches to language pedagogy that have emerged over the years. It concludes by acknowledging the potential of TBLT to provide a balanced, holistic approach to language pedagogy. Chapters 2 and 3 then focus on theoretical rationales for TBLT, alongside exploration of the central construct of *task* for purposes of TBLT.

Part II turns to the *practice* of TBLT. Chapter 4 begins with a brief overview of several contexts across the globe where TBLT ideas have been utilised, leading to the crucial issue of how teachers can put TBLT into action. The chapter goes on to focus on the syllabus as the overall framework that sets the agenda for what happens in classrooms. Then, and drawing on both theory and practice, Chapters

5 and 6 explore several key matters for the implementation of TBLT, organised around the three stages of a task-based lesson (pre-task / task / post-task) and including how language learners may be supported to carry out tasks effectively (Chapter 5) and how attention to grammar (or focus on form) can occur in the task-oriented classroom (Chapter 6).

The focus of Part III is on the *evaluation* of TBLT. Part III ranges from using tasks for classroom assessment purposes (Chapter 7) to a broader consideration of how evidence can be gathered about how TBLT in practice is working (Chapter 8). The concluding chapter (Chapter 9) looks at factors that impact on stakeholders as they wrestle with theoretical perspectives that influence TBLT as innovation and as they consider TBLT's implementation in classrooms. The chapter acknowledges that there are on-going challenges for TBLT that need to be addressed and explores what these mean for those who wish, as theorists, researchers and/or practitioners, to advance the cause of TBLT.

Who Is this Book For?

Although this book presents the foundational principles of TBLT from the perspective of teachers and learners, the book has several audiences in mind. On the one hand, and drawing on the contexts that have given rise to the issues I explore, the book is designed for university undergraduate and graduate students currently undertaking study in applied linguistics, language teaching and education, especially those who have been, are or will become teachers of languages themselves, and who wish to increase their knowledge and understanding of TBLT. On the other hand, it will be of interest not only to those conducting research in language teaching and learning but also to practising teachers who would like to gain a research- and theory-informed foundation in TBLT.

This book sits at the intersection between academic texts that explain the phenomenon of TBLT, often in complex ways that can seem elaborate and inaccessible, or simply too detailed, and practitioner-focused texts or course books that aim to be a how-to guide, but that may offer little by way of theorising or research, and are therefore not detailed enough. The book thus steers a middle path.

In framing itself as a "back-to-basics" text, there is a risk that it may reduce key arguments to the extent that their importance, their inter-relatedness and their theoretical and practical challenges become over-simplified or overlooked. Yes, that is a risk of the reductionism that guides this text. However, the fact that misunderstandings and apprehensions about TBLT persist indicates the need for a text that can return us to the basics. To mitigate the limitations inherent in simplification, I pose questions to encourage readers to reflect on the issues I raise and what they mean for theory and practice. Furthermore, I make reference, at the end of each chapter, to further readings that can help to take readers more deeply into those aspects of theory, research and practice that particularly interest them and about which they would like to know more.

I hope that readers will find the approach I have taken to be valuable and informative, especially those who are just making a start on the TBLT journey, whether as students, researchers or teachers, and that this book will provide some useful steps on the way.

Martin East
Auckland, New Zealand
December 2020.

References

Bygate, M. (2020). Some directions for the possible survival of TBLT as a real world project. *Language Teaching*, 53(3), 275–288.

Littlewood, W. (2004). The task-based approach: Some questions and suggestions. *ELT Journal*, 58(4), 319–326.

Van den Branden, K. (2016). The role of teachers in task-based language education. *Annual Review of Applied Linguistics*, 36, 164–181.

PART I
Theorising TBLT

1

LANGUAGES

How Are They Learned and How Should They Be Taught?

Introduction

Across the world, there is now widely held agreement that the fundamental goal of teaching and learning in languages programmes should be to help students to develop their communicative competence in the target language. The communicative agenda has been realised in classrooms in a range of ways. Task-based language teaching (hereafter TBLT) is one such realisation. As its name suggests, central to TBLT is the notion of *task* as something that language learners carry out for themselves as a means to drive second language acquisition (SLA) forward.

TBLT has been growing in momentum since the 1980s as part of the communicative agenda, and has caught the attention of a wide array of people working in a wide variety of settings. These people have included: teachers of a range of additional languages (L2), including English as L2, whether in so-called second language (ESL) or foreign language (EFL) contexts; teacher educators; curriculum designers; educational administrators; policy makers; language testers; SLA researchers; and textbook writers. Van den Branden et al. (2009) concluded on this basis that TBLT is being advocated in many contexts across the globe as "a potentially very powerful language pedagogy" (p. 1). The evidence is increasing that there is global uptake of TBLT ideas, and TBLT is now officially endorsed in a number of countries.

Interest in the power of TBLT to enhance L2 learners' communicative competence has led many people over the years to investigate TBLT's claims. Bygate (2020) informed us that TBLT's on-going potential is evidenced by the fact that, four decades after the earliest publications, it remains "a topic of lively interest and debate" (p. 284). TBLT also remains a "contested endeavour" (East, 2017, p. 412), seen by several stakeholders as "still a relatively recent innovation" (Long, 2016, p. 28).

The perception of TBLT as an innovation to be questioned lies in its essentially learner-centred and experiential pedagogical approach, which stands in contrast to more traditional approaches to language pedagogy. The student-focused methods advocated by TBLT enthusiasts can often appear to clash with received wisdom that suggests that the teacher should remain in charge of what happens in the classroom. Practitioner uncertainty about TBLT is further compounded by confusion about what TBLT actually is, leading Hall (2018), for example, to claim that "significant differences can be seen in the way its various proponents have conceptualized the approach" (pp. 106–107).

In light of on-going questions and concerns, this book explores the theoretical and practical *foundational principles* of TBLT. At different points, I pose questions for reflection so that readers can link the ideas I present back to their own experiences with language pedagogy, whether as learners or teachers of an L2. At the end of each chapter, I present suggestions for further reading where these are helpful in illuminating and developing readers' understanding of the phenomenon of TBLT. Fundamentally, my aim is to lay a foundation, indeed several foundations, as springboards from which readers can launch themselves, should they wish to go deeper in their exploration of any aspect of TBLT.

My principal concern in this book is the instructed context (i.e., what goes on inside a language classroom in contrast to more naturalistic environments for L2 learning). In this opening chapter, I go back to some very fundamental principles that have informed various approaches to classroom-based L2 teaching and learning. Some of the concepts I present may be well known to many readers. Others may be less familiar. However, presenting these fundamental principles will help to lay an important initial foundation for subsequent chapters where I will explore TBLT, and how TBLT has developed over the last 40 years.

Language Learning and Teaching in the Classroom

When considering how L2 learners' communicative competence can best be advanced in the language classroom, there are two key questions to address at the outset:

1. How do students learn languages?
2. How should we teach languages?

The second question is contingent on answers to the first. That is, if we can answer the first question around how students *learn*, we will have some valuable information about how we might *teach*. These two fundamental questions exercise both teachers and scholars. Classroom practitioners want to be effective in their work and ensure that the students in their care have the best opportunities to make progress in their learning. Educational researchers are likewise concerned to investigate and pinpoint effective practices that will enhance learning. When it comes to L2 teaching and learning, language teachers' reflections on practice and SLA researchers' empirical investigations aim to identify the processes involved in learning a new language and what appears to have the most beneficial impact in and for the classroom. Several foundational theoretical perspectives on learning help to inform our thinking about effective instruction.

How Do Students Learn Languages?

Mitchell et al. (2019) argued that discussions about SLA have always been influenced by broader and more general discussions about human learning. One such discussion is the so-called *nature–nurture* debate. This debate raises an important question in response to the initial question, how do students learn languages? As Mitchell et al. put it, "[h]ow much of human learning derives from innate predispositions, that is, some form of genetic pre-programming, and how much of it derives from social and cultural influences as we grow up?" (p. 11). The classic text by Lightbown and Spada (2013) provided an excellent and detailed overview of various ways in which people have theorised and aimed to enhance language learning, whether as L1 (i.e., first language) or L2. Drawing on several of the key domains they explored, in what follows I outline three foundational but contrasting theoretical perspectives on learning. These have informed researchers' and educationalists' thinking, not only about language acquisition, but also, more broadly, about the acquisition of any knowledge or skill:

1. behaviourism, or, "it's all about nurture"
2. innatism, or, "it's all about nature"
3. interactionism, or, "it's a bit of both."

Behaviourism

The psychological theoretical perspective known as behaviourism was particularly influential in the 1940s and 1950s, predominantly in the United States, and formed a strong basis for understanding how effective learning might be constructed and developed. It owed much to the work of Burrhus Frederic Skinner (1904–1990), a well-known American psychologist, although the concept and its advocates predated Skinner's work.

Experiments with rats and pigeons helped Skinner to formulate the notion of reinforcement. The experiments enabled him to determine that he could control the animals' behaviour through introducing rewards and punishments. The animals quickly learned which behaviours led to rewards, leading to what Skinner termed *positive* reinforcement. When certain behaviours were rewarded, the behaviour was repeated (or strengthened). Conversely, behaviour that was not reinforced tended to be less frequently repeated over time (or became weakened). Punishment was designed to reduce unwanted behaviour or strengthen a preferred outcome. Skinner's theory of reinforcement and punishment became known as operant conditioning based on rewards and sanctions.

With regard to L1 acquisition, traditional behaviourists believed that children come into this world as *blank slates* (*tabula rasa*) on which knowledge can be written. Their L1 is acquired as a result of imitation, practice, feedback on success and habit formation. From this perspective, children imitate the sounds and language patterns they are exposed to in the environments around them, and when they receive positive reinforcement on their language use, such as being praised for saying something, or obtaining something they want, the patterns of language that led to the successful communication become ingrained and habitual. If, for example, a young child wants to have a cup of milk, that child learns through imitation how to ask for the milk. When children are successful in getting what they ask for, this reinforces children's language use. They continue to imitate and practise the sounds and patterns until they form habits of correct language use that enable them to develop their language proficiency.

According to the behaviourist view, both the quality and the frequency of the language the child hears, alongside consistent reinforcement, are important. In other words, young children need to be presented with accurate quality language on a regular and consistent basis. It is only through frequently hearing and imitating accurate language that children can receive reliable reinforcement about their use of language and thereby succeed in acquiring language.

Translating the behaviourist perspective to the phenomenon of SLA, behaviourist-informed teaching approaches would be teacher-led and expository. In the behaviourist L2 classroom, the teacher would be the expert and leader who imparts knowledge and explains principles, for example, grammar rules and how they work. In this top-down approach, the students would sit passively, absorbing the knowledge that the teacher presents to them, and then practising the content through a range of activities such as grammar exercises, with positive reinforcement achieved through students' (accurate) performances. Important elements of classroom work would include drilling, repetition, memorisation and rote learning, with the teacher explaining and presenting examples of language that the students need to acquire, and providing feedback on language use. Thus, in a very real sense, a behaviourist view on SLA would be predicated on the necessity for teachers to teach students all that they need to know.

Lightbown and Spada (2013) noted that behaviourism appears to present a reasonable explanation for how children acquire aspects of their L1, particularly the more frequent or pedestrian aspects, and at the earliest stages of acquisition. The behaviourist view of language acquisition, and a behaviourist take on learning and instruction, do have a level of intuitive appeal, and there is no doubt that they can give us a partial explanation of language acquisition. Lightbown and Spada went on to assert, however, that behaviourism cannot offer a satisfactory explanation of how children acquire and demonstrate command of more complex grammatical features.

Innatism

The 1960s witnessed a move away from behaviourism towards a more cognitive approach that took into account learners' ability to work things out for themselves, leading to a contrasting theoretical framework for language acquisition – innatism. The innatist (or nativist) perspective owed a great deal to the work of the American theoretical linguist Noam Chomsky (1928–date), who became "one of behaviorism's most successful and damaging critics" (Graham, 2019, §7, para. 12).

Critiquing Skinner's (1957) book on verbal behaviour, Chomsky (1959) made the assertion that the behaviourist perspective cannot account for what came to be known as "the logical problem of language acquisition" (see, e.g., Baker & McCarthy, 1981) – or "the fact that children come to know more about the structure of their language than they could reasonably be expected to learn on the basis of the samples of language they hear" (Lightbown & Spada, 2013, p. 20). That is, children might be exposed to parts of language – sometimes complete phrases in themselves, sometimes partially complete, sometimes accurate, sometimes not. However, just like individual dominoes that can be put together in specific combinations, children learn how to put these isolated components of language together both successfully and correctly (i.e., assemble the dominoes in the correct order) so as to form a complete whole without necessarily having been exposed to all the linguistic permutations. (Cook, 1985, pp. 2–3, provided some interesting illustrative examples of this.) Chomsky argued that, if it is the case that L1 users can do this successfully, language acquisition cannot simply be put down to imitation or repetition. Something else must be contributing. Chomsky concluded that this "something else" is the child's innate ability – children can think and reason for themselves; they can construct correct patterns out of the individual bits that they have been exposed to.

The innatist position as posited by Chomsky was built on the belief that children have been biologically programmed to acquire language – that they possess a Language Acquisition Device (LAD) – and that language proficiency develops in a similar way to other biological functions. Graham (2019) stated Chomsky's hypotheses in these words: "the rules or principles underlying linguistic behavior are abstract (applying to all human languages) and innate (part of our native psychological endowment as human beings)" (§7, para. 12).

Chomsky was therefore reacting to what he saw as the inadequacy of the behaviourist theory of learning based purely on imitation and habit formation through positive reinforcement. As Graham (2019) explained, language learning appears to occur without the need for explicit or detailed teaching, and behaviourism cannot explain how this might be so. From a Chomskyan perspective, children's minds are not blank slates on which can be written all the words, phrases and permutations that they need to imitate. Rather, children are born with an innate ability to work out the rules for themselves based on the limited examples of natural language they receive, somehow aligning them to an underlying internal template that contains the rules that underpin all language systems – what Chomsky termed Universal Grammar (UG). From an innatist perspective, the child's innate ability is fundamental to L1 development.

Translating this perspective to the phenomenon of SLA, instruction in the language itself would effectively be unnecessary and therefore non-existent. It would not just be up to the students to sit in class and absorb passively what they are being taught; they would actually need to play a central part in the learning process. Learning from an innatist perspective would therefore rely on the students' ability to think through for themselves the rules of the language they are receiving and are required to process as they engage in language learning. Immersion in the L2 would be fundamental.

However, although Lightbown and Spada (2013), for example, conceded that progress could be made through immersion without direct instruction, there is also evidence that progress can be hindered without some level of guided input. From an SLA perspective, innatism, like behaviourism, has its limitations.

Two Mutually Exclusive Extremes

Skinner's behaviourist operant conditioning influenced early twentieth-century thinking about how languages are learned. Chomsky's innatist theorising motivated fundamental rethinking in this regard. Thus began a "cognitive revolution" (Atkinson, 2011, p. 6) as "a direct response to American behaviorism" (p. 8). In summary, behaviourism and innatism represent two very contrasting approaches that inform teaching and learning – with the behaviourist approach being top-down, teacher-led and expository (teach students everything they need to know) and the innatist approach being bottom-up, learner-centred and experiential (let students work it all out for themselves). In other words, behaviourism represents a theory of learning dependent solely on nurture, or the influence of the environment, and innatism represents a theory of learning dependent solely on nature, or a child's or student's innate abilities. Both approaches may be critiqued on the basis of only partially explaining the complex phenomenon of human learning (and therefore of language learning, whether L1 or L2).

Reflection Point

Behaviourism and innatism as theories to explain language acquisition are now generally regarded as incomplete. Nevertheless, their legacies live on in L2 classrooms.

Think about your own experiences of learning an L2:

1. Which learning activities do you think were more influenced by a behaviourist standpoint, and which by an innatist perspective?
2. Which activities did you find more useful?
3. Which theoretical influence seemed to be more dominant in your experience?

Interactionism

Lightbown and Spada (2013, p. 24) spoke of a third theoretical perspective which they labelled as interactionist. In essence, interactionism may be regarded as standing between the behaviourist and innatist positions – a kind of half-way house position that takes into account both nurture and nature.

It is important to make clear at this point that interactionism as an approach to learning is not black and white in the way that behaviourism and innatism might be seen to be, and an interactionist stance on learning can be viewed from several perspectives. In this book, I use the words *interactionism* and *interactionist* as umbrella labels under which a range of positions and orientations necessarily sit. Their unifying feature, however, is that they allow room and space for what the teacher does as well as what the students do. (Another appropriate label is *constructivism*, and I will use that label in Chapter 9.)

At its simplest, interactionist approaches to L1 learning essentially focus on the role of the linguistic environment *in interaction with* the capacities of the child in determining language development, suggesting that both elements (environmental stimuli and innate ability) are important. Interactionist positions suggest that language proficiency develops as a result of the complex interplay between the environment to which the child is exposed and the uniquely human characteristics of the child.

Unlike the innatists, who would argue that children's innate ability will enable them ultimately to process language samples as experienced in the real world, one interactionist claim would be that language that is adapted to fit the capability of the learner is a crucial element in the language acquisition process. As a consequence, some interactionists have emphasised so-called child-directed speech (CDS), the language which is not only addressed to children but is adjusted in ways that make it easier for them to understand. Its purpose would be to foster social interaction between parent and child, that is, "shared attention … in adult-child discourse" (Saxton, 2009, p. 64), and "negotiation between caregiver(s) and infant" (Matychuk, 2005, p. 301). In one form or another, repetition and recasts of simplified language (i.e., repeating an error back to the speaker, but in a corrected form) would be components of CDS, and would support infants' early attempts to communicate.

Two very early influential players in the development of an interactionist perspective on learning, including children's acquisition of their L1, were Jean Piaget (1896–1980), a Swiss psychologist, and the Soviet psychologist Lev Vygotsky (1896–1934). The work of these two illustrates somewhat different positions on the nature–nurture interface.

Piaget's perspective on learning was that cognitive development emerges from children's in-built predisposition to adapt themselves to new experiences, and that children learn through active self-discovery. Hence, children take an active role in the learning process. As children interact with their environment, they construct their own understandings of the world, and their developing language reflects the growth of their logical thinking and reasoning skills (see, e.g., Piaget, 1926).

Vygotsky's observations of children relating to other children and adults led him to the conclusion that language develops primarily from interactions with others. Vygotsky's sociocultural theory of human learning (see, e.g., Vygotsky, 1978) thus attributes learning to a social process, and communal collaboration plays a fundamental role in the development of knowledge and understanding. From Vygotsky's perspective, children need help and social interaction to fully develop their knowledge. A parent or other more experienced adult is able to provide the child with *scaffolding* to support the child's evolving language development.

In essence, and with regard to L1 development, Piaget appeared to place more emphasis on children's internal processing ability, whereas Vygotsky appeared to be more concerned with the influence of the environment on language acquisition. When it comes to L2 development, the phenomenon of interaction for purposes of SLA may also essentially be viewed from two perspectives that are informed by different theoretical stances on the inter-relationship between nature and nurture. These may be labelled as cognitive-interactionist and sociocultural-interactionist. I will unpack dimensions of these positions in Chapter 2. For now, I provide a brief overview.

The cognitive-interactionist perspective is concerned with the interplay between learners' internal cognitive processes and what they notice about the L2 as they participate in communicative interaction. This psycholinguistic perspective focuses on the classroom activities in which learners engage collaboratively, and the cognitive demands these activities place on learners. A sociocultural standpoint places emphasis on opportunities for learner–teacher and learner–learner collaborations that will foster SLA. Both perspectives, the cognitive-interactionist and the sociocultural-interactionist, therefore see a role for interactions between learners. Both will emphasise promoting meaningful inter-learner exchanges to foster SLA. However, both have different understandings about their significance for L2 learning.

In practice, interactionist-informed L2 classrooms would maintain a balance (or interaction) between teacher-led moments of both exposition and feedback, and learner-centred moments of exploration and experimentation. The interactionist position allows for both these dimensions to be occurring alongside each other. Interactionists thus place considerably greater importance on the environment than would have been the case for innatists. The position also accommodates the reality that each learner is unique, that each has their own individual biological make-up and capacity to learn, and that teachers will ideally accommodate those individual differences. Group work may be a prominent feature. Guided collaborative or discovery learning would support the developing intellectual knowledge and skills of learners.

In summary, an interactionist theoretical perspective on learning aims to deal with the limitations inherent in the contrasting theoretical perspectives emerging from distinguishing between nature and nurture. The interactionist standpoint does not, however, represent one single or coherent approach. When it comes to the phenomenon of L2 learning, if we regard interactionism as a kind of mix and match that addresses the limits of a nature-informed viewpoint (such as innatism) or a nurture-oriented position (such as behaviourism), this raises several challenges in practice. Its implication is that learner-centred and experiential approaches find themselves at one end of a continuum of theoretical positions, and teacher-led and expository approaches are located at the other end.

When conceptualised as a continuum, this would suggest that interactionism represents a range of stances on the relative learning contributions of both biological and environmental factors. As a consequence, and in practice, some teachers working within an interactionist understanding of learning may lean more towards the learner-centred end and put more emphasis on the learners and what they are doing; others may position themselves more towards the teacher-led end and put more emphasis on what the teacher does. Teachers' positioning may well vary with different classes and at different times. This continuum of practice will become important in subsequent chapters where I explore the phenomenon of TBLT. At this point, however, I turn from how students learn a language to how we might teach a language.

How Should We Teach Languages?

In light of the three theoretical perspectives on learning that I have presented in the first part of this chapter – behaviourism, innatism and interactionism – the second important question to address is, how should we teach languages? In what follows, I outline, for illustrative purposes, some contrasting approaches to language pedagogy that have emerged as a consequence of engagement with different theoretical perspectives. This presentation does not provide a full historical account of the rich and varied experimentation with a range of approaches and methods over many years (see Richards & Rodgers, 2014, for a more exhaustive overview). It will, however, provide some insight into how different theories about learning have been played out in L2 classrooms.

I begin with three contrasting approaches. The first two exemplify realisations, in different ways, of a behaviourist-informed theory of learning, and the third represents an attempt to build L2 learning from an innatist perspective:

1. grammar-translation, or, "focus on the rules with an emphasis on reading and writing"
2. audio-lingualism, or, "focus on the rules with an emphasis on listening and speaking"
3. the Natural Approach, or, "get them immersed in communicating."

Grammar-translation

The approach to L2 teaching and learning that ultimately came to be known as grammar-translation has a very long history, stretching way back into the 1800s. Its antecedent can be found within the UK and European school systems as a way of teaching Latin and Greek as classical languages. Both Latin and Classical Greek were "dead" languages (i.e., languages that were no longer spoken by any L1 speakers and therefore no longer used for any communicative purposes). The emphases for teaching the classical languages came to be on the study of grammar and the reading and translation of texts written in the original languages. The development of oral proficiency was quite unnecessary.

As the so-called Modern Foreign Languages (MFLs) slowly began to be introduced in schools, the emphases and approaches to teaching Latin and Greek were subsequently transferred to the MFLs. Grammar-translation emerged as a popular and influential model, dominating from the 1840s to the 1940s. Although it replicated the basic procedures for teaching Latin and Greek in a living language context, it actually began in MFL teaching, first applied in a French as L2 textbook for learners in Germany (Kirk, 2018). However, teachers who wanted the MFLs to be acknowledged as reputable subjects of study alongside the classics found themselves having to accept that "grammar and translation were not negotiable" (Howatt, 2009, p. 471), and grammar-translation emerged as a "methodological compromise" (p. 467) that retained features of traditional language teaching and significantly curtailed the role of spoken language. As a consequence, the move to incorporating the MFLs carried with it the emphases on literature, grammar and translation.

In grammar-translation, the literature became the gateway to the understanding of a new culture, and translation continued as a primary means of demonstrating proficiency in the target language. Grammar-translation was essentially a teacher-led, top-down expository way of teaching, with a strong focus on grammar instruction and practice. On these bases, the method reflected dimensions of a behaviourist theory of learning. Writing was also an important skill to be developed, but the focus was on accuracy. Grammar-translation courses were underpinned by structural syllabi that defined the grammar and structures to be taught, graded according to arbitrary levels of complexity.

Fundamentally, in the grammar-translation model there was no emphasis on real communication in real contexts and no interest in students learning how to communicate meaningfully in the target language. As a consequence, those studying an MFL through grammar-translation might have ended up being able to read and understand works of literature, and even write beautifully accurate and complex prose. Opportunities to learn how to communicate authentically and fluently in real-world contexts were significantly limited.

Audio-lingualism

The US context for language learning witnessed the emergence of a quite different behaviourist-informed model. As early as the 1940s, linguists at the University of Michigan began to develop an oral approach to L2 learning from which a distinctive method emerged – audio-lingualism. This method proved to be very popular in both the United States and Canada during the 1950s and 1960s, built on the perceived need to enhance L2 learning so as to maintain connections across the globe.

In contrast to grammar-translation, audio-lingualism was an attempt to bring more authentic language use into classrooms, informed by the belief that, if learners of an MFL could pay attention to what they hear and what they say, this would help them to learn how to communicate in real-world contexts. The claim of audio-lingualism was that it would enable students to achieve proficiency in an MFL effectively and efficiently.

The focus of audio-lingualism was on repeated listening and speaking drills. It was around this time that we saw the development of the phenomenon of the language laboratory. These were rooms filled with rows of desks, separated into individual booths that contained listening consoles with headphones with attached microphones and a tape recorder or cassette player. Students would sit at their own individual booths and would listen to the recordings. Essentially, they listened to phrases that might be used in everyday conversations (such as greetings, personal introductions, social interactions) and they repeated and mimicked the phrases that they heard. The teacher, sitting at a central control booth, was able to listen to any individual student in the room without the student knowing, monitoring what the student was doing, and able to provide feedback or comment via the student's headphones.

As with grammar-translation, audio-lingual courses were underpinned by structural syllabi. The approach relied on a typical behaviourist stimulus–response–feedback pattern, drawing on the drilling and repetition of grammatically accurate samples of language and leading to the formation of habits of language use. It was therefore top-down and teacher-led, with emphasis again placed on linguistic accuracy – this time through saying the words correctly by mimicking sentences.

Thus, students learning an MFL through audio-lingualism might have ended up being able to understand and say accurately the words and phrases they had been exposed to, but spontaneous expression was delayed. That is, despite the authentic contexts of the dialogues students listened to, students did not learn how to focus on interaction with others in an unrehearsed way. In real situations beyond the classroom they may have been confident in using the phrases they had learned, and could use these quite successfully, but as soon as the person they were talking to stepped outside the phrases that had been learned in the dialogue, they could become completely lost and not know how to respond. As with grammar-translation, opportunities to learn how to communicate authentically and fluently in real-world contexts were considerably restricted.

Although grammar-translation and audio-lingualism echo key elements of a behaviourist theoretical orientation, there were two essential differences in practice. The first of these related to grammar instruction. Within grammar-translation, the focus was on *teaching* (and *then* practising) the rules – a so-called deductive approach which relied on direct teacher input. Within audio-lingualism, by contrast, the focus was on *mimicking* (and *thereby* practising the rules) – a so-called inductive approach which relied on students' noticing of rules and patterns, and working these out for themselves. The second difference related to target language use. In grammar-translation, the L1 was often used as the vehicle for instruction; in audio-lingualism, by contrast, predominant use of the L2 was encouraged. Furthermore, the emphases on listening and speaking in audio-lingualism may well have been perceived as beneficial for L2 learning in comparison with the reading and writing emphases of grammar-translation. Nevertheless, moving into the 1970s, and partly in reaction to Chomsky's critique of a behaviourist explanation for language learning, there was, at least in the Unied States, a decline in popularity of audio-lingualism, and a decline in use of language laboratories.

At this point, it is important to acknowledge that components of both grammar-translation and audio-lingualism, alongside the behaviourist-informed elements that influenced them, still have considerable impact in the present day. (I will revisit this reality and explore its implications in subsequent chapters.) The direct teaching and practice of grammatical rules remains a core element of many L2 courses across the globe, as does a focus on memorisation of vocabulary. Furthermore, repeating phrases and sentences, drilling for pronunciation and intonation, and rote-learned dialogues remain commonplace activities. The language lab may have diminished in popularity, but language labs still exist (now often equipped with multimedia computers), and so-called self-access centres provide similar opportunities for listening and speaking practice.

The Natural Approach

One approach to language learning which emerged in the 1970s presents a stark contrast to grammar-translation and audio-lingualism. The Natural Approach was originally proposed by Tracy Terrell (1943–1991), an education theorist and teacher of Spanish at the University of California. In a footnote to the first of two papers, Terrell (1977) explained his experience-driven rationale for exploring what, in that paper, he described as an approach to language teaching that would be "strikingly different" from behaviourist-informed methods. He framed his argument for a radically different approach by the belief that "it is possible for students in a classroom situation to learn to communicate in a second language" (p. 325).

Terrell's experiences with behaviourist-oriented pedagogies led him to recognise that many students of an L2 in programmes with which he was familiar did not reach even a minimal level of being able to communicate in the target language. Thus, the Natural Approach shifted the emphasis from a model that was top-down, teacher-led and accuracy-focused to one that was bottom-up, learner-centred and fluency-oriented, to the extent that Terrell (1977) suggested, "if we are to raise our expectations for oral competency in communication we must lower our expectations for structural accuracy" (p. 326). This did not mean that accuracy should be regarded as unimportant for effective communication; it did mean that communication could be achieved even when accuracy was imperfect.

Furthermore, if communication was seen as more important than the learning of grammatical rules and patterns, it naturally followed that the major or exclusive focus of classroom activities should be "to evoke real communication" (p. 330). For this to be achieved, it was necessary for entire lessons to be built around communicative activities, with students encouraged to recognise their own role in working out the rules and thereby improving the quality of their language, and with more formal learning activities taking place outside of class.

What made the Natural Approach innatist? Terrell (1977, 1982) made no reference to Chomsky. He did, however, make clear reference to the distinction between acquisition (a sub-conscious process) and learning (a deliberate process) advocated by his innatist-influenced contemporary Stephen Krashen (1941–date), working at that time in the Linguistics Department at the University of Southern California, and an early very influential figure in the development of communicative approaches to L2. (I will explore some of Krashen's ideas in Chapter 2.) Essentially, Terrell (1982) rejected behaviourist notions that students develop "skills that match exactly what is taught," and learning relies on "memorized prefabricated patterns" and a "habit-drill based approach" (p. 121). Furthermore, Terrell believed that effective L2 learning was better achieved when it mirrored how children might acquire their L1, that is, through "natural acquisition processes" as understood from an innatist perspective (p. 122).

At least according to Terrell's accounts, the Natural Approach was considerably more successful than behaviourist-influenced methods when the fundamental goal of teaching and learning in L2 programmes should be to help students to develop their ability to communicate in the target language. Being innatist in orientation, the syllabus in the Natural Approach focused on communicative activities that Terrell perceived would promote sub-conscious SLA and that reflected the perceived communicative needs of the students (e.g., participate in a conversation with one or more others; read and write personal letters).

Accuracy versus Fluency

The three approaches to language pedagogy that I have thus far presented illustrate an important distinction that appeared to emerge – that between *accuracy* and *fluency*. Michel (2017, p. 50) succinctly defined accuracy as "the target-like and error-free use of language," and fluency as "the smooth, easy, and eloquent production of speech with limited numbers of pauses, hesitations, or reformulations." She further added complexity, or "the size, elaborateness, richness, and diversity of the L2 performance," as an additional variable of importance for effective and successful communication, the so-called complexity-accuracy-fluency (CAF) triad. Furthermore, the ultimate goal of increasing proficiency is automaticity, or language users' ability to utilise their knowledge of the target language spontaneously and without conscious effort. In due course, *automatic* language users will be able to "perform a complex series of tasks very quickly and efficiently, without having to think about the various components and subcomponents of action involved" (DeKeyser, 2001, p. 125).

It would seem that the three pedagogical approaches I have presented so far were incomplete in addressing all aspects that might make communication effective or automatic. Teacher-led behaviourist approaches to learning reflected in both grammar-translation (with its emphases on reading and writing) and audio-lingualism (with its emphases on listening and speaking) appeared to undermine L2 learners' ability to develop skills in undertaking genuine communication for authentic purposes. The underlying emphases of the Natural Approach – that most students of an L2 wish to acquire the ability to communicate effectively in the L2, and that this can be achieved if students are given adequate in-class opportunities to communicate (Terrell, 1977) – are significant and (from a communicative perspective) warrant a close look. However, it would seem that accuracy, although important, was viewed as a less essential component of communicative effectiveness – a position that could be interpreted as an "'anything-goes-as-long-as-you-get-the-message-across' approach to second language teaching" (Savignon, 1983, p. 1).

The questions become whether, how and to what extent the CAF triad can be integrated effectively in classroom-based language teaching contexts in ways that lead to automaticity in language use. In other words, how is the goal of communicative competence to be realised more holistically in contemporary language classrooms?

Reflection Point

Grammar-translation, audio-lingualism and the Natural Approach represent three different classroom realisations of aspects of behaviourist or innatist theories. As with these two contrasting theoretical perspectives, the legacies of these teaching approaches live on in L2 classroom practices.

1. Which elements of the three approaches have you drawn on (or might you consider drawing on) in your own L2 teaching?
2. Which elements do you think are potentially beneficial for language teaching?
3. Which elements do you think are a potential hindrance?

Advancing the Communicative Agenda: Communicative Language Teaching

As Terrell (1982) reflected back on five years of classroom experimentation with his Natural Approach, he concluded that the approach he was advocating was not the only means of L2 teaching that could enhance students' ability to communicate with L1 speakers of the target language. He argued that any approach that focuses on genuine communication as the basis for classroom activities will lead to this outcome within a very short space of time.

So-called Communicative Language Teaching (CLT) has emerged as a significant and enduring approach to developing L2 learners' communicative competence, and, furthermore, one that, potentially at least, might be able to reconcile the limitations of strongly behaviourist- or strongly innatist-influenced pedagogies – a more interactionist-informed perspective on teaching and learning. Benson and Voller (1997, p. 10) succinctly described the advent of CLT in these words:

> From time to time, a new concept enters the field of language education as an alternative method or approach, but rapidly grows in significance to the point where it comes fundamentally to condition thinking throughout the field. Such was the case with Communicative Language Teaching … which began life in the late 1960s as an alternative to "structural" and "grammar translation" models of teaching, but rapidly became an axiom of language teaching methodology. The question ceased to be, "Should we be teaching languages communicatively?", and became, "How do we teach languages communicatively?". As part of this paradigm shift, other concepts (authenticity, learner-centredness, negotiation, etc.) began to cluster around a "communicative" core.

CLT emerged as a response to calls for greater emphasis on genuine communication in L2 classrooms. When considered against the backdrop of the considerable history of language teaching approaches stretching back to and beyond grammar-translation, CLT has come to be viewed by many as the most influential approach to have emerged, and is, furthermore, a paradigm that continues to dominate in language learning classrooms (see, e.g., Spada, 2007, 2018). In the CLT paradigm, "what it means to know a language," as Hedge (2000) expressed it, underwent a significant pedagogical shift towards enhancing learners' ability to "*put that knowledge to use in communicating* with people in a variety of settings and situations" (p. 45, my emphasis). In East (2008, p. 14), I described CLT in these terms:

> The distinguishing feature of CLT approaches is that they have led to a distinct move away from artificiality of language with its emphasis on frequently decontextualized grammatical structures and vocabulary learning common within earlier frameworks such as "grammar-translation". Instead there has been a move towards an understanding that language exists for purposes of *real* communication with *real* individuals in *real* contexts.

Savignon (1991) made clear that the CLT movement must be seen as an *international* initiative to respond to the perceived needs of language learners in a variety of contexts. Its genesis, she noted, was traceable to concurrent developments both in

Europe and the United States, even though, as Byram and Méndez García (2009) put it, the two strands of development were "surprisingly independent" (p. 492).

Chomsky's theories on language acquisition were, of course, influential in a movement away from strongly behaviourist models of teaching and learning. However, as a reaction to what was perceived as "Chomsky's somewhat limiting definition of the scope of linguistic theory" (Spolsky, 1989, p. 138), other theorists began to articulate communicative competence as an underlying theoretical framework for what it means to communicate successfully in a language. This "rival notion" (p. 138) was also significant in framing and informing the dimensions that were becoming important for CLT.

Hymes (1972) was among the first to use the term communicative competence. One early influential model of this competence was published back in the early 1980s by Canale and Swain, based at that time at the Ontario Institute for Studies in Education (OISE) in Canada (Canale, 1983; Canale & Swain, 1980). Their model arose from an Ontario Ministry of Education funded research project into the acquisition of French as L2. Canale and Swain based their model on what they argued were already accepted principles of communicative approaches that had clearly been emerging since the late 1960s. Theirs was an attempt to test these principles and provide a more comprehensive theoretical framework. Although the Canale and Swain model has been developed by others (for a useful overview, see the introductory chapter in Walker et al., 2018), the model remains a succinct articulation of what Canale and Swain described as "the content and boundaries of communicative competence" which, in their view, would "lead to more useful and effective second language teaching, and allow more valid and reliable measurement of second language communication skills" (1980, p. 1). The model entailed four dimensions, concisely presented by Canale (1983):

1. *Grammatical or formal competence*: it is important to develop knowledge of systematic features of grammar, word formation and sound patterns – knowing the rules, knowing how words are put together in sentences, knowing how to pronounce words.
2. *Sociolinguistic competence*: it is also important to develop knowledge of the varieties of language that are suitable for different kinds of people interacting in different contexts about different topics, that is, to know the appropriate language for the context.
3. *Discourse competence*: it is one thing to know individual words and phrases and to be able to have basic conversations, but communicative competence must ultimately entail being able to deal with extended language use in context – for example, being able to read and understand a newspaper article, or listen to and understand a lecture.
4. *Strategic competence*: it is important to develop skills in knowing what to do when you do not know something in the language, and how you can maintain the communication. Strategies may include guessing the meaning

of an unknown word from the context, using a dictionary to locate a meaning or asking somebody to slow down when speaking or to repeat or rephrase what they have said.

The Canale and Swain model has provided one useful theoretical framework on which communicative approaches to L2 teaching that allow for equal attention to complexity, accuracy and fluency might be built.

Putting CLT into Practice

The 1970s and 1980s were the beginnings of what Richards (2006) labelled the "classic" CLT phase. In this phase, several realisations of CLT became apparent, reflecting the influences of the three perspectives on learning I presented earlier, and signalling different standpoints on how the goal of communicative competence might be realised. Two polarisations illustrate the different influences.

At the teacher-led end of the learning continuum, a communicative model that had already emerged by the 1970s became known as weak CLT. Weak CLT essentially reflected certain principles of the grammar-translation and audio-lingual traditions, and would typically have been underpinned by a structural syllabus (albeit one that might have begun to include *situations or contexts* for communicative language use [café, hotel, airport, classroom, etc.], and/or different *functions* to which language might be put [requesting, apologising, justifying, etc.]).[1] In weak CLT, teachers (having most likely learned a language themselves from a strongly teacher-led perspective) tended to foreground grammar teaching, often through what might be called the "classic lesson structure" of Presentation-Practice-Production or PPP (Klapper, 2003).

Under a PPP model, teachers would begin by presenting a particular grammar point to the class. Students would then practise the grammar point, utilising a range of grammar practice activities (e.g., fill-in-the gap; matching; transformation). Once the grammar point had been practised, students would be asked to produce or proceduralise the rule in a pseudo-communicative context, often through some kind of structured role-play that was intended to replicate a real-world scenario, such as buying something in a café or asking for directions. The main purpose of the communicative activity was to utilise the practised rule. There was minimal (if any) scope for creative use of language that went beyond the confines of the language that had been practised. Thus, weak CLT favoured accuracy over fluency.

The model of CLT emerging at the learner-centred and experiential end of the learning continuum became known as the strong form. Strong CLT arose essentially as a reaction by teachers against what were perceived as the limitations of methods such as grammar-translation and audio-lingualism, or a strongly grammar-oriented PPP sequence, in particular due to their emphases on grammar and accuracy, and constrained and controlled language. In strong CLT, structure-based syllabi were replaced by syllabi that, as with the Natural Approach, foregrounded the kinds of *communicative activities* in which it might be anticipated that learners might need to engage in different contexts. (These became effectively the forerunners of syllabi based on communicative *tasks*.)

In the strong CLT classroom, emphasis was placed solely on communication, and overt attention to formal aspects of the language was negated, based on principles of immersion in the target language and an understanding that language users would be able to work out the rules for themselves. Consequently, strong CLT resembled in several key respects the Natural Approach. The approach favoured fluency over accuracy.

By the 1980s, weak CLT had emerged as "more or less standard practice" (Howatt, 1984, p. 279), and continues into the present as such. Furthermore, PPP (albeit in modified forms that might now place greater emphasis on more spontaneous communication in the final stage) still persists into the present as a dominant procedure, and one with which many teachers of languages across the world are familiar. By contrast, strong CLT has shown itself over time not to be as popular as the weak model predicated on PPP.

Reflection Point

I noted that two polarisations became apparent during what Richards (2006) referred to as the classic CLT phase (1970s to 1990s) – weak CLT and strong CLT. Think about your own experiences of learning and/or teaching an L2:

1.   Which elements of CLT have you encountered?
2.   Which polarisation has seemed to be the more prominent, in your experience?
3.   What do you think may be the benefits and drawbacks of the PPP sequence?

Conclusion

This initial chapter has considered two historically influential theories of learning – behaviourism and innatism – alongside their enactment in contrasting language teaching approaches. I also began to explore the interactionist perspective, and made a claim that CLT held out potential as a possible outworking of interactionist stances on teaching and learning. This begs an important question: where does interactionism fit into a polarised (weak versus strong) view of CLT? It is important, in closing, to recognise that, when it comes to communicative approaches in practice, there have been, as Van den Branden et al. (2009) put it, "gradations of pedagogical choice" rather than two "mutually exclusive extremes" (p. 3). CLT-oriented teachers now draw in practice on a range of teaching techniques and learning opportunities that reflect, whether consciously or not, these teachers' positionings on a continuum from teacher-led to learner-centred. In this sense, therefore, and among the different approaches to language teaching that have been presented in this chapter, CLT is arguably the most balanced or the most flexible in its ability to accommodate a range of perspectives on learning.

That said, and as I have already mentioned, the PPP model as a key component of weak CLT remains very entrenched in many communicatively oriented teachers' practices. This is particularly a weakness in cases where the presentation stage still focuses on grammar instruction and the production stage is the vehicle for utilising the targeted rule. This has implications for controlling and constraining the language that learners use and limiting their opportunities to be creative with language as part of their own self-efficacy. However, strong CLT is not necessarily a solution because it takes no account of any place for instruction.

Long (2015) neatly summarised the dilemma: the "two major traditional language teaching orthodoxies" represented in the polarised versions of CLT were "excessively interventionist, on the one hand, and irresponsibly, wholly non-interventionist, on the other" (p. 20). As I intimated in East (2012), CLT, in both its strongest and weakest forms, has been found wanting. The scene is set for a consideration of TBLT. Chapter 2 provides an introduction to the theoretical arguments that have informed the emergence and development of a task-based approach.

Suggested Further Reading

Lightbown, P., & Spada, N. (2013). Second language learning in the classroom. In *How languages are learned* (4th ed., pp. 153–199). Oxford University Press.

Richards, J. C., & Rodgers, T. S. (2014). Communicative Language Teaching. In *Approaches and methods in language teaching* (3rd ed., pp. 83–115). Cambridge University Press.

Note

1 See Chapter 4 for a discussion of how the structural syllabus developed in different ways as a consequence of the on-going communicative agenda. See also Richards (2006) for a useful overview of syllabus development in the classic CLT phase.

References

Atkinson, D. (2011). Cognitivism and second language acquisition. In D. Atkinson (Ed.), *Alternative approaches to second language acquisition* (pp. 1–23). Routledge.

Baker, C. L., & McCarthy, J. J. (1981). *The logical problem of language acquisition*. MIT Press.

Benson, P., & Voller, P. (Eds.). (1997). *Autonomy and independence in language learning*. Longman.

Bygate, M. (2020). Some directions for the possible survival of TBLT as a real world project. *Language Teaching*, 53(3), 275–288.

Byram, M., & Méndez García, M. C. (2009). Communicative language teaching. In K. Knapp & B. Seidlhofer (Eds.), *Handbook of foreign language communication and learning* (pp. 491–516). De Gruyter.

Canale, M. (1983). On some dimensions of language proficiency. In J. W. J. Oller (Ed.), *Issues in language testing research* (pp. 333–342). Newbury House.

Canale, M., & Swain, M. (1980). Theoretical bases of communicative approaches to second language teaching and testing. *Applied Linguistics*, 1(1), 1–47.

Chomsky, N. (1959). Review of Skinner's Verbal Behavior. *Language*, 35(1), 26–58.

Cook, V. (1985). Chomsky's Universal Grammar and second language learning. *Applied Linguistics*, 6(1), 2–18.

DeKeyser, R. (2001). Automaticity and automatization. In P. Robinson (Ed.), *Cognition and second language instruction* (pp. 125–151). Cambridge University Press.

East, M. (2008). *Dictionary use in foreign language writing exams: Impact and implications*. John Benjamins.

East, M. (2012). *Task-based language teaching from the teachers' perspective: Insights from New Zealand*. John Benjamins.

East, M. (2017). Research into practice: The task-based approach to instructed second language acquisition. *Language Teaching*, 50(3), 412–424.

Graham, G. (2019). *Behaviorism*. Stanford University. https://plato.stanford.edu/archives/spr2019/entries/behaviorism.

Hall, G. (2018). *Exploring English language teaching: Language in action* (2nd ed.). Routledge.

Hedge, T. (2000). *Teaching and learning in the language classroom*. Oxford University Press.

Howatt, A. P. R. (1984). *A history of English language teaching*. Oxford University Press.

Howatt, A. P. R. (2009). Principles of approach. In K. Knapp & B. Seidlhofer (Eds.), *Handbook of foreign language communication and learning* (pp. 467–490). De Gruyter.

Hymes, D. (1972). On communicative competence. In J. B. Pride & J. Holmes (Eds.), *Sociolinguistics* (pp. 269–293). Penguin.

Kirk, S. (2018). Grammar-translation: Tradition or innovation? In N. McLelland & R. Smith (Eds.), *The history of language learning and teaching II: 19th-20th century Europe* (pp. 21–33). Legenda.

Klapper, J. (2003). Taking communication to task? A critical review of recent trends in language teaching. *The Language Learning Journal*, 27, 33–42.

Lightbown, P., & Spada, N. (2013). *How languages are learned* (4th ed.). Oxford University Press.

Long, M. (2015). TBLT: Building the road as we travel. In M. Bygate (Ed.), *Domains and directions in the development of TBLT: A decade of plenaries from the international conference* (pp. 1–26). John Benjamins.

Long, M. (2016). In defense of tasks and TBLT: Nonissues and real issues. *Annual Review of Applied Linguistics*, 36, 5–33.

Matychuk, P. (2005). The role of child-directed speech in language acquisition: A case study. *Language Sciences*, 27(3), 301–379.

Michel, M. (2017). Complexity, accuracy, and fluency in L2 production. In S. Loewen & M. Sato (Eds.), *The Routledge handbook of instructed second language acquisition* (pp. 50–68). Routledge.

Mitchell, R., Myles, F., & Marsden, E. (2019). *Second language learning theories* (4th ed.). Routledge.

Piaget, J. (1926). *The language and thought of the child*. Harcourt, Brace, & Co.

Richards, J. C. (2006). *Communicative language teaching today.* Cambridge University Press.

Richards, J. C., & Rodgers, T. S. (2014). *Approaches and methods in language teaching* (3rd ed.). Cambridge University Press.

Savignon, S. (1983). *Communicative competence.* Addison-Wesley.

Savignon, S. (1991). Communicative language teaching: State of the art. *TESOL Quarterly,* 25(2), 261–277.

Saxton, M. (2009). The inevitability of child directed speech. In S. Foster-Cohen (Ed.), *Language acquisition* (pp. 62–86). Palgrave Macmillan.

Skinner, B. F. (1957). *Verbal behavior.* Copley Publishing Group.

Spada, N. (2007). Communicative language teaching: Current status and future prospects. In J. Cummins & C. Davison (Eds.), *International handbook of English language teaching* (pp. 271–288). Springer.

Spada, N. (2018). Isolating or integrating attention to form in communicative instruction: A dilemma? *Babel,* 53(1), 7–12.

Spolsky, B. (1989). Communicative competence, language proficiency, and beyond. *Applied Linguistics,* 10(2), 138–156.

Terrell, T. D. (1977). A natural approach to second language acquisition and learning. *The Modern Language Journal,* 61(7), 325–336.

Terrell, T. D. (1982). The Natural Approach to language teaching: An update. *The Modern Language Journal,* 66(2), 121–132.

Van den Branden, K., Bygate, M., & Norris, J. (2009). Task-based language teaching: Introducing the reader. In K. Van den Branden, M. Bygate, & J. Norris (Eds.), *Task-based language teaching: A reader* (pp. 1–13). John Benjamins.

Vygotsky, L. S. (1978). *Mind in society: The development of higher psychological processes.* Harvard University Press.

Walker, I., Chan, D., Nagami, M., & Bourguignon, C. (Eds.). (2018). *New perspectives on the development of communicative and related competence in foreign language education.* De Gruyter.

2

INPUT, OUTPUT AND INTERACTION – CRUCIAL FOUNDATIONS FOR TBLT

Introduction

In Chapter 1, I drew attention to the stark contrasts represented in behaviourist- and innatist-informed approaches to language pedagogy, and also to the inadequacies of this historical learning binary for language learning. I went on to propose the potential of interactionist approaches that would provide roles for both the teacher and the learners in the L2 classroom. In this light, I introduced the notion of Communicative Language Teaching (CLT) as a possible means of reconciling these roles. I noted, however, that as CLT unfolded, it became subject to polarisations in practice. These polarisations emerged as CLT's proponents grappled, on the one hand, with maintaining a traditional teacher-led stance that had historically been influenced by behaviourist principles (and was found in so-called weak CLT) and, on the other, with learner-centred experiential ideas that had been informed by aspects of innatist thinking (and was realised in so-called strong CLT).

It would seem that conservatism won out. Weak CLT appeared over time to become the more dominant model in practice. This led to the continuance of structural syllabi, and, as I pointed out in Chapter 1, the persistence of the classic lesson structure of Presentation-Practice-Production (PPP), albeit a structure that might nowadays allow greater room for more spontaneous communicative opportunities. The potential for a balanced holistic approach to enhancing L2 learners' communicative competence appeared to have been constrained in practice.

Thus, in the 1980s, and largely as a reaction to the perceived shortcomings of structural approaches, including weak CLT, the notion of TBLT as a development aligned to the communicative agenda began to be promulgated (Van den Branden et al., 2009). As Robinson (2011) explained, "TBLT was, initially, a proposal for improving pedagogy with only a slight foundation in empirical research into ... SLA processes," with teacher concerns arising from a perceived need for "a greater emphasis on communicative activities in language teaching" (p. 4). Nevertheless, second language acquisition (SLA) theorists and researchers also embraced the proposal, and the phenomenon of task use and its implications for effective SLA have been extensively investigated.

The essential *theoretical* driver for TBLT, as Nunan (2004) put it, was that "learners learn to communicate by communicating" (p. 8). This was the premise underpinning the innatist-oriented Natural Approach (Terrell, 1977, 1982), and influencing strong CLT. The proponents of TBLT were, however, keen to avoid the limitations of a pure focus on communication. As I explained in East (2012, pp. 22–23):

> TBLT is a logical development to the CLT paradigm that might address some of the apparent weaknesses of CLT. This is because it aims to reconcile, on the one hand, the primary importance of *fluency* ... with due attention, on the other hand, to *accuracy* ... Unlike weak CLT, grammar is not fore-grounded in a teacher-dominated way. Unlike strong CLT, grammar is not ignored and learners are not left entirely to their own devices to work out the rules.

Moving on from the historical antecedents I presented in Chapter 1, the purpose of Chapter 2 is to focus on some of the key theoretical perspectives that have been influential in the advancement of communicative approaches to language teaching and that, in turn, have informed TBLT as a "logical development" to CLT. As with the theories of learning I presented in Chapter 1, some of the theories I outline here may be well known to readers, and others may be less familiar. However, exploring some of the fundamental theoretical drivers for TBLT will help to continue to build the foundation I started to lay in Chapter 1 and, in particular, will provide a clearer picture of how and why TBLT has developed over the last 40 years.

What, then, are the key theoretical perspectives on SLA that underpin Nunan's (2004) claim that communication fosters communication? I start with a presentation of three cognitivist models:

1. the input hypothesis, or, "it's all about the language learners receive"
2. the output hypothesis, or, "it's all about the language learners create"
3. the interaction hypothesis, or, "it's all about the language learners share."

The Input Hypothesis

In Chapter 1, I noted Krashen as an early influential figure in the development of communicative emphases in L2 teaching and learning. In the course of the 1980s, Krashen published and discussed, in three books, an early model of SLA whose hypotheses came to influence several dimensions of thinking (Krashen, 1981, 1982, 1985). The three books expanded on ideas he had begun to explore, and publish, earlier (Krashen, 1976, 1977). Krashen's hypotheses are often referred to as the Monitor Model, a framework that, according to Atkinson (2011), was "highly cognitivist" (p. 13) and informed by the perspective of "learning as information processing" (p. 18).

It is important to acknowledge that, influenced by Chomsky's perspective on L1 learning, Krashen's standpoint on SLA was essentially innatist, and dimensions of his proposals have been subject to substantial critique since their original introduction (see, e.g., McLaughlin, 1987, for one early example). Nonetheless, Krashen has argued that his position, to which it seems he has continued to adhere (e.g., TELF Training Institute, 2019), can be supported by research evidence (e.g., Mason & Krashen, 1997; Rodrigoa et al., 2004). Furthermore, we often look back to Krashen's model as a means of gaining some *initial* understanding of several important dimensions of SLA.

With regard to the fundamental processes involved in SLA, Krashen made an important distinction between two components – acquisition and learning. Essentially drawing on the concept of the Language Acquisition Device that Chomsky claimed was accessible to children learning their L1, Krashen argued that learners acquired the L2 in much the same way. This was a natural and subconscious process, with no conscious attention to the grammatical rules.

Learning was conceptualised as a contrasting component which, Krashen argued, was achieved via a deliberate process of studying and attention to the grammar and rules of language, leading to conscious knowledge of the L2 and explicit knowledge of the rules. This was the process that was going on in the traditional L2 classroom where teachers explained grammatical rules, and students learned these rules through instruction and practice.

Krashen maintained that only acquired language was available for communicative purposes. On this basis, all that would be necessary for SLA to occur would be to immerse learners in language. Learners would acquire the language for themselves without there being any necessity to teach them the rules. A further argument was that language was acquired in only one way, that is, by exposure to what Krashen described as *comprehensible input* – language that, overall, learners can understand, even if they do not necessarily understand every individual word. In other words, learners make progress with their knowledge of the L2 when they understand language input (through listening and/or reading) that is slightly more advanced than their current level.

Krashen represented comprehensible input with the formula I +1. In the formula, I represents the language that a learner currently knows. This language may be inaccurate or incomplete, that is, it is the learner's interlanguage, or the bridge between L1 and L2 where learners draw on their L1 to compensate for what they do not yet know in the L2. The +1 component represents language that learners have not yet understood or acquired. As learners understand more of the input they are exposed to, they progress through the sequence of acquisition of grammatical structures determined by what Krashen termed the natural order of acquisition, and become more competent in understanding the L2. In practice, I + 1 becomes a cycle, a process of gradual acquisition.

The input hypothesis Krashen proposed was essentially concerned with *comprehending* (not *producing*) language. Nevertheless, in Krashen's view, comprehending leads to acquisition, and when input is comprehensible, acquisition will naturally occur. Once language is *acquired*, it can be *produced*. As Ellis (2018) put it, from Krashen's perspective acquisition was "entirely input-driven" to the extent that "speech cannot be taught" (p. 7). Furthermore, if sufficient input was available, the required grammar was also automatically available, negating the requirement to teach grammar explicitly. From this theoretical standpoint, and in particular at the beginning stages of the SLA process, learners should be provided with extensive opportunities to process reading and listening input, before proceeding to speak and write.

There can be no doubt that Krashen's model offers us some valuable insights into, and a partial explanation of, key elements in the SLA process, particularly in light of the transition from largely behaviourist-influenced structure-based teaching to approaches that emphasised meaningful communication. Indeed, Krashen's theorising had considerable impact on Terrell and the development of the Natural Approach (see Chapter 1), and a jointly authored book presenting the approach was subsequently published (Krashen & Terrell, 1983). Nevertheless, significant critique of the hypothesis has led to development and refinement.

The Output Hypothesis

In what Nunan (2004) described as "an eloquent assault upon the input hypothesis" (p. 80), Swain took the argument about successful SLA further when, based on a considerable amount of research undertaken in Canada into the outcomes of immersion and content-based instruction, she proposed the comprehensible output (CO) hypothesis.

Swain's observations from the Canadian French immersion context demonstrated to her that, despite ample exposure to comprehensible input, input alone was not sufficient to ensure that learners developed communicative competence, particularly where accurate use of language was concerned. Swain (1985) argued that, in addition to input, learners required opportunities to create output. That is, "the act of *producing* language (speaking or writing) constitutes, under certain circumstances, part of the process of second language learning" (Swain, 2005, p. 471, my emphasis). This was because active use of the L2 requires a different psycholinguistic process from comprehension (Nunan, 2004).

Swain's initial argument (1985) was that learning and acquisition take place when learners encounter a limit in their linguistic knowledge – when they try to communicate something but fail to get their message across. Swain (1995) explained that, as learners begin to produce language, they may "*notice a gap* between what they *want* to say and what they *can* say, leading them to recognize what they do not know, or know only partially" (pp. 125–126, my emphases). When learners become aware that they do not know something, they seek to change the way they are trying to express themselves to overcome the barrier they have encountered and to get their message across more adequately, to make it more comprehensible. They are modifying output.

According to the CO hypothesis, successful SLA will occur when learners are *pushed* to produce both written and spoken language more accurately – where "pushed" here suggests a necessity to perform in language beyond a learner's comfort level. As Swain (1985) put it, pushed output is a means to give learners opportunities to focus on meaningful and contextually appropriate use of language, and thereby "to test out hypotheses about the target language, and to move the learner from a purely semantic analysis of the language to a syntactic analysis of it" (p. 252). Pushed output, alongside the feedback that language users may receive on the output they are attempting to create, enables learners to notice when they do not know something and work to make up the gap. This process stretches learners' interlanguage, causing them to acquire more language and develop more accurate use of language because they learn something new about how language works. Ultimately, they develop accuracy, fluency and automaticity in language use.

It would be useful at this juncture to mention the noticing hypothesis, an SLA concept proposed by Schmidt (e.g., 1990, 1993, 2001). Schmidt's argument was that learners cannot acquire grammatical features in an L2 unless they first notice them and how they are being used. This is not to suggest that noticing *alone* helps learners to acquire language; rather, in Schmidt's view, noticing is the essential starting point for SLA to occur. The grammatical features that are noticed, either directly by the learner or by having the learner's attention brought to these features in some way, become available for acquisition – that is, "what learners notice in input is what becomes intake for learning" (Schmidt, 1995, p. 20).

Considered together, Swain's and Schmidt's positions propose that noticing entails learners recognising what they do not yet know, and still need to discover, and/or registering particular forms in the input and the functions they are fulfilling. The noticed forms can then be acquired. (Debate has occurred over whether learners need to notice something consciously, or whether the noticing can to some extent be subconscious.)

As with Krashen's input hypothesis, there can be no doubt that Swain's CO hypothesis, including the necessity to push learners to create output beyond what they currently know, contributes some key elements to explaining SLA. Also, Swain's perspective creates greater space for teacher input in the acquisition process, through, for example, feedback on language use. However, Swain did not make the claim that CO is responsible for all (or even most) acquisition of language, but, rather, that "*sometimes*, under *some* conditions, output facilitates second language learning in ways that are different from, or enhance, those of input" (Swain & Lapkin, 1995, p. 371, my emphases). Moreover, Krashen's counter-arguments were that several studies have demonstrated that high levels of linguistic proficiency can be developed without having to produce language, and that pushing learners to create output can be uncomfortable and stressful (Krashen, 1994). Comprehensible and pushed output become part of the broader mix of theories that inform successful SLA.

The Interaction Hypothesis

Several key researchers and theorists in the field of SLA, arguably beginning with Hatch (1978), and including others such as Pica (1994), Gass (1997) and Long (1981, 1983a, 1983b, 1985, 1996), extended the role and necessity of output by arguing that conversational *interaction* is an essential, or perhaps even sufficient, condition of SLA. The so-called interaction hypothesis is therefore built on the premise that the development of language proficiency is essentially promoted by face-to-face interaction and communication. It is an extension of both the input and the output hypotheses.

Pica (1994) described Hatch as making "a pivotal and indelible mark on the field of second language acquisition" through seminal work which, in Pica's view, led to interaction becoming "a major focus of debate and discussion" (p. 494). Furthermore, Pica acknowledged Long's work as adding substantially to our understanding from a research perspective. Indeed, Long has been described as "one of the founders of the modern Cognitive-Interactionist Tradition" (Markee, 2015, p. 23). Long's interaction hypothesis evolved not only from Krashen's claims regarding comprehensible input as a necessary condition for SLA, but also from Hatch's work on the importance of conversation to developing grammatical accuracy.

Long agreed with Krashen's stance that input is important for language learning and that, for input to be effective for purposes of SLA, it must be *comprehensible*. Long was concerned, however, with the question of how that input could actually be made comprehensible. What if the input contained elements that are simply above the comprehension level of learners? How could the meaning in the input be made clearer? Long proposed the notion of the *negotiation of meaning* in communicative interaction.

Meaning negotiation occurs when there is a breakdown in communication, that is, when a gap in the communication occurs which interlocutors attempt to overcome. Pushed output helps to enable an interlocutor to close the gap, but interaction, or, to be more precise, *modified* interaction, enables the negotiation process; it helps to identify and then solve the communication problem. Meaning negotiation is essentially the process where one interlocutor in an interaction seeks to make their meaning clearer or tries to understand what the other interlocutor is saying, by adjusting the language they use or by asking questions about the language that has been used. Hence, they negotiate meaning by trying to bridge the gap through modifying their output.

In his original presentation of the interaction hypothesis, Long (1983b) compared L1 and L2 speaker input and argued that interactional modification makes input comprehensible, thereby promoting acquisition. In some respects, this might resemble Child Directed Speech, that is, language that is not only addressed to children but also adjusted to make it easier for them to understand (see Chapter 1). This does not, however, necessarily have to involve choosing simpler language, as might be the case when addressing a child. Modifications may be achieved through using gestures or contextual clues (indeed Krashen also maintained that input could be made more comprehensible in these ways). It may furthermore involve communicative strategies. These may be on the part of the initiator of the input, such as comprehension checks ("did you understand me?"), or repeating key elements of an utterance. They may also be on the part of the receiver of the input in the form of clarification requests ("can you say that again please?") or requests to change the tempo ("can you slow down please?"). In a later iteration of the interaction hypothesis, Long (1996) placed more emphasis on the need for corrective feedback that might be offered, for example, by a teacher or by a more capable peer, that would enable output to be modified and meaning more successfully negotiated.

In essence, Long's interaction hypothesis is built on the premise that, as learners engage in interaction, they receive input which they process and they create output which they monitor. Through the interaction (including the output modifications and feedback that occur), they increase their acquisition of the language. The interactionist perspective creates room, not just for peer-to-peer interactions, but also for interactions where the teacher has a guiding role to play. In turn, it is important to consider a different take on interaction – the sociocultural.

Interactionism – The Sociocultural Perspective

As I previously stated, the model proposed by Long may be referred to as contributing to a cognitive-interactionist theory of SLA in the instructed context (Long, 2015; Markee, 2015). In Chapter 1, I introduced the cognitive-interactionist model as one theoretical approach. I also presented a different stance on interaction, which may be referred to as the sociocultural-interactionist position. This leads to a complementary theoretical framework through which to view the processes of SLA. The sociocultural position looks at input, output and interaction from the perspective of learners working in collaboration with, and interacting socially with, others. By this argument, input, output and interaction are socially mediated and occur in social contexts.

As I outlined in Chapter 1, the sociocultural perspective owes much to early work by Vygotsky. Essentially, Vygotsky's observations led him to conclude that language develops primarily from social interaction. Vygotsky (1978) argued, "[e]very function in the child's cultural development appears twice: first, on the social level, and later, on the individual level; first, between people (interpsychological) and then inside the child (intrapsychological)" (p. 57). Vygotsky's sociocultural theory of human learning thus attributes learning to a social process. In this theory, interpersonal relationships are crucial to the development of knowledge and understanding. Vygotsky conceptualised the space between the inter- and the intrapsychological as the Zone of Proximal Development (ZPD), which represents "the distance between the actual developmental level as determined by independent problem solving and the level of potential development as determined through problem solving under adult guidance, or in collaboration with more capable peers" (p. 86).

Lantolf and Thorne (2006) presented a substantial theoretical overview of sociocultural theory as it pertains to SLA. More recently, Lantolf and Poehner

(2014) attempted to bridge the gap between research and practice with regard to Vygotskian-informed SLA principles. They succinctly summarised the socio-cultural-interactionist stance with these words:

> The central principle of Vygotsky's theory is that human consciousness arises through the dialectical unity of our biologically endowed brain and "auxiliary stimuli" appropriated during participation in social practices. The stimuli enable us to intentionally control, or regulate, our mental functioning.
>
> *(Lantolf and Poehner, 2014, p. 8)*

The stimuli Lantolf and Poehner (2014) referred to include the mediatory influence of others, whether peers or teachers, but could also include artefacts (such as books or the Internet) that provide knowledge that learners currently do not have. A socio-cultural perspective on SLA would suggest that, as learners produce language collaboratively, negotiate meaning as they interact and receive feedback on their language use (from a teacher or more capable peer), they acquire language. Vygotsky's ZPD provides the space within which (through scaffolding, language modification and feedback) learners move from what they are only able to accomplish with help and support to what they can ultimately accomplish independently. Interaction therefore serves as a form of mediation. Eventually, the forms and functions of language are internalised – leading in due course to linguistic automaticity.

Reflection Point

I have suggested that input, output and interaction have roles to play in successful SLA and the development of communicative competence.

Imagine two groups of language learners, one at the very beginning stages of L2 learning, and the other at a more advanced stage:

1. Can you give an example of *input* and *output* that you think would be beneficial for learners to receive or create at these two stages?
2. What *interactional* opportunities may be possible and beneficial at these stages?
3. In what different ways do you think the *negotiation of meaning* might occur in learner–learner interactions?

Input, output and interaction represent three key dimensions that are said to contribute to SLA. In what follows, I present two further contrasting theoretical standpoints that represent different emphases with regard to SLA processes and I relate them to the interactionist standpoint.

Skill Acquisition Theory

Skill Acquisition Theory or SAT (DeKeyser, 2001, 2015, 2017) finds its basis in a range of viewpoints on learning, including both cognitive and behaviourist perspectives. Chapelle (2009) noted that this theory focuses on "language learning as a *process* of human learning" (p. 747, my emphasis). On this basis, learning an L2 may be compared to learning any other skill, such as learning to play a musical instrument or learning to drive. Practice, which may broadly be defined as "engaging in an activity with the goal of becoming better at it" (DeKeyser, 1998, p. 50), is a significant component.

SAT represents a kind of multi-stage cognitive stimulus–response theory that involves a gradual progression from initial *declarative* knowledge that might involve controlled processing, through *procedural* knowledge, and ultimately to a final stage of *automaticity* (Ellis & Shintani, 2014). The model begins, for example, with conscious or explicit knowledge of grammar rules (the declarative) which may occur through some form of pre-teaching. Through practice, this becomes unconscious or implicit knowledge of how the rules are applied (the procedural), leading, as I explained in Chapter 1, to language users' ability to utilise their knowledge of the target language spontaneously and without conscious effort (the automatic). As Lyster and Sato (2013) put it, the L2 acquisitional process begins to occur for learners "through explicit information provided to them about how grammar works." Where this is successful, "proceduralization is attained as automatized knowledge through practice" (p. 76).

Crucially, SAT presents the principle that both explicit (declarative) and implicit (procedural) knowledge of the grammar are important components of developing the skill of using language. Its claim as a general theory of learning is, however, that learners begin to learn something by means of largely explicit processes. Challenging the notion that this is essentially an outmoded behaviourist-informed teacher-led approach, DeKeyser (2010) noted that practice is "a time-tested and commonsensical idea for most teachers and learners," despite its having "taken a beating in recent decades" (p. 156). Furthermore, the kind of practice anticipated goes beyond "drill-and-kill" – that is, the grammar practice exercises or substantial pattern repetitions that may have been present in earlier behaviourist-influenced approaches. Rather, it represents *communicatively linked* systematic practice that is not available when the focus is purely on input-processing and meaning, as might have been the case in the innatist-informed classroom.

SAT might also be interpreted as a linear and sequential model of acquisition, operating from explicit to implicit, that supports the process of PPP as found in weak CLT. However, as I have already noted, a tendency of the PPP model, at least as practised in the early days of CLT, was to place strong emphasis on the development of declarative knowledge through the presentation and practice stages, *potentially* proceduralising this knowledge in the final production stage, but often through controlled (and limited) communicative activities. As a consequence, the ultimate goal of automaticity may have been hindered. In this regard, Bange et al. (2005), for example, suggested that more opportunities were needed for contextualised practice so that students could proceduralise their declarative knowledge more adequately. To accomplish this, students required extensive opportunities to interact with each other in communicative contexts and to receive guidance and feedback on their language use from a teacher or more capable peer.

Conversely, Lyster and Sato (2013) asserted that, in contexts where primary emphasis has been placed on immersion in language (such as may have been apparent in strong CLT), teacher scaffolding and feedback may have roles to play in helping learners to *develop* declarative knowledge from the procedural knowledge that they may have acquired in "more or less naturalistic ways" (p. 77). Thus, SAT from this perspective exemplifies how "controlled and automatic processes constantly interact" (p. 73) and "declarative and procedural knowledge can coexist" (p. 74) and can be bidirectional, allowing for "guided practice *and* communicative practice" (p. 78, my emphasis).

Importantly as a theoretical perspective, SAT is built on the premise that extensive interactional practice coupled with feedback will provide the means to turn explicit knowledge into implicit, leading to the ultimate goal of automaticity in language use. SAT moves beyond a behaviourist-informed approach to explicit knowledge, sees roles for both what the teacher does and what the learners do, and provides a complement to both cognitive-interactionist and sociocultural-interactionist perspectives on SLA.

Usage-based Theories

A different stance on SLA is provided through usage-based theories of language acquisition, based on the premises that "L2 learning is primarily driven by exposure to L2 input, and that learners 'induce' the rules of their L2 from the input by general learning mechanisms" (Mitchell et al., 2019, p. 14). From this theoretical stance, the acquisition process is largely implicit and incidental. Consequently, exposure to input is a necessary condition for language acquisition to occur, and rules that are acquired in one context can be applied more broadly to other contexts. Fundamentally, language acquisition emerges over time from language in use.

Primarily proposed as a theory of L1 acquisition, Tomasello (2003) argued that, from a usage-based perspective, "all constructions may be acquired with the same basic set of acquisitional processes" (p. 6). He labelled the first of these processes as intention-reading. That is, very young children communicate initially through "reading the intention" of an interlocutor. For example, even before they can speak, and having early learned to follow a finger pointing to a specific object or occurrence, children will start to point at things to direct others' attention to objects and events.

For Tomasello (2003), the second L1 acquisitional process was pattern-finding. He argued that children do not learn words and grammar directly or abstractly. Rather, they try to comprehend complete utterances, or chunks of language, that carry specific meanings. Simply put, language is made up of collections of words and structures; each of these has meaning; we learn these meanings by using them. The ability to spot patterns is all that is necessary for acquisition to occur.

For example, the important issue for subsequent correct use of language is recognising the patterns in, and understanding the meaning behind, "throw me the ball," rather than knowing the rules of imperative (throw), direct object (ball) and indirect object pronoun (me). Thus, learners of an L1 do not learn the sentence structure as "verb + object(s)"; they learn the sentence structure by associating meaning to the language chunk and beginning to respond accordingly.

At first view, a usage-based theory of acquisition may appear to be innatist in that it is built on a learner's innate ability to process language input – as Tomasello (2000) put it, there can be "no question that human children are biologically prepared to acquire a natural language" (p. 247). However, Tomasello rejected fundamental tenets of Chomsky's theorising, such as the notion that humans are born with an in-built grammatical system that includes the general principles of language and that informs the development of a child's L1. According to Marchman and Thal (2004), from an innatist perspective "children are special because they 'have' something" – that is, an innate ability to acquire language by drawing on the Language Acquisition Device and Universal Grammar. From a usage-based perspective, by contrast, "children are special because what they have enables them to *do something*" – that is, "they construct an impressive system of grammar using domain-general skills in the context of doing everyday, ordinary things" (p. 144).

A usage-based account of language acquisition has implications for SLA. The most direct implication is that learners must have frequent opportunities to engage with and process language input. This input will include "the provision of good quality positive evidence" (MacWhinney, 2004, p. 911), or accurate language samples. The input must also be sufficiently rich for learners to be able to detect and notice regular patterns in language use from the examples given to them. Furthermore, and given the limited time that is often available for L2 learning in comparison with L1 learning, the teacher has a role to play in drawing learners' attention to grammatical structures, particularly in cases where these structures are unusual or irregular (Dolgova & Tyler, 2019).

Importantly, in a usage-based model grammar is treated as "a contextually based, rather than a context-independent phenomenon," placing importance on "recreating communicative context in language instruction" (Dolgova & Tyler, 2019, p. 947). Usage-based theories are built on the premise that actual language use is the primary mechanism for learning about the structure of language. As with SAT, the ultimate goal is automaticity in language use, which may be evidenced linguistically as competence in communication. In Tomasello's (2000) words, communicative competence ultimately derives not only from the need to "be conventional" and "use language the way that other people use it" (p. 209), that is, follow the rules so as to be understood, but also to "be creative" and "formulate novel utterances tailored to the exigencies of particular communicative circumstances" (pp. 209–210), that is, be automatic.

Dolgova and Tyler (2019) also pointed out that there is no single usage-based model of language or language learning. Rather, the approach includes a range of standpoints. Furthermore, a usage-based approach moves beyond an innatist-informed understanding of implicit knowledge, sees roles for both what the teacher does and what the learners do, and, as with SAT, provides a complement to both cognitive-interactionist and sociocultural-interactionist perspectives on SLA.

Reflection Point

Nunan (2004) claimed, "learners learn to communicate by communicating" (p. 8).

1. To what extent do you agree with Nunan's claim?
2. What specific contributions do you think the cognitive-interactionist and sociocultural-interactionist perspectives can make with regard to the claim?
3. What do you see as the essential differences between Skill Acquisition Theory and usage-based accounts of SLA, bearing this claim in mind?

Relating Theoretical Perspectives to TBLT

In what I have presented so far, the foundational theoretical groundwork has been laid for a closer and deeper exploration of what TBLT is and how it might be enacted in classrooms. Essentially, TBLT represents the emergence of a communicative approach that sits within an interactionist perspective on learning, based on the theoretical premise that "language is best learned and taught through interaction" (Pica et al., 1993, p. 10). Furthermore, unlike strongly behaviourist approaches that might have emphasised accuracy to the detriment of fluency, or strongly innatist approaches that might have done the opposite, the interactive stance on SLA informing TBLT accommodates attention to *both* fluency (meaning) *and* accuracy (form). Fluency is attended to through ample opportunities for learners to interact in the target language. Accuracy is attended to not only through meaning negotiation but also through input and feedback from a more proficient collaborator.[1] This dual attention, which can be viewed from both cognitive and sociocultural perspectives, will be underscored in subsequent chapters as I explore the phenomenon and outworkings of TBLT.

Ellis et al. (2019) highlighted the importance of both cognitive and sociocultural perspectives for TBLT, particularly in facilitating dual attention to meaning and form. In their view, cognitive-interactionist theories support TBLT by highlighting both that SLA takes place both incidentally and implicitly when learners focus on meaning as they undertake a task, and that, at the same time, a focus on form (grammar) is needed to make sure that learners pay attention to the grammatical forms they encounter in the input. Interaction thus "facilitates learning when it promotes noticing and noticing-the-gap" (p. 61). From a sociocultural perspective, learning is mediated, and occurs when learners have opportunities to interact with different kinds of artefact, with social interaction being an essential means of mediation. Hence, learning "commences *within* an interaction between an expert (a teacher or a more advanced learner) and a learner, resulting in the co-construction of a ZPD" (p. 105). In this context, scaffolding takes place when one speaker (the one with the greater level of expertise) supports another speaker (the less proficient interlocutor) to perform a skill or use a linguistic feature that they are (initially) unable to perform or use on their own.

Before moving on to consider some of the practical outworkings of TBLT (and some of the challenges they bring), there is one more major theoretical issue that needs to be tackled – what exactly is a task for the purposes of TBLT? In Chapter 3, I explore the task construct in some depth by drawing on a range of different theoretical definitions of task that have emerged over the years. In the remainder of this chapter, I begin the exploration of the task construct, but from the specific perspective of the underlying theoretical frameworks of input, output and interaction that I have presented earlier, with particular focus on interaction and meaning negotiation.

Tasks for Purposes of Input, Output and Interaction

Willis and Willis (2007) asserted, "the most effective way to teach a language is by engaging learners in real language use in the classroom." This, they suggested, is "done by designing tasks – discussions, problems, games, and so on – which require learners to use language for themselves" (p. 1). According to Cook (2010), TBLT "sees second language learning as arising from particular tasks that students do in the classroom" (p. 512). In Robinson's words, TBLT "places the construct of 'task' at the center of curricular planning" (2011, p. 4). Returning to the foundational theoretical principle underpinning TBLT expressed by Nunan (2004) – that learners learn to communicate by communicating – tasks become the means through which, in Nunan's words, there can be "an emphasis on learning to communicate through *interaction* in the target language" (p. 1, my emphasis).

How, then, is *task* to be defined? And how is a task to be differentiated from the many activities that might be found in the typical communicative language classroom, thus making it a distinct construct?

A succinct and focused definition of the task construct was provided by Bygate et al. (2001) as follows: a task is "an activity which requires learners to use language, with emphasis on meaning, to attain an objective" (p. 11). Van den Branden (2006) essentially replicated this core definition in these words: a task is "an activity in which a person engages in order to attain an objective, and which necessitates the use of language" (p. 4). Van den Branden went on to align this essential definition with the three theoretical perspectives on SLA with which I opened this chapter:

According to this definition, using language is a means to an end: by understanding language *input* and by producing language *output* i.e. by *interacting* with other people in real-life situations through the use of language, the goals that the learner has in mind can be (better) achieved.

(p. 4, my emphases)

Drawing on Van den Branden's (2006) description, we could come up with an initial, straightforward working definition of a task:

A task has a goal which requires processing input, creating output and interacting with others to meet it.

Below, I present and discuss a task example that might fulfil this basic operational definition.[2]

Example: A Two-way Interactive Speaking Task

How do input, output and interaction work together to compel the negotiation of meaning that Long had suggested was crucial to SLA or that Vygotsky asserted was fundamental to learning? In other words, what kinds of tasks compel language learners to find a way through to a goal, using language?

For input, output and interaction to become components of what happens between two interlocutors, there needs to be, at a minimum, some kind of information that must be exchanged between the two. Interaction takes place when two or more interlocutors try to communicate with each other. Furthermore, interaction can be one-way or two-way. In one-way communication, one interlocutor creates output and the other receives it, whereas, in two-way communication, both interlocutors have opportunities to receive input and create output. This leads to the distinction between one-way tasks (where one interlocutor has all of the information needed to achieve the goal and the other interlocutor has to discover that information) and two-way tasks (where the two interlocutors have unique information to contribute that is not known to the partner).

A simple two-way task follows a straightforward format. Two students work in a pair. Both have different pieces of information, known only to them. The goal is to find out all the information. The individual pieces of information must be exchanged in some way so that the goal can be reached successfully. Partner A needs to pass on information to Partner B, and vice versa. This requires language (processing input, creating output and interacting), and that language needs to be made understandable to both partners.

An example of a two-way task that could be used with relative beginners in an L2 could run along the following lines. This task example fits the immediate context in which I work, but is easily cross-transferable to other contexts. New Zealand is a country of two islands (North and South). The weather across both islands can be very different, with bright sunshine and warm weather in the north, and rain and strong winds in the south. A task that might emerge from this context is as follows:

> Work with a partner. Partner A has a map of the whole country, but only has weather information for the North Island (weather symbols, temperature, etc.). Partner B has the same map of the whole country, but only weather information for the South Island. Work together to identify and note on your map what the weather is like in six different locations in both islands (twelve pieces of information in total).

The goal of the task – what Van den Branden (2006) would refer to as the objective that necessitates the use of language – is to complete the whole map so that the weather across the whole country has been identified. Sitting opposite each other, and having their own information guarded by some kind of barrier so that their partner cannot see it (a school bag might suffice), the students may take turns to ask questions of each other to fill in their part of the map.

Gathering the information to fill in the map requires understanding input (comprehending what the partner is saying) – at the very least understanding a straightforward formulaic expression such as "what's the weather like in …?" It also requires producing output – making statements about the weather in a range of places across the island ("it's sunny in …"; "it's raining in …"). Most crucially, it requires interaction – clarifying utterances, requesting repetition, and so on – so that, through the use of language, the goal of completing the map is reached. The task is also arguably real-life – a criterion that Van den Branden (2006) suggested was important – in that people do typically want to find out information about what the weather is like in different locations. Thus, this basic two-way task maps onto Van den Branden's operational definition. It also maps onto several of the theoretical concepts I explored earlier in this chapter – comprehensible input; comprehensible output; meaning negotiation through interaction.

The "complete the weather map" task is very straightforward. It might be difficult to see how the task will necessarily push learners towards higher levels of language acquisition. There are, however, ways in which the task could be embellished. Perhaps the partners need to consider which items of clothing might be the most appropriate for a particular location, or where they would most likely go to complete a particular activity, given the weather conditions. In this way, the questioning moves beyond a simple formulaic "what's the weather like in …?" It requires greater reasoning and constructing somewhat more complex language. Alternatively, instead of having a map, perhaps the two partners have independent access to the Internet and are required to seek out, and then explain to their partner, what a longer-term forecast for the weather is suggesting in different locations across the country, and what those forecasts might mean for making future plans to undertake different activities. Thus, as originally framed, the map exercise is a typical two-way task that requires interaction involving straightforward language. Long (2018) noted, however, that "[s]uch tasks range from simple picture-matching and 'spot-the-difference' tasks for beginners, to complex business simulations and academic research projects for more advanced learners" (p. 5).

The important issue here, in light of the theory I have presented in this chapter, is that the sharing and gathering of information in a two-way task ultimately requires a process of negotiation of meaning. The participants are required to be active negotiators. They can initiate interactional exchanges, not only to offer the information they have, but also to ask for the information they do not have. Long argued that, in these ways, two-way tasks necessarily force more meaning negotiation into play than one-way tasks, and also enhance comprehension and SLA.

Reflection Point

The "complete the weather map" task represents a so-called information gap task – something needs to be found out.

1. Have you come across or used information gap tasks in your own learning or teaching of an L2? What different kinds have you encountered?
2. What value do you think information gap tasks might have in light of the claim that learners learn to communicate by communicating?
3. Can you come up with your own example of a straightforward information gap task?

Conclusion

The first two chapters of this book have aimed to lay several basic theoretical foundations for the exploration of the phenomenon of TBLT. Chapter 1 considered three theoretical perspectives on learning – behaviourism, innatism and interactionism. The interactionist perspective on learning was further differentiated to bring out both its cognitive and its sociocultural dimensions. I went on to demonstrate how different theories of learning found expression in different approaches to language teaching in instructed contexts. Chapter 2 considered three cognitive approaches to SLA – hypotheses concerning input, output and interaction. Furthermore, interaction was again differentiated in both cognitive and sociocultural terms. The chapter also presented Skill Acquisition Theory and usage-based theories of learning as contrasting theoretical perspectives on SLA.

Importantly, Chapters 1 and 2 lead to the assertion that, as Pica et al. (1993) had put it, language is most effectively learned and taught through interaction. It is not surprising, therefore, that it has been argued that interaction is not only advantageous for SLA, but also has a central role to play in SLA theory and language pedagogy. Indeed, it is important to acknowledge that the cognitive-interactionist approach, and the role of feedback within it, have been subject to substantial empirical investigation (see, e.g., Mackey, 2007, 2012; Mackey & Polio, 2007; Philp & Gurzynski-Weiss, 2020). More broadly, both the cognitive and the social dimensions of interaction continue into the present as significant theoretical drivers for tasks and TBLT (see, e.g., Mackey, 2020). TBLT holds the potential for a language learning approach that capitalises on interaction.

I concluded this chapter by illustrating how interaction finds expression in a simple two-way information gap task. Chapter 3 continues the theoretical journey, but now also begins to relate theory more concretely to practice. Chapter 3 explores in more depth the construct of task for the purposes of TBLT.

Suggested Further Reading

Loewen, S., & Sato, M. (2018). Interaction and instructed second language acquisition. *Language Teaching, 51*(3), 285–329.

Robinson, P. (2011). Task-based language learning: A review of issues. *Language Learning, 61*(s1), 1–36.

Notes

1 I consider the role of direct instruction for the purpose of developing grammatical competence in Chapter 6.
2 This working definition, considered alongside the theories I have presented in this chapter, might lead to the perception that SLA and tasks must involve spoken interaction. In practice, tasks can exploit a range of skills. I look more closely at this important matter in Chapter 3.

References

Atkinson, D. (2011). Cognitivism and second language acquisition. In D. Atkinson (Ed.), *Alternative approaches to second language acquisition* (pp. 1–23). Routledge.

Bange, P., Carol, R., & Griggs, P. (2005). *L'apprentissage d'une langue étrangère: Cognition et interaction.* L'Harmattan.

Bygate, M., Skehan, P., & Swain, M. (Eds.). (2001). *Researching pedagogic tasks: Second language learning, teaching and testing.* Longman.

Chapelle, C. (2009). The relationship between second language acquisition theory and computer-assisted language learning. *The Modern Language Journal, 93*(s1), 741–753.

Cook, V. (2010). Linguistic relativity and language teaching. In V. Cook & A. Bassetti (Eds.), *Language and bilingual cognition* (pp. 509–518). Psychology Press.

DeKeyser, R. (1998). Beyond focus on form: Cognitive perspectives on learning and practicing second language grammar. In C. Doughty & J. Williams (Eds.), *Focus on form in classroom second language acquisition* (pp. 42–63). Cambridge University Press.

DeKeyser, R. (2001). Automaticity and automatization. In P. Robinson (Ed.), *Cognition and second language instruction* (pp. 125–151). Cambridge University Press.

DeKeyser, R. (2010). Practice for second language learning: Don't throw out the baby with the bath water. *International Journal of English Studies*, 10(1), 155–165.

DeKeyser, R. (2015). Skill acquisition theory. In B. VanPatten & J. Williams (Eds.), *Theories in second language acquisition* (pp. 94–112). Routledge.

DeKeyser, R. (2017). Knowledge and skill in ISLA. In S. Loewen & M. Sato (Eds.), *The Routledge handbook of instructed second language acquisition* (pp. 15–32). Routledge.

Dolgova, N., & Tyler, A. (2019). Applications of usage-based approaches to language teaching. In X. Gao (Ed.), *Second handbook of English language teaching* (pp. 939–961). Springer.

East, M. (2012). *Task-based language teaching from the teachers' perspective: Insights from New Zealand*. John Benjamins.

Ellis, R. (2018). *Reflections on task-based language teaching*. Multilingual Matters.

Ellis, R., & Shintani, N. (2014). *Exploring language pedagogy through second language acquisition research*. Routledge.

Ellis, R., Skehan, P., Li, S., Shintani, N., & Lambert, C. (2019). *Task-based language teaching: Theory and practice*. Cambridge University Press.

Gass, S. (1997). *Input, interaction, and the second language learner*. Lawrence Erlbaum.

Hatch, E. (1978). Discourse analysis and second language acquisition. In E. Hatch (Ed.), *Second language acquisition: A book of readings* (pp. 401–435). Newbury House.

Krashen, S. (1976). Formal and informal linguistic environments in language acquisition and language learning. *TESOL Quarterly*, 10, 157–168.

Krashen, S. (1977). Some issues relating to the Monitor Model. In H. Brown, C. Jorio, & R. Crymes (Eds.), *Teaching and learning English as a second language: Some trends in research and practice* (pp. 144–148). TESOL.

Krashen, S. (1981). *Second language acquisition and second language learning*. Pergamon Press.

Krashen, S. (1982). *Principles and practice in second language acquisition*. Pergamon Press.

Krashen, S. (1985). *The input hypothesis: Issues and implications*. Longman.

Krashen, S. (1994). The input hypothesis and its rivals. In N. Ellis (Ed.), *Implicit and explicit learning of languages* (pp. 45–77). Academic Press.

Krashen, S., & Terrell, T. D. (1983). *The Natural Approach: Language acquisition in the classroom*. Pergamon.

Lantolf, J. P., & Poehner, M. E. (2014). *Sociocultural theory and the pedagogical imperative in L2 education: Vygotskian praxis and the research/practice divide*. Routledge.

Lantolf, J. P., & Thorne, S. L. (2006). *Sociocultural theory and the genesis of second language development*. Oxford University Press.

Long, M. (1981). Input, interaction, and second language acquisition. *Annals of the New York Academy of Sciences*, 379(1), 259–278.

Long, M. (1983a). Linguistic and conversational adjustments to non-native speakers. *Studies in Second Language Acquisition*, 5(2), 177–193.

Long, M. (1983b). Native speaker/non-native speaker conversation and the negotiation of comprehensible input. *Applied Linguistics*, 4(2), 126–141.

Long, M. (1985). Input and second language acquisition theory. In S. Gass & C. Madden (Eds.), *Input in second language acquisition* (pp. 377–393). Newbury House.

Long, M. (1996). The role of the linguistic environment in second language acquisition. In W. Ritchie & T. Bhatia (Eds.), *Handbook of second language acquisition* (pp. 413–468). Academic Press.

Long, M. (2015). *Second language acquisition and task-based language teaching.* Wiley-Blackwell.

Long, M. (2018). Interaction in L2 classrooms. In J. I. Liontas (Ed.), *The TESOL Encyclopedia of English Language Teaching.* John Wiley & Sons.

Lyster, R., & Sato, M. (2013). Skill Acquisition Theory and the role of practice in L2 development. In M. P. García Mayo, M. Junkal Gutierrez Mangado, & M. Martínez Adrián (Eds.), *Contemporary approaches to second language acquisition* (pp. 71–91). John Benjamins.

Mackey, A. (Ed.). (2007). *Conversational interaction in second language acquisition: A collection of empirical studies.* Oxford University Press.

Mackey, A. (2012). *Input, interaction and corrective feedback in L2 classrooms.* Oxford University Press.

Mackey, A. (2020). *Interaction, feedback and task research in L2 learning: Methods and design.* Cambridge University Press.

Mackey, A., & Polio, C. (Eds.). (2007). *Multiple perspectives on interaction in second language acquisition.* Routledge.

MacWhinney, B. (2004). A multiple process solution to the logical problem of language acquisition. *Journal of Child Language, 31*(4), 833–914.

Marchman, V., & Thal, D. (2004). Words and grammar. In D. I. Slobin & M. Tomasello (Eds.), *Beyond nature-nurture: Essays in honor of Elizabeth Bates* (pp. 141–164). Lawrence Erlbaum.

Markee, N. (Ed.). (2015). *The handbook of classroom discourse and interaction.* John Wiley & Sons.

Mason, B., & Krashen, S. (1997). Extensive reading in English as a foreign language. *System, 25*(1), 91–102.

McLaughlin, B. (1987). *Theories of second-language learning.* Edward Arnold.

Mitchell, R., Myles, F., & Marsden, E. (2019). *Second language learning theories* (4th ed.). Routledge.

Nunan, D. (2004). *Task-based language teaching.* Cambridge University Press.

Philp, J., & Gurzynski-Weiss, L. (2020). On the role of the interlocutor in second language development: A cognitive-interactionist approach. In L. Gurzynski-Weiss (Ed), *Cross-theoretical explorations of interlocutors and their individual differences* (pp. 20–50). John Benjamins.

Pica, T. (1994). Research on negotiation: What does it reveal about second language acquisition? Conditions, processes, and outcomes. *Language Learning, 44*(3), 493–527.

Pica, T., Kanagy, R., & Falodin, J. (1993). Choosing and using communication tasks for second language instruction and research. In G. Crookes & S. Gass (Eds.), *Task and language learning: Integrating theory and practice* (pp. 9–34). Multilingual Matters.

Robinson, P. (2011). Task-based language learning: A review of issues. *Language Learning, 61*(s1), 1–36.

Rodrigoa, V., Krashen, S., & Gribbons, B. (2004). The effectiveness of two comprehensible-input approaches to foreign language instruction at the intermediate level. *System 32(1), 53–60, 32*(1), 53–60.

Schmidt, R. (1990). The role of consciousness in second language learning. *Applied Linguistics, 11*(1), 17–46.

Schmidt, R. (1993). Consciousness, learning and interlanguage pragmatics. In G. Kasper & S. Blum-Kulka (Eds.), *Interlanguage pragmatics* (pp. 21–42). Oxford University Press.

Schmidt, R. (1995). Consciousness and foreign language learning: A tutorial on the role of attention and awareness. In R. Schmidt (Ed.), *Attention and awareness in foreign language teaching and learning (Technical Report No. 9)* (pp. 1–64). University of Hawaii at Manoa.

Schmidt, R. (2001). Attention. In P. Robinson (Ed.), *Cognition and second language instruction* (pp. 3–32). Cambridge University Press.

Swain, M. (1985). Communicative competence: Some roles for comprehensible input and comprehensible output in its development. In S. Gass & C. Madden (Eds.), *Input in second language acquisition* (pp. 235–256). Newbury House.

Swain, M. (1995). Three functions of output in second language learning. In G. Cook & B. Seidlhofer (Eds.), *Principles and practice in applied linguistics: Papers in honour of H. G. Widdowson* (pp. 125–144). Oxford University Press.

Swain, M. (2005). The output hypothesis: Theory and research. In E. Hinkel (Ed.), *Handbook of research in second language teaching and learning* (pp. 471–484). Routledge.

Swain, M., & Lapkin, S. (1995). Problems in output and the cognitive processes they generate: A step towards second language learning. *Applied Linguistics*, 16(3), 371–391.

TELF Training Institute. (2019). What teachers need to know (and what's stopping them) (with Stephen Krashen). http://www.tefltraininginstitute.com/podcast/2019/1/29/what-teachers-need-to-know-and-whats-stopping-them-with-stephen-krashen.

Terrell, T. D. (1977). A natural approach to second language acquisition and learning. *The Modern Language Journal*, 61(7), 325–336.

Terrell, T. D. (1982). The Natural Approach to language teaching: An update. *The Modern Language Journal*, 66(2), 121–132.

Tomasello, M. (2000). Do young children have adult syntactic competence? *Cognition*, 74(3), 209–253.

Tomasello, M. (2003). *Constructing a language: A usage-based theory of language acquisition.* Harvard University Press.

Van den Branden, K. (2006). Introduction: Task-based language teaching in a nutshell. In K. Van den Branden (Ed.), *Task-based language education: From theory to practice* (pp. 1–16). Cambridge University Press.

Van den Branden, K., Bygate, M., & Norris, J. (2009). Task-based language teaching: Introducing the reader. In K. Van den Branden, M. Bygate, & J. Norris (Eds.), *Task-based language teaching: A reader* (pp. 1–13). John Benjamins.

Vygotsky, L. S. (1978). *Mind in society: The development of higher psychological processes.* Harvard University Press.

Willis, D., & Willis, J. (2007). *Doing task-based teaching.* Oxford University Press.

3

THE CONSTRUCT OF TASK FOR THE PURPOSES OF TBLT

Introduction

In Chapter 2, I made the case that communicative interaction offers considerable potential for enhancing second language acquisition (SLA). Philp et al. (2014), for example, underscored the beneficial learning potential of peer-to-peer collaborations. They did this from two standpoints. From a cognitive perspective (Long's interaction hypothesis), participants in interaction "adjust how they express meaning in response to communication difficulties (e.g., through repetition, restructuring, or rephrasing of language)." From a sociocultural perspective (Vygotsky's ZPD), learning is co-constructed and seen as "a jointly developed process and inherent in participating in interaction" (p. 8). Interactions are not limited to peer-to-peer work; teachers may be components of the collaboration. From an interactionist perspective, it is theorised that language proficiency develops through learners' participation in collaborative interactions, alongside the opportunities for scaffolding, negotiation of meaning and feedback that such collaborations create.

TBLT is an approach to SLA that capitalises on interactionist theories of learning. As the name suggests, in TBLT *task* is the central construct through which interaction is facilitated and the central focus of TBLT's learner-centred and experiential orientation. Towards the end of Chapter 2, I defined a task as follows:

A task has a goal which requires processing input, creating output and interacting with others to meet it.

The purpose of this chapter is to expand on this essential definition. This chapter presents a range of theoretical definitions of task, alongside several examples of tasks, with a view to developing a more comprehensive understanding of this fundamental construct for the purposes of TBLT.

Task – Broadly Defined

One issue that emerges from a consideration of the literature on TBLT is that the construct of task has been subject to a range of definitions over the years. Overviews are provided, for example, in Bygate et al. (2001, pp. 9–10), Ellis (2003, pp. 4–5) and Van den Branden (2006, p. 4). By way of initial exploration of the task construct, I present some of the earliest definitions that appeared during the 1980s and 1990s and I draw out the distinctions between them. I go on to consider a somewhat more consolidated position that began to emerge in the late 1990s and 2000s.

Task – Early Definitions

Long (1985) provided one of the earliest definitions of what might constitute a task. He saw the task concept in very broad terms as "a piece of work undertaken for oneself or for others, freely or for some reward" (p. 89). He went on to present a range of everyday examples, including painting a fence, filling out a form, buying a pair of shoes, making an airline reservation or taking a driving test.

Some of the tasks Long listed were clearly linguistic in orientation, whereas others were not. For example, we cannot make an argument that fence painting is likely to promote SLA (unless this activity is occurring concurrently with a conversation with someone else). Similarly, taking a driving test does not *necessarily* contribute to SLA or necessitate the use of language, although there are clearly linguistic elements that require negotiation – including being able to interpret road signs (many of which would be symbols), and, more particularly, responding to the requests of the examiner (which requires, at least, understanding of input).

However, other examples in Long's early definition have clear linguistic potential, including filling out a form (requires the processing of input and the creation of written output), or buying a pair of shoes and making an airline reservation (requires interaction with written instructions for on-line purchases, or interactions in real time with a salesperson or a travel agent – whether by phone or in person).

Thus, although some of Long's (1985) examples can be turned into linguistic opportunities, others do not require attempts to communicate. However, the concept of task that Long wished to put across here was essentially that tasks relate to real-world activities, or "the hundred and one things that people *do* in everyday life at work and play, and in between" (p. 89, my emphasis). Considerably more recently, Long (2015) reiterated a similar list to define tasks as "the real-world activities people think of when planning, conducting, or recalling their day." As Long noted, "[s]ome tasks are mundane, some complex. Some require language use, some do not; for others, it is optional" (p. 6).

Crookes, an early contemporary of Long, suggested that a task was "a piece of work or an activity, usually with a specified objective, undertaken as part of an educational course, at work, or used to elicit data for research" (Crookes, 1986, p. 1). As with Long (1985), therefore, Crookes provided quite a wide-ranging definition of a task in relation to real-world activities. However, he included in his definition higher-order tasks which would require the use of language and the transmission of meaning. Reaching an objective (e.g., producing some kind of report or output) was an important element.

In contrast to Long's (1985) broad task definition which focused on real-world activities, another broad, but this time clearly linguistically oriented, task definition was proposed by Breen (1987). Breen argued that a task was "any structured *language learning* endeavour which has a particular objective, appropriate content, a specified working procedure, and a range of outcomes for those who undertake the task" (p. 23, my emphasis). He went on to suggest that a task was therefore represented by "a range of workplans" whose overarching purpose was to enable language learning, "from the simple and brief exercise type, to more complex and lengthy activities such as group problem-solving or simulations and decision-making" (p. 23). Once more, outcome was seen as important. Furthermore, Breen's view on tasks to facilitate language learning included straightforward exercises at one end of a continuum, as well as more complex activities at the other end that would require significant communicative interaction.

Two early task definitions proposed respectively by Nunan (1989) and by Willis (1996) were more focused on what might be happening in the communicative L2 classroom. Nunan proposed that tasks "involve communicative language use in which the user's attention is focused on meaning rather than linguistic structure" (p. 10). Willis suggested that tasks are "activities where the target language is used by the learner for a communicative purpose … in order to achieve an outcome" (p. 23). In both cases, the emphasis is on using language in classrooms to reach a communicative goal.

Bygate et al. (2001) argued that several of the definitions emerging during the 1980s and 1990s were "interestingly similar but also interestingly different … [and with] distinctive emphases" (p. 10). Furthermore, these early definitions of task appeared to relate to both tasks in general and tasks for communication. However, definitions that began to appear in the late 1990s and beyond started to crystallise thinking around particular core elements of the task construct for communicative purposes. Below I present four task construct definitions that demonstrate a level of synergy.

Task – More Narrowly Defined

Skehan (1998, p. 47) proposed a definition that brought together the perspectives of a range of authors and synthesised the task construct into five components – a task is an activity in which:

1. meaning is primary
2. learners are not given other people's meanings to regurgitate
3. there is some sort of relationship to comparable real-world activities

4.   task completion has some priority
5.   the assessment of the task is in terms of outcome.

Ellis (2003, 2009b) similarly proposed a four-component definition of task – a task is an activity where:

1.   the primary focus should be on meaning
2.   there should be some kind of gap
3.   learners should principally be dependent on their own resources to complete the activity
4.   there is a clearly defined outcome over and above the use of language.

Ellis and Shintani (2014, pp. 135–136) usefully expanded on this four-fold categorisation in ways that map the task construct onto the central components of input, output and interaction:

1.   Meaning focus: learners should principally be focused on processing input and creating output, rather than on grammatical form.
2.   Gap: there is a requirement to express information, give an opinion or deduce meaning.
3.   Own resources: learners are not specifically taught or directed to the language they need to complete the task (i.e., they are free to use any language they wish to reach the task outcome, rather than being constrained by a requirement to produce specific language, although they may be able to take some language directly from any provided input to help them complete it).
4.   Outcome: the language is the means to reach the outcome, but not an end in itself (i.e., learners undertaking the task are not primarily focused on having to use language correctly but, rather, on reaching the goal anticipated in the task).

The above four characteristics are, in the words of Ellis and Shintani (2014), "directed at ensuring that a task results in language use where learners treat the language as a 'tool' for achieving a communicative outcome rather than as an 'object' to be studied, analysed and displayed" (p. 136), as might have been the case in a more traditional realisation of the Presentation-Practice-Production (PPP) sequence (see Chapter 1).

Willis and Willis (2007, p. 13) suggested that teachers could pose six questions to evaluate the extent to which a given activity could really be called a task:

1.   Does the activity engage learners' interest?
2.   Is there a primary focus on meaning?
3.   Is there an outcome?
4.   Is success judged in terms of outcome?
5.   Is completion a priority?
6.   Does the activity relate to real world activities?

All the above definitions (Ellis, 2003, 2009b; Skehan, 1998; Willis & Willis, 2007) have in common an emphasis on the primacy of meaning. It is important here to distinguish between two types of meaning – semantic (sentence-level) and pragmatic (more broadly contextual). Ellis and Shintani (2014), for example, explained that semantic meaning encompasses "the specific lexical and grammatical meanings encoded by words and grammatical structures," whereas pragmatic meaning incorporates "the functional meanings that arise when language is used to describe, request, apologize and so on" (p. 136). In each of the task definitions above, meaning should be interpreted in its pragmatic (communicative) sense.

Finally, Samuda and Bygate (2008) proposed a succinct definition that linked input, output and interaction to SLA: a task for the purposes of TBLT may be defined as "a holistic activity which engages language use in order to achieve some non-linguistic outcome while meeting a linguistic challenge, with the overall aim of promoting language learning, through process or product or both" (p. 69).

Taking these later definitions into account, it can be seen that, over time, some level of unity appears to emerge around the task construct. Key identifiable characteristics are:

1. a relationship to real-world activities (a dimension of authenticity)
2. a primary focus on communicative meaning and fluency (rather than grammatical form and accuracy)
3. a gap (something that learners have to work out)
4. an outcome beyond the use of language (language is not used as an end in itself).

It is possible to relate these four key characteristics (and the definitions that have led to them) to the original working definition of task I have already proposed: a task has a goal which requires processing input, creating output and interacting with others to meet it.

Tasks in Practice

Having presented several theoretical definitions of the task construct and brought out the essential features of tasks as they might be utilised in the communicative L2 classroom, in what follows I present a range of task types that reflect these definitions. I begin with some categories and go on to provide examples.

Tasks as Means to Overcome a Gap

The so-called Bangalore project, or, more precisely, the Bangalore Communicational Teaching Project or CTP, ran from 1979 to 1984 in what is now formally Bengaluru, the capital of the Indian state of Karnataka. It owes its genesis to Neiman Stern (N. S.) Prabhu, who was working at that time as the English Language Officer at the British Council in Madras (now officially Chennai). Prabhu's plan was to devise a communicative syllabus for school-based learning of English as L2, a central component of which was a set of tasks, or, "what is to be done in the classroom rather than what parts of the content are to be learnt" (Prabhu & Carroll, 1980, p. 2).

The Bangalore project was essentially a reaction to a structural approach to English Language Teaching that had been introduced on a wide scale in South India from the 1960s. The project was largely influenced by a rejection of behaviourist-informed approaches to teaching, alongside an acceptance of an innatist perspective on the distinction between acquisition and learning (see Chapter 2). The project thus rejected the assumption that teachers needed to attend to grammar rules in a top-down teacher-led way, and instead supported the supposition that learners could work out rules for themselves as they engaged in language use. In taking this stance, Prabhu was attempting to meet the specific needs of the local context as he perceived them. This was therefore, in Brumfit's (1984) words, "a locally-based experiment, arising directly from a dissatisfaction with existing methods" (p. 235). The experiment, as Brumfit noted, was in several respects a process of trial and error, and a working out of hunches about what might be effective in the classroom.

To facilitate SLA, Prabhu designed materials which were not based on any overt pre-selection of grammatical rules that needed to be taught and practised. Rather, the materials he designed promoted, in his own words, (1) learners' "natural desire to meet a challenge" (i.e., solve a problem in some way); (2) the "preoccupation with meaning or thinking which such problem-solving necessarily brings about"; and (3) the "incidental struggle with language-use which such activity engenders" (Prabhu, 1982, p. 3).

Early evaluations of the project used the label *task* to describe the activities that Prabhu developed – the project consisted of "specific tasks" (Brumfit, 1984, p. 235) or "a series of tasks in the form of problem-solving activities" (Beretta & Davies, 1985, p. 121), in what essentially became a "task-based syllabus" (Beretta, 1990, p. 321).

Specifically, Prabhu (1987) proposed three categories of task, each of which has in common the requirement to *overcome a gap*, that is, to work out and/or provide information that is initially unknown:

1. information gap, or, "find something out"
2. reasoning gap, or, "work something out"
3. opinion gap, or, "express what you think."

The three task categories with which Prabhu experimented became early prototypes of tasks in action. It should be noted, however, that Prabhu's tasks were not designed to promote peer-to-peer interaction. As Brumfit (1984) noted, curiously Prabhu did not encourage pair or group work. This was ostensibly on the basis of its lack of fit with the immediate context, alongside apprehension that learners might resort to using their L1 or might embed linguistic errors into their language. On the contrary, the tasks were strongly input-based and teacher-led, with the teacher first interacting with the whole class around a sample of language (thereby providing a model, and also, through asking individual learners to respond in some way, helping to make the input comprehensible). Once this had been done, the learners would work on the activities by themselves.

Nevertheless, from an interactionist perspective, the task prototypes do have the potential to provide opportunities for paired or group interactions, that is, for making input comprehensible through negotiation of meaning (modifying language, asking questions) and receiving feedback on task performance. In this respect, Prabhu had arguably, as Brumfit (1984) put it, "developed a set of materials which, with adjustments, can be used as a basis for fluency activities in any language teaching" (p. 235).

Reflection Point

In Chapter 2, I presented a "complete the weather map" task as an example of a straightforward information gap task, which is arguably suitable for near beginner L2 learners working in a pair. Prabhu (1987) suggested three kinds of "overcome the gap" task.

1. In what ways do you think that reasoning gap and opinion gap tasks might be more linguistically and cognitively demanding than information gap tasks?
2. Can you come up with example scenarios for a *reasoning gap* task and an *opinion gap* task that may be suitable for L2 students at intermediate to advanced level working in a pair?
3. Setting up a whole-class debate about a controversial issue may provide a useful means of promoting interaction. Can you come up with an example of a debate that requires overcoming both reasoning and opinion gaps?

Developing the Task Gap Concept

Building on the tripartite task model emerging from Prabhu's work, Pica et al. (1993) presented an early typology of task types that could be used for interactional purposes. They proposed five essential types which they labelled as jigsaw, information gap, problem-solving, decision-making and opinion exchange.

Pica et al. (1993) began from the premise that tasks for interactional communicative purposes are both goal-oriented (there is an outcome for which the learners are aiming) and activity-inducing (the learners must do something collaboratively to reach the outcome).

The jigsaw and information gap tasks proposed by Pica et al. (1993) parallel Prabhu's information gap tasks. They are typically paired tasks where two interlocutors "hold portions of a totality of information which must be exchanged and manipulated, as they work convergently toward a single task goal" (p. 20). Pica et al. argued, however, that jigsaw tasks differ from information gap tasks in terms of the roles interactants play and their access to the information they need to complete the task. By their definition, in a jigsaw task both interlocutors hold different pieces of the information and both must interact to share that information (two-way). In an information gap task, by contrast, only one partner has the information which the other partner needs to find out (one-way). In their view, in comparative terms a jigsaw task (two-way information exchange) is the type of task "most likely to generate opportunities for interactants to work toward comprehension, feedback, and interlanguage modification processes related to successful SLA" (p. 21).

Problem-solving, decision-making and opinion exchange tasks parallel Prabhu's reasoning gap and opinion gap tasks. Pica et al. (1993) suggested that, in all three of their proposed task types (and in contrast to information gap tasks), the two interlocutors would hold the same information in common (e.g., information about a problem to be solved; input that provokes a decision to be reached or opinions to be shared). In each case, a two-way *requester–supplier* relationship exists (both partners can talk with each other about the same information). However, interaction is not a pre-requisite for being able to complete the task because one participant could choose to work individually, drawing on the input to suggest a solution to the problem, come to a decision or formulate and provide an opinion. Also, such tasks may be divergent in the sense that more than one outcome (solution, decision, opinion) can be reached. Nevertheless, such tasks can usefully provoke interaction, particularly in cases where (as with reasoning gap tasks) a single solution may need to be proposed or a single decision may need to be negotiated and reached (convergence).

Pica et al. (1993) concluded that there are differences in the effectiveness of these five task types as means to provide learners with opportunities for "comprehension, feedback, and interlanguage modification" (p. 23). In their view, the most effective task types for these purposes appeared to be jigsaw and information gap, whereas the least effective appeared to be opinion exchange.

When considering the relative effectiveness of these task types to promote SLA, Pica et al. (1993) spoke of their fluidity. That is, each task type could be modified in ways that would move it out of one category and into another, depending on what was required in the task. For example, if the two-way information in a jigsaw task were assigned to only one participant, it would become an information gap task. If participants undertaking a problem-solving or decision-making task were only given pieces of the problem and could only solve the problem by sharing information, the problem-solving or decision-making task becomes a jigsaw task. If the goal of a task that encourages expression of divergent opinions also, or ultimately, requires a single mutually agreed judgment, an opinion exchange task becomes a decision-making task. None of this should be seen as problematic; rather, it points to the flexibility with which tasks can be designed and utilised for a range of purposes in the communicative classroom.

Overcome the Gap Tasks in Practice

A useful way of illustrating the kinds of tasks that might align with the typologies proposed by Prabhu (1987) and by Pica et al. (1993) is to consider some examples. As with the information gap task I presented in Chapter 2, a reasoning gap or problem-solving/decision-making task essentially requires the sharing of information. However, a conclusion needs to be reached on the basis of thinking through the information "through processes of inference, deduction, practical reasoning, or a perception of relationships or patterns" (Nunan, 2004, p. 57). For example, a reasonably straightforward task for reasoning purposes may be as follows:

> You are looking for a job and have been offered an interview for a job you would love – but the interview is tomorrow and in a city 200 miles away. You can get there by bus, train or flight. You have timetables in front of you, alongside information on cost and travel duration for each mode of transport. Work with a partner/group and use the available information to come up with the most logical travel plan, taking into account factors such as cost, time and efficiency.

A potentially more complex reasoning/problem-solving/decision-making task may be this:

> A young couple are preparing their wedding reception. Each has a group of four friends who do not know each other, but who all need to be seated at the same eight-seat table for the reception. To help with planning, you have some information on each of the friends (for example, age, where the person comes from, what the person does for a living, interests, likes and dislikes). Work with a partner/group and use the available information to come up with a suitable seating plan that will (hopefully) maximise the opportunity for everyone at the table to get on with the people they will be sitting next to.

Tasks such as the ones presented above require understanding the given input (details provided on the transport options or the eight people) and the ability to work out from that input, in collaboration with others, the best solution to the problem. As Nunan (2004) explained, the task "necessarily involves comprehending and conveying information" – as in a typical information gap task – "but the information to be conveyed is not identical with that initially comprehended. There is a piece of reasoning which connects the two" (p. 57).

An opinion gap or opinion exchange task involves each interlocutor's ability to identify and then present (and perhaps justify) a personal viewpoint, feeling or attitude in the context of processing a particular situation. Nunan (2004) clarified that the task may require "using factual information and formulating arguments to justify one's opinion, but there is no objective procedure for demonstrating outcomes as right or wrong, and no reason to expect the same outcome from different individuals or on different occasions" (p. 57). Consequently, although a reasoning gap task may involve some level of objective logic, an opinion gap task takes account of more subjective or individual perspectives.

The two reasoning gap task scenarios presented above may, with simple adaptation, become opinion gap tasks. For example, disagreement about the best travel option to get to an interview or the most suitable seating combination at a wedding reception may give rise to opportunities to state, and argue for, a particular perspective. However, in both cases it should be possible to reach an objective outcome (even though that outcome may to some extent be open to debate) – one route to the interview is likely to be the most expedient and economical; one seating plan will likely maximise a harmonious gathering. An opinion gap/exchange task whose outcomes are more unpredictable is this:

> The country where you live is debating the legalisation of cannabis, on either medicinal or recreational grounds, or both. You have been given an article that outlines some of the benefits and drawbacks, both medicinally and recreationally. Read the article, and then debate with your partner/group what you think about the legalisation of cannabis. Decide who presents the most convincing perspective.

The emphasis in the above task scenario is on what individuals actually think about a subject that is controversial and on which a range of justifiable opinions may be held. Not all opinion gap tasks need to deal with such hot topics. What is potentially challenging with the above opinion exchange task is that, depending on the scenario, some students may feel uncomfortable about expressing their own opinion. One way to mitigate this problem might be to assign students to different roles (e.g., Person A: in favour of medicinal cannabis but against recreational cannabis; Person B: vehemently against both; and so on). Students are then required to give an opinion based on an assigned perspective, rather than having to reveal their own viewpoints. (See East, 2018, pp. 40–41, for an example of how this kind of opinion gap task might be structured.)

What I have presented above represents different ways in which the archetypical information gap/reasoning gap/opinion gap conceptualisations of tasks might be put into practice from an interactionist perspective. I turn now to a different classification of task types presented by Willis (1996).

Other Task Types in Practice

Willis (1996) broadly classified tasks into six types which arguably demonstrate some level of increasing difficulty:

1.   listing
2.   ordering and sorting

3. comparing
4. problem-solving
5. sharing personal experiences
6. creative tasks.

As the name suggests, a listing task is essentially a task whose outcome is to generate some kind of list. A typical listing task could be something like this:

> You and a partner/group are planning a class party for the end of the semester. Make a list of all the items you need to buy to make the party a success.

A listing task may seem very straightforward and pedestrian, and, indeed, it could be very suitable for beginner learners of an L2 who lack an extensive vocabulary repertoire. Willis (1996) suggested, however, that listing tasks can generate a good deal of interaction as the interlocutors may be required to present and perhaps justify their ideas, thereby bringing in elements of reasoning and opinion exchange. Paired or group listing tasks promote processes such as brainstorming, where students tap into what they may already know, or fact-finding, where students seek out additional or unknown information by asking others or utilising resources such as books or the Internet. Listing tasks can be made more challenging where a level of justification is required for why particular items need to make it on the list.

An ordering and sorting task may, at its simplest, also have as its outcome some kind of list, but here the list needs to have been arranged according to at least one specific criterion. A straightforward ordering and sorting task could be something like this:

> You would like to find out when your classmates have their birthdays. Carry out a survey to find out how many classmates have a birthday in each month from January to December.

Willis (1996) suggested that several essential processes are involved in students' collaboration in an ordering and sorting task: sequencing of items, actions or events in a logical or chronological order; ranking of items according to the stated criteria or personal viewpoints; and placing items into specific groups for which the categories may or may not have been given.

A comparing task is essentially an information gap task. Information from at least two sources is provided (e.g., two different versions of a map), and this information is compared to identify similarities or differences (e.g., what the weather is like in different places) – see Chapter 2. An alternative could be a simple spot-the-difference task:

You and a partner each have a picture of the same room in a house, but there are eight differences between your picture and your partner's picture. Talk with your partner to see if you can find the differences.

The required processes to complete a comparing task include: identifying specific pieces of information and relating these to other pieces of information, and identifying similarities and differences.

A problem-solving task is essentially a reasoning gap/decision-making task. Such tasks require the interlocutors to think through some kind of problem and reason out a solution (see the examples given earlier). Willis (1996) proposed that these tasks might, at their most straightforward, include short puzzles such as logic problems. At a more complex level, students may be required to solve some kind of real-life problem through processes such as "expressing hypotheses, describing experiences, comparing alternatives and evaluating and agreeing a solution" (p. 27). As Willis noted, the processes and length of time required for task completion will vary in accordance with the nature and complexity of the problem to be solved.

Somewhat analogous to opinion gap/opinion exchange tasks are tasks that require students to talk about personal experiences. These provide spaces for students to talk more openly about themselves and share something of them-selves with others. Willis (1996) suggested that the interaction that results from these opportunities reflects elements of casual social conversation and is not so directly goal-oriented. This does not, however, have to be the case. Where an experience-sharing task is more closely aligned with an opinion gap task, it is possible to imagine scenarios for which an outcome is anticipated (e.g., sharing opinions to reach consensus on the best course of action). Since personal experience tasks (like opinion gap tasks) may provoke a level of discomfort for some interlocutors in some contexts, tasks can be constructed such that experi-ences are shared "in role" rather than "in fact" (as I suggested earlier for opinion gap tasks).

Willis's (1996) final category of creative tasks provides scope, as the name suggests, for students to be creative, linguistically and non-linguistically, in a range of ways. Willis referred to these as projects. They might involve pairs or groups collaborating around some kind of goal which could include, for example, creative writing, social/historical research or multi-media projects, spanning anything from a series of lessons to several weeks. An outcome might be to present a summary of the project to the whole class. As Willis noted, such tasks are more open-ended and may tend to include more stages than other tasks, or even combine a range of task types. Students may need to spend time outside class researching aspects or gathering information that will contribute to the project's completion.

Reflection Point

Pica et al. (1993) and Willis (1996) presented two taxonomies of proposed task types. Both taxonomies arguably run from more straightforward to more challenging tasks.

1. How useful do you think these taxonomies would be for a teacher wishing to plan tasks for L2 classes?
2. What similarities or overlaps can you identify between the two taxonomies?
3. Which task types, in your view, represent the least and the most challenging for students?

Task Types – Broadening the Considerations

So far in this chapter, and taking into account the theoretical frameworks for SLA I presented primarily in Chapter 2, I have outlined several theoretical definitions of communicative language use tasks alongside a range of different task types that illustrate and give substance to those definitions. I did this in relation to the work of several theorists and practitioners who have worked in different contexts. The task types I presented are not mutually exclusive, and it is possible to see several areas of overlap. In the final part of this chapter, I outline some broader and more general considerations for task design, task implementation and task use.

Closed versus Open Tasks

In addition to the range of task types that Willis (1996) proposed, Willis also differentiated between closed and open tasks, suggesting that, in practice, tasks can operate on a continuum between the two.

Closed tasks are highly structured and set a very specific goal, with precise instructions, only one outcome and only one way of achieving it. These tasks are therefore, to use Pica et al.'s (1993) terminology, convergent, and interactants will work towards the same ultimate goal. Jigsaw tasks and information gap tasks will often be closed. Open tasks are more open-ended and the goal is less definite. Reasoning and opinion gap tasks are necessarily more open. Although in some cases only one solution may be reached or one decision may be appropriate (i.e., they are also convergent), in other cases the tasks are divergent in that several outcomes are possible. As Willis (1996) explained it, "real-life problem-solving tasks have specific goals, too (e.g. to agree on a prioritised list or on a solution), but each pair's outcome might be different, and there will be alternative ways of reaching it" (p. 28). The earlier examples of deciding on the best way to get to an interview, or the best seating plan for good social interactions at a wedding reception, represent tasks where one outcome may be the most logical, but where several may be possible. Long (2018) suggested that there is "some evidence that closed two-way tasks produce more negotiation for meaning, more feedback, more uptake, and greater fluency than open tasks" (p. 5).

Focused versus Unfocused Tasks

Whereas closed and open tasks refer principally to outcome (which may be convergent or divergent), focused and unfocused tasks refer principally to grammar. A focus on grammar is a whole issue in itself for TBLT, which I tackle in more detail in Chapter 6. At this stage, it is useful to make the focused/unfocused distinction with regard to putting tasks into operation.

According to Ellis et al. (2019), for example, unfocused tasks are designed to prompt more general samples of language, whereas focused tasks are constructed so as to direct learners to using a particular linguistic feature or grammatical structure (even though focused tasks do need to satisfy the general criteria for being a task). García Mayo (2018) similarly commented that, in an unfocused task, "learners use the language freely and no particular grammar form is needed to complete the task." Focused tasks, by contrast, "have been designed in such a way that learners will need to use a specific grammar form in order to complete them" (p. 2). Such tasks do need, in her words, to focus on something meaningful or authentic. That is, they are not simply grammar practice activities. Nevertheless, they need to be designed so that language users are compelled to use a specific linguistic feature. García Mayo presented a useful illustrative example:

> Work with a partner. You are both real-estate agents. Each of you has information on one house that you wish to sell. Convince your partner that your property is better than your partner's property.

The target structure here is comparative – "my house is bigger than / newer than / in a better location than …" The task is focused because (all being well) it compels the interlocutors to use these comparative structures. Problematic, of course, is that, if tasks allow students to use any language they wish to complete the task (see, e.g., Ellis & Shintani, 2014), it would be acceptable if students found a way to complete this task without using the comparative – by simply saying, for example, "my house is big / new / well-located" – although hopefully students would see the comparative as the most useful grammatical structure to fulfil the task outcome. Thus, the key issue when devising a focused task is that the task can force a particular structure into use.

Real-world versus Pedagogic Tasks

The notion of a focused task designed to target a particular grammar construction, alongside some of the task examples I have presented in this chapter, might raise questions about how real-world a task can or should be. The extent of authenticity in classroom-based tasks, such as planning how to get to an interview, organising a wedding reception seating plan or discussing which house is a better buy, depends on who the students are, and their anticipated language learning goals (a classroom-based interaction between two "real-estate agents" would clearly be more authentic for those who are, or plan to become, such agents than for those who are not).

Nunan (2004) distinguished between real-world tasks and pedagogical tasks. Long (2015) similarly argued that real-world tasks (what he referred to as target tasks) need to be transformed, at the level of the classroom, into tasks that he termed pedagogic. In turn, pedagogic tasks might focus on discrete dimensions of the target task. If, for example, the real-world (target) task is "attending a job interview" (a scenario that may well be very relevant, depending on the students), a pedagogic task may draw on language required for one component of that target task (plan how best to get there). A sequence of pedagogic tasks may simulate dimensions of the interview experience. However, the pedagogic tasks are limited in their authenticity, and, in turn, the level of authenticity will be determined by the students and their target task needs (which is why Long argued for needs analysis at the start of planning a task-based course, an issue I take up in Chapter 4).

Although a pedagogically oriented task may lack a level of authenticity with regard to the *situation* it aims to replicate, another dimension of authenticity is important. The task may arguably be real-world if it draws on the kinds of *language* that may be used in outside-of-class real-life contexts, regardless of the situation (e.g., offering an opinion; suggesting alternatives), or the kinds of *skills* that L2 users might draw on in a real-life interactional situation beyond the task (e.g., co-operating and collaborating; making themselves understood). It is therefore important to make the distinction between *situational* and *interactional* authenticity (Bachman, 1990). For pedagogical purposes, several of the tasks I have presented in this chapter may be regarded as *interactionally* authentic, even if they may lack a level of *situational* authenticity.

Face-to-Face versus Technologically Mediated Tasks

Situational and interactional authenticity also have implications for the *medium* through which interactive tasks are enacted. The considerable expansion of technology over the past few decades means that authentic interaction is now no longer limited to real-time physically present face-to-face contexts, and, in the real world, interactions between people are frequently technologically mediated.

Computers, hand-held devices and smartphones, equipped with cameras and video-conferencing applications, have created countless opportunities for virtual face-to-face interactions. Video conferencing provides considerable scope for authentic synchronous exchanges where close physical proximity is not a pre-requisite. There are several positive implications for TBLT, and the literature that focuses on the interface between technology and TBLT is expanding (see, e.g., González-Lloret, 2016, 2017, 2020; González-Lloret & Ortega, 2014; Ziegler, 2016).

González-Lloret (2020), for example, argued that a key benefit of technologically mediated tasks is that they enable L2 speakers who are geographically remote to communicate with each other in ways that align with TBLT in theory and practice – that is, they facilitate "active participation and interaction as well as opportunities for negotiation of differing perspectives and opinions, disagreement, resolution and consensus building" (p. 67). In the context of presenting several examples of successful technology-facilitated tasks utilised by researchers in a range of situations, González-Lloret noted that telecollaborative projects remain popular avenues for these kinds of L2 interaction, where the outcome may be to create some kind of artefact (e.g., a poster presentation for a conference or a travel itinerary).

Even asynchronous (not in real time) on-line exchanges provide opportunities for meaning negotiation. In comparison with synchronous interactions, such communications provide greater space to process input and create output. Furthermore, the input and output processing may be in written form (e.g., an email exchange or discussion thread between students in two different locations to reach a goal, rather than spoken interactions). In turn, this raises a final – and significant – consideration for the task construct: that tasks are more than just about speaking.

Input-based versus Output-based Tasks

The tasks that I have so far presented in this chapter lend themselves particularly to spoken interaction, and it is certainly very important to acknowledge that spoken interactive tasks do have a central and significant place for SLA, seen from both cognitive and sociocultural perspectives. As I illustrated in Chapter 2, theoretical rationales for task use are more clearly articulated for spoken production than they are for other skills such as writing, reading and listening (Robinson, 2011). Also, a great deal of research work in the TBLT space over several decades has focused on "interaction … to provoke negotiation for meaning" (Bygate et al., 2001, p. 3) and, as a consequence, oral tasks (e.g., Ahmadian, 2012; Ellis, 2009a; Skehan & Foster, 1998).

It would be remiss, however, to allow a perception to persist that interaction must necessarily be *spoken*, and, *ipso facto*, that tasks for the purposes of TBLT must be *speaking* tasks. From a learning perspective, the interaction anticipated, for example, as learners operate within their ZPDs, could involve peer/group collaborations that draw on a range of skills (e.g., collaborative writing or reading). As I noted in Chapter 2, scaffolding support can also be mediated as individuals (or groups) interact with printed or Internet-based artefacts. These might include dictionaries, word lists or textbooks, and other on-line support resources. Interaction may be primarily mediated through face-to-face collaborations, but it is certainly not limited to such collaborations. Tasks for purposes of TBLT can therefore be constructed not only as *output*-based (tasks focused on language production, through both speaking and writing) but also as *input*-based (tasks focused on processing input through listening and/or reading).

A range of research has investigated tasks in relation to skills other than speaking. In their edited collection of studies, Byrnes and Manchón (2014) focused exclusively on writing and framed several writing activities from a task-based perspective. Green (2005) and Mounts and Smirnova (2011) have discussed reading tasks. Ellis (2003) and Ellis et al. (2019) underscored the value of, for example, so-called listen–and–do tasks where students listen to instructions or descriptions and then perform actions that will demonstrate their comprehension of the input. Furthermore, East (2017) asserted that "an understanding that communicative approaches should foster an *integrated* skills approach acknowledges the reality that, when speaking for example, listening is a necessary important component" (p. 420). Indeed, Hinkel (2010) has suggested that TBLT is perhaps "the most widely adopted model of *integrated* language teaching today" (p. 115, my emphasis). That tasks can be focused on skills other than speaking, or can be integrated, means that they can also be conducted in modes other than pairs/groups. There is also scope for tasks to be undertaken individually or as a whole class. (I talk more about this in Part II.)

The interaction anticipated with output-based tasks may be with the medium of the task itself, rather than with an interlocutor. For example, giving a speech (a monologic speaking task) is arguably interactive in that it may require processing input and creating output in the preparation stage. The speech itself is a one-way output, although it may additionally require interacting with an audience in some kind of question-and-answer scenario. Creating written output (e.g., writing a letter of complaint about a faulty product) can be conceptualised as an interactive task, where an individual creates output, but perhaps in interaction with support resources such as a dictionary that require the processing of input.

Input-based tasks also require some kind of interaction, although, as Ellis (2012) put it, they may be "non-reciprocal" in that (as with some output-based tasks) they do not necessarily require interaction with an interlocutor. Rather, the interaction is between learners and "oral or written input in the form of instructions or descriptions." These interactions may require learners to "demonstrate understanding non-verbally (e.g. by an action, selecting the right picture, finding the differences between two pictures, completing a map, or making a model)" (p. 211).

The rationale for input-based tasks, as noted by Ellis (2012), is found in theoretical frameworks such as Krashen's (1985) comprehensible input hypothesis (see Chapter 2). Also, input-based tasks can operate beneficially as focused tasks. As Loschky and Bley-Vroman (1993) observed, it can be challenging to make output-based tasks focused because, as I previously stated, learners are free to complete the task using any language they wish, and could therefore potentially avoid using the target structure. It is more straightforward to design input-based tasks that require the targeted structure. Furthermore, and in line with Krashen's argument that input leads to acquisition (which is subsequently demonstrated in output), Ellis et al. (2019) suggested that, initially, TBLT should be input-driven.

With regard to technology-mediated TBLT, the Internet is a rich source of language input – written, aural and visual – and technology provides "many opportunities for listening and reading tasks, and even writing tasks also," and can enable learners to "go well beyond the limitations of their own particular learning context" (Ellis et al., 2019, p. 365).

Reflection Point

Notwithstanding central roles in TBLT for speaking and collaborative work in line with interactionist theories of learning, East (2017) indicated two persistent misunderstandings – that "tasks are all about speaking," and that "pair and group work must be central to the task-based classroom" (p. 420). This does not have to be the case.

Can you come up with straightforward (beginner/intermediate level) examples of:

1. an individual output-based writing task?
2. an individual input-based reading task?
3. an individual input-based listen-and-do task?

Note: what you come up with should reflect the essential characteristics of a task (real-world relationship; focus on meaning; gap; and outcome).

Conclusion

The purpose of this chapter has been to introduce a range of task types and task considerations in order to develop a more comprehensive understanding of the central task construct for TBLT. Provided that the task meets essential task characteristics as outlined earlier in this chapter, tasks may be output-based or input-based, carried out in pairs or groups, or undertaken individually or as a whole class.

One concluding matter to consider is that, however carefully designed against theoretical task criteria, and however carefully planned for students, tasks in practice may end up looking quite different from tasks in theory. This is not necessarily problematic but, rather, reflects (and respects) learner autonomy in what is essentially a learner-centred pedagogical approach.

Breen (1989), for example, differentiated between what he labelled *task-as-workplan* and *task-as-process*. Task-as-workplan represents the task as presented to students. This includes, for example, any input to be provided, the task instructions and anticipated task outcome. Task-as-workplan thus conceptualises what *should* occur as students undertake the task. Task-as-process represents the activities that *actually* occur and what the students actually do when they perform the task as students interpret what is required and negotiate what should happen. What students do with the task may end up looking different from what teachers planned for the task. That said, the definitions of task given in this chapter typically refer to task-as-workplan and represent what teachers, as the task-setters, intend to happen. This arguably needs to be the starting point for task and course design considerations (Ellis et al., 2019).

It is time now to consider how TBLT in theory becomes TBLT in practice. In Part II, I explore how all the theory I have presented, in particular in Chapters 2 and 3, might be realised in classrooms.

Suggested Further Reading

East, M. (2018). How do beginning teachers conceptualise and enact tasks in school foreign language classrooms? In V. Samuda, M. Bygate, & K. Van den Branden (Eds.), *TBLT as a researched pedagogy* (pp. 23–50). John Benjamins.

Willis, J. (1996). Aspects of tasks. In *A framework for task-based learning* (pp. 23–37). Longman Pearson Education.

References

Ahmadian, M. J. (2012). The effects of guided careful online planning on complexity, accuracy and fluency in intermediate EFL learners' oral production: The case of English articles. *Language Teaching Research*, 16(1), 129–149.

Bachman, L. F. (1990). *Fundamental considerations in language testing*. Oxford University Press.

Beretta, A. (1990). Implementation of the Bangalore Project. *Applied Linguistics*, 11(4), 321–337.

Beretta, A., & Davies, A. (1985). Evaluation of the Bangalore Project. *ELT Journal*, 39(2), 121–127.

Breen, M. (1987). Learner contributions to task design. In C. Candlin & D. Murphy (Eds.), *Language learning tasks* (pp. 23–46). Prentice-Hall.

Breen, M. (1989). The evaluation cycle for language learning tasks. In R. K. Johnson (Ed.), *The second language curriculum* (pp. 187–206). Cambridge University Press.

Brumfit, C. (1984). The Bangalore procedural syllabus. *ELT Journal*, 38(4), 233–241.

Bygate, M., Skehan, P., & Swain, M. (Eds.). (2001). *Researching pedagogic tasks: Second language learning, teaching and testing*. Longman.

Byrnes, H., & Manchón, R. M. (Eds.). (2014). *Task-based language learning: Insights from and for L2 writing*. John Benjamins.

Crookes, G. (1986). Task classifications: A cross-disciplinary review. In *Technical report no. 4*. Center for Second Language Classroom Research, Social Science Research Institute, University of Hawaii.

East, M. (2017). Research into practice: The task-based approach to instructed second language acquisition. *Language Teaching*, 50(3), 412–424.

East, M. (2018). How do beginning teachers conceptualise and enact tasks in school foreign language classrooms? In V. Samuda, M. Bygate, & K. Van den Branden (Eds.), *TBLT as a researched pedagogy* (pp. 23–50). John Benjamins.

Ellis, R. (2003). *Task-based language teaching and learning*. Oxford University Press.

Ellis, R. (2009a). The differential effects of three types of task planning on the fluency, complexity, and accuracy in L2 oral production. *Applied Linguistics*, 30(4), 474–509.

Ellis, R. (2009b). Task-based language teaching: Sorting out the misunderstandings. *International Journal of Applied Linguistics*, 19(3), 221–246.

Ellis, R. (2012). *Language teaching research and language pedagogy*. Wiley-Blackwell.

Ellis, R., & Shintani, N. (2014). *Exploring language pedagogy through second language acquisition research*. Routledge.

Ellis, R., Skehan, P., Li, S., Shintani, N., & Lambert, C. (2019). *Task-based language teaching: Theory and practice*. Cambridge University Press.

García Mayo, M. P. (2018). Focused versus unfocused tasks. In J. I. Liontas (Ed.), *The TESOL Encyclopedia of English Language Teaching* (pp. 1–5). John Wiley & Sons.

González-Lloret, M. (2016). *A practical guide to integrating technology into task-based language teaching*. Georgetown University Press.

González-Lloret, M. (2017). Technology and task-based language teaching. In S. Thorne & S. May (Eds.), *Language, education and technology. Encyclopedia of language and education* (3rd ed., pp. 193–205). Springer.

González-Lloret, M. (2020). Using technology-mediated tasks in second language instruction to connect speakers internationally. In C. Lambert & R. Oliver (Eds.), *Using tasks in second language teaching: Practice in diverse contexts* (pp. 65–81). Multilingual Matters.

González-Lloret, M., & Ortega, L. (Eds.). (2014). *Technology-mediated TBLT: Researching technology and tasks*. John Benjamins.

Green, C. (2005). Integrating extensive reading in the task-based curriculum. *ELT Journal*, 59(4), 306–311.

Hinkel, E. (2010). Integrating the four skills: Current and historical perspectives. In R. Kaplan (Ed.), *The Oxford handbook of applied linguistics* (2nd ed., pp. 110–123). Oxford University Press.

Krashen, S. (1985). *The input hypothesis: Issues and implications*. Longman.

Long, M. (1985). A role for instruction in second language acquisition: Task-based language teaching. In K. Hylstenstam & M. Pienemann (Eds.), *Modelling and assessing second language acquisition* (pp. 77–99). Multilingual Matters.

Long, M. (2015). *Second language acquisition and task-based language teaching*. Wiley-Blackwell.

Long, M. (2018). Interaction in L2 classrooms. In J. I. Liontas (Ed.), *The TESOL encyclopedia of English language teaching* (pp. 1–7). John Wiley & Sons.

Loschky, L., & Bley-Vroman, R. (1993). Grammar and task-based methodology. In G. Crookes & S. Gass (Eds.), *Tasks and language learning: Integrating theory and practice* (pp. 123–163). Multilingual Matters.

Mounts, E., & Smirnova, L. (2011). *A task-based approach to teaching reading*. Proceedings of the 5th International Technology, Education and Development Conference (INTED 2011), 7–9 March, Valencia: Spain, 4046–4050.

Nunan, D. (1989). *Designing tasks for the communicative classroom*. Cambridge University Press.

Nunan, D. (2004). *Task-based language teaching*. Cambridge University Press.

Philp, J., Adams, R., & Iwashita, N. (2014). *Peer interaction and second language learning*. Routledge.

Pica, T., Kanagy, R., & Falodin, J. (1993). Choosing and using communication tasks for second language instruction and research. In G. Crookes & S. Gass (Eds.), *Task and language learning: Integrating theory and practice* (pp. 9–34). Multilingual Matters.

Prabhu, N. (1987). *Second language pedagogy*. Oxford University Press.

Prabhu, N. S. (1982). *The Communicational Teaching Project, South India*. The British Council.

Prabhu, N. S., & Carroll, D. J. (1980). Syllabus design and methodology. *Newsletter (Special Series), Bangalore Regional Institute of English*, 1(4), 1–20.

Robinson, P. (2011). Task-based language learning: A review of issues. *Language Learning*, 61(s1), 1–36.

Samuda, V., & Bygate, M. (2008). *Tasks in second language learning*. Palgrave Macmillan.

Skehan, P. (1998). *A cognitive approach to language learning*. Oxford University Press.

Skehan, P., & Foster, P. (1998). Task type and task processing conditions as influences on foreign language performance. *Language Teaching Research*, 1(3), 185–211.

Van den Branden, K. (2006). Introduction: Task-based language teaching in a nutshell. In K. Van den Branden (Ed.), *Task-based language education: From theory to practice* (pp. 1–16). Cambridge University Press.

Willis, D., & Willis, J. (2007). *Doing task-based teaching*. Oxford University Press.

Willis, J. (1996). *A framework for task-based learning*. Longman Pearson Education.

Ziegler, N. (2016). Taking technology to task: Technology-mediated TBLT, performance, and production. *Annual Review of Applied Linguistics*, 36, 136–163.

PART II
Practising TBLT

4

PUTTING TBLT INTO PRACTICE

The Bigger Picture

Introduction

Part I of this book has focused on the theoretical underpinnings of TBLT. In particular, I have considered an interactionist stance on teaching and learning, with roles and expectations for both teachers and learners in the L2 classroom. I have also looked in some detail at the construct of task, and considered several examples of tasks that might be utilised in the task-oriented classroom. In Part II, I explore issues regarding the practical implementation of TBLT. This does not mean that I will leave the theory behind. There are some aspects of theory that I will revisit, and others that need to be introduced. However, the emphasis in Part II is on issues pertaining to putting TBLT into practice. In particular, in this chapter I look at the bigger picture with regard to implementing TBLT and consider some of the implications for TBLT implementation that arise from how it has been put into practice in different circumstances.

The chapter begins by presenting brief illustrative examples of some of the contexts where TBLT ideas have been utilised. There are other situations that could have been chosen. The ones I present have been selected to illustrate several of the different motivations for, and outworkings of, TBLT across the globe. They serve to illustrate that TBLT ideas are being entertained in diverse contexts internationally. They also illustrate that the TBLT endeavour is not straightforward or easy, and that TBLT in practice is subject to both meaningful steps forward and challenging steps back. Later in the chapter, and building on some of the issues emerging from the contexts I present, I consider different types of syllabus that may inform language teaching and learning programmes. I go on to look at what these syllabus types might look like in the hands of individual teachers who may wish to explore task-based ideas.

Some Contexts Where TBLT Ideas Have Been Introduced

India

The Bangalore Communicational Teaching Project (CTP), which I referred to in Chapter 3, was a school-based programme in South India, implemented by N. S. Prabhu, to improve learners' acquisition of English as L2. The project's impact has been reasonably extensively documented. Prabhu himself provided a valuable summative book-length discussion (Prabhu, 1987).

The project represented an early attempt to devise a learning programme based on tasks. It arose from dissatisfaction with the prevailing accuracy-oriented practices that were then in play, which included the so-called Structural-Oral-Situational (SOS) syllabus. This kind of syllabus aimed to be communicative, but was strongly teacher-led, graded according to perceived hierarchies of complexity of grammar and lexis, and placed emphasis on controlled practice of discrete language items through structural drilling.

The CTP ran for five years between 1979 and 1984. Eight classes of children aged between 8 and 13, and in a range of schools in different towns and districts, took part. The project involved, in total, 18 teachers and 390 students. There were no pre-conceived ideas about how the teaching should go. There was, rather, a general idea of what the project wanted to achieve, but, as I noted in Chapter 3, it was really a process of trial and error to see what might work and what might not work. There was, however, a continued two-way engagement between theory and practice, and opportunities for the unfolding findings to be discussed in several fora.

It is reported that, in practice, there was minimal deviation from the schools' normal (teacher-led) modes of operation. There was also a strong focus on individual processing of language input, rather than opportunities for collaborative interaction. However, perhaps the most major step forward to come out of this seminal project was the articulation of three archetypal task types (information gap, reasoning gap and opinion gap) which have informed the repertoire of types that are often drawn on in the TBLT-oriented classroom (see Chapter 3).

Belgium

A more recent interesting case of TBLT implementation was the introduction of TBLT into programmes for Dutch as L1 or L2 in Flanders, the Dutch-speaking region of Belgium, beginning in 1990. This was a large-scale and long-term initiative targeted at learners in primary, secondary and adult education contexts. One target group was adult speakers of Dutch as L2. Many of these had immigrated into Flanders from the 1960s as a consequence of changes in immigration policies, or held refugee status. There was a perceived need to enhance these learners' proficiency in Dutch in order to help them to integrate more fully into Flemish society. Moreover, the children of these groups were often under-achieving in school. They thereby became a strong focus of the initiative.

As with the Bangalore project, the Flanders case arose out of a perceived dissatisfaction with the efficacy of more traditional structural approaches. Van den Branden (2006) noted that, up to the time of the project, language education in Flanders had tended to utilise a top-down, behaviourist-informed, audio-lingual approach. He went on to explain that many teachers, policy makers and educationalists did not see this technique as responding sufficiently to the language needs that immigrants were presenting. In this light, TBLT was perceived as having "much potential" due to "its emphasis on needs analysis, primacy of functional, meaningful tasks and its link to real-world objectives" (p. 14).

Unlike in the Bangalore project, which was largely intuitive in nature, in the Flanders case task-based syllabi, materials and extensive teacher professional development initiatives were put in place to support the introduction of the programmes. Teacher support initiatives for teachers in schools ran from 1994 to 2003, and during this period different iterations were tried out, evaluated and adapted (Norris, 2015). These factors were among those influencing the relative success of the implementation of TBLT in the context. Indeed, several publications emerging from the project have demonstrated the level of success that was achieved (e.g., Van den Branden, 2006, 2009; Van den Branden et al., 2007).

Hong Kong

Carless (2003, 2007, 2009) described an initiative to introduce TBLT for the teaching of English as L2 into primary and secondary schools in Hong Kong. This was essentially, as with Flanders, a top-down initiative whereby, since the late 1990s, TBLT became officially adopted through prescribed syllabi, both at the primary school level (Curriculum Development Council, 1997) and at the secondary school level (Curriculum Development Council, 1999). These documents were subsequently updated (Curriculum Development Council, 2002, 2007), but continued to advocate for a task-based approach.

The earlier (1999) secondary document, for example, supported TBLT on the following basis:

> The task-based approach aims at providing opportunities for learners to experiment with and explore both spoken and written language through learning activities which are designed to engage learners in the authentic, practical and functional use of language for meaningful purposes.
>
> *(Curriculum Development Council, 1999, p. 41)*

This emphasis continued in the newer 2007 document:

> The task-based approach to language learning emphasizes learning to communicate through purposeful interaction. Through the use of tasks, learners are provided with purposeful contexts and engaged in processes that require

them to exercise critical thinking and creativity, explore issues and solutions, and learn to use the language skills and functions, grammar items and structures, vocabulary, and tone, style and register for meaningful communication.

(Curriculum Development Council, 2007, p. 73)

The Hong Kong context usefully illustrates both the potential and the challenges of TBLT. The context is, as Carless (2012) explained, "a predominantly conventional teaching culture in which grammar has generally been taught through explicit explanation and controlled practice" (p. 349). TBLT, then, was once more viewed as a reaction to traditional structural approaches. Nevertheless, in its context, the innovation represented by TBLT has met with some resistance in practice, and explicit exploration of grammar remains a key component. As a consequence, and as Chan (2019) commented, the curriculum documents in the Hong Kong context illustrate a "hybrid" version of TBLT which demonstrates "a transition from a linguistic and lexical syllabus to one oriented towards communicative functions, that uses tasks as the main activities *and* considers language forms as equally important" (p. 13, my emphasis).

China

Within a highly centralised education system, China's Ministry of Education is responsible for proposing the curriculum for all public schools and universities. Furthermore, English is mandated by the Ministry of Education as a compulsory course starting from primary school and through to tertiary level. Students have historically been taught mainly through a grammar-translation approach, influenced by a Confucian Heritage Culture which emphasised the teacher's role in the classroom endeavour and principles such as memorisation and repetition.

However, support for the implementation of TBLT in Chinese primary and secondary schools can be found in the Chinese National English Curriculum Standards (NECS) (see, e.g., Chinese Ministry of Education, 2001, 2011). TBLT is also promoted at tertiary level in the College English Curriculum Requirements (CECR) (see, e.g., Chinese Ministry of Education, 2007).

With regard to the NECS, revised standards have shifted the emphasis onto students' ability to use English for communicative purposes. The 2001 document, for example, stated, "[t]he main task for the new English curriculum is to shift from overemphasizing the transmission mode of teaching and learning based on grammar and vocabulary to the development of students' overall ability in language use." TBLT was seen at the time as one means to develop "students' comprehensive language competence" through promoting learning as "a process during which students develop language proficiency" (Chinese Ministry of Education, 2001, p. 1, cited in Wang, 2009, pp. 280–281).

Despite the mandatory nature of learning English in China, and an encouragement towards TBLT, the NECS did not make any particular teaching approach mandatory. Nevertheless, performance descriptors reflected a meaning-focused, task-oriented pedagogy, and additionally, from 2001 textbooks were subject to review by the National Textbook Review Committee of China's Ministry of Education (Wang, 2009). Once reviewed positively, books could be recommended for use. The endorsement of textbooks became one means of encouraging the pedagogical approaches that were being recommended at the level of curriculum.

In practice, however, having to deal with large classes and grammar-oriented examinations have tended to be two reasons why otherwise positive teachers might shy away from implementing task-based ideas, especially in a context where grammar instruction has continued to be seen as a valued component of teaching English as L2 (Ji & Pham, 2020; Skehan & Luo, 2020; Xiongyong & Samuel, 2011; Zheng & Borg, 2014).

New Zealand

As a final illustrative example, I present a brief overview of the New Zealand case. A communicative approach to language teaching has been in evidence in New Zealand's schools sector for several decades. However, the publication of a revised national curriculum (New Zealand Ministry of Education, 2007), mandated from 2010, brought the communicative agenda to the fore in a newly established learning area, *Learning Languages*. A revised curriculum statement made expectations of the new learning area clear: "[t]his learning area puts students' ability to communicate at the centre by making Communication the core strand [central focus]. ... In the core Communication strand, students learn to use the language to make meaning" (p. 24). Additionally, the revised curriculum encouraged, across all curriculum areas, learner-centred and experiential pedagogical approaches.

As a consequence of the new learning area and the pedagogical directions being signalled, TBLT became highlighted as one means of fulfilling curricular expectations in school L2 classrooms. To support teachers with implementing task-based ideas, a range of support initiatives was put in place, including explanatory documents and professional development opportunities. In particular, teachers' attention was drawn to effective principles for enhancing second language acquisition (SLA), including input, output and interaction (see Chapter 2), alongside Ellis's four-fold classification of a task (see Chapter 3) (New Zealand Ministry of Education, 2017). Furthermore, interactionist perspectives on learning (both cognitive and sociocultural – see Chapter 2) were emphasised and promoted (New Zealand Ministry of Education, 2011).

However, a principle embedded in curriculum delivery in the New Zealand context is that schools are to be regarded as individual and independent entities, and school leaders are free to interpret the expectations of the curriculum according to their local contexts and perceived priorities. In this regard, although the curriculum itself is mandatory in government-funded schools, and its communicative emphasis for language learning is therefore also an expectation, its modes of delivery are not prescribed. Thus, TBLT itself has not been mandated and teachers are free to borrow TBLT ideas (or not) depending on their own local circumstances and interpretations of the communicative agenda.

Implications for Implementing TBLT

The above illustrative cases make it apparent that a decision may be made to implement TBLT for a range of reasons. These may include bottom-up reasons – one or more practitioners working in a local context express dissatisfaction with more teacher-oriented, accuracy-focused pathways and syllabus expectations, decide that they would like to try something new, and start looking into how they might experiment with task-based ideas; top-down reasons – a particular educational jurisdiction makes the decision to introduce TBLT as the officially sanctioned approach, and educational establishments within that jurisdiction are required to implement it by virtue of authorised syllabi; or a combination of both – recommended from those in authority, with implementation in the hands of local teachers. In contexts where TBLT is being considered or introduced, teachers may be able to access, in addition to syllabi, professional development opportunities, support resources, course outlines and textbooks to help them in their endeavour.

It is also apparent that, as I previously stated, the process of implementing TBLT ideas is not necessarily smooth and unproblematic. Both advances and challenges will be encountered in the process of putting TBLT into practice. This suggests that, regardless of the approach to or reasons for adoption, all contexts in which TBLT is being entertained as an option or expectation require certain elements to be considered above and beyond the construct of *task*. In other words, a key question to be addressed, regardless of context, is: how can teachers put TBLT into practice? When it comes to answering that question, it is important to say at the outset that, whereas there is generally broad agreement about the essential characteristics of a task (real-world relationship; focus on meaning; gap; and outcome), there is considerable debate about where, when and how tasks fit into the bigger picture of effective pedagogical practice (as can be seen in some of the tensions emerging in, for example, Hong Kong and mainland China).

Reflection Point

The varied cases of TBLT implementation I have introduced show several distinct differences, but also some commonalities.

1. What perceived benefits for TBLT can be seen in these cases?
2. What hindrances to successful TBLT implementation are apparent?
3. In your own context (or a context you are familiar with), can you identify which benefits and hindrances might be in evidence if task-based ideas were being considered?

Recapping a Bit of History

It would be useful at this point briefly to review some of the central tensions I explored in some depth in Part I of this book. Essentially, and going back to the theories of learning I presented in Chapters 1 and 2, the pedagogical bigger picture has been shaped by different understandings of what makes learning effective. Indeed, as I explored in those chapters, these different understandings on learning have influenced the kinds of methods for and approaches to language teaching that have emerged over the years.

Earlier and essentially behaviourist-informed approaches such as grammar-translation and audio-lingualism focused on accuracy, with strong components being the explicit teaching of grammar (in grammar-translation), or memorisation and repetition of grammatically accurate phrases (in audio-lingualism). By contrast, the essentially innatist-informed Natural Approach emphasised using language for genuinely communicative reasons, but there was no direct teaching of grammar, and therefore no overt attention paid to accuracy. Communicative Language Teaching (CLT) held out some promise as a means of reconciling these polarisations, allowing room for both what the teacher does and the learners do.

Despite the potential for greater integration, polarisations within CLT itself became evidenced by stronger forms (learner-centred and experiential, at the expense of explicit teaching of rules) and weaker forms (teacher-led and expository, at the expense of opportunities for learners to be creative with language). Furthermore, weak CLT early became embedded as more favoured in instructed contexts (Howatt, 1984). TBLT emerged as a learner-centred and experiential response to structure-based approaches such as weak CLT. Nonetheless, it sought (in line with interactionist theories of learning) to reconcile and take into account not only the different but important roles of the teacher and the learner, but also a balanced focus on both fluency and accuracy. Its central component was the communicative task.

Polarisations within TBLT

The contrasting cases of TBLT implementation that I presented at the start of this chapter demonstrate that, in spite of its learner-focused, experiential underpinnings, TBLT itself has been subject to different emphases (in particular with regard to the teacher's role) as it has developed in different contexts over the decades. This is perhaps inevitable as practitioners have grappled with various challenges in diverse contexts. For example, Prabhu's (1987) early reactionary experimentation was essentially driven by innatist-informed ideas; by contrast, the version of TBLT that began to emerge in Hong Kong was strongly influenced by behaviourist-oriented teacher-led elements. As with CLT, TBLT, it seems, is also subject to stronger and weaker variants.

Seen from the perspective of an interactionist continuum (see Chapter 1), largely learner-centred practices would be located at the stronger end, with mainly teacher-led practices at the weaker end. Variants to TBLT find themselves at different points. This means that, in practice, adherents who lean more towards the learner-centred end would place greater emphasis on inherent cognitive processes, and on what the learners are doing; others who place themselves more towards the teacher-led end would place greater emphasis on the external environment which provides samples of the language to be learned, and on what the teacher does. There is, as I noted in Chapter 1, not simply one interactionist perspective on learning. This leads to complexity when it comes to the implementation of TBLT.

In the strongest form of TBLT, engaging in tasks may be seen as "the *necessary and sufficient* condition of successful second language acquisition" (Nunan, 2004, p. 21, my emphasis) and "the need to transact tasks is seen as adequate to drive forward language development" (Skehan, 1996, p. 39) in much the same way as people learn their L1. As Bygate (2016) explained, in strong TBLT both the syllabus/curriculum and the pedagogic procedures advocated within it revolve around tasks, the core learning and teaching processes in the programme are directly derived from the tasks, and there is no initial selection of the language to be prioritised. From this perspective, learners in the strongest TBLT classroom would essentially be required to engage in a series of tasks. Processing the rules of language use would be implicit and unconscious. The learning assumption would be that, provided that the tasks are set up adequately and appropriately, learning and acquisition will take place without the need for direct teacher intervention.

In East (2012), I proposed an argument against the claims of the strongest form of TBLT because it seems to be built on the premise that TBLT is "effectively a teacher-free zone, in which tasks work their effect without any need for mediation." I concluded that, seen from an interactionist standpoint, "teacher input and direction have crucial roles to play in helping students to execute tasks successfully" (p. 82).

In strong forms of TBLT positioned further along the continuum, a learner-centred and experiential perspective would still place solid emphasis on the tasks as the central components and would also emphasise the learners' ability to derive the rules of language use from the interactions. However, some form of mediation from the teacher, for example, in terms of feedback on language use, would play a part (see the comprehensible output and interaction hypotheses presented in Chapter 2, and also how grammar may be attended to, Chapter 6). In these cases, the teacher becomes "a crucial interactional partner in task-based language classrooms" (Van den Branden, 2009, p. 284), but emphasis is still placed on learners' ability to notice for themselves how language works. In some instances, this perspective would not preclude, in Bygate's (2016) words, "the use of non-task-like activities to develop formal control, fluency or understanding of particular formal features." However, these activities would "act as adjuncts to the main [task-based] elements of the programme" (p. 387).

Skehan (1996) also presented a weaker view of TBLT where tasks, although necessary, were *not* sufficient, and where tasks were "a vital part of language instruction, but … embedded in a more complex pedagogic context" (p. 39). In a more dominantly teacher-led perspective on TBLT towards the other end of the continuum, tasks would also be important elements, but the teacher would have a more central role to play, offering direct instruction where this is perceived to be necessary, either before the task, or after the task, or both. Again, non-task-like activities may (and probably will) feature. These weaker forms of TBLT do not involve task-based syllabi or a task-exclusive curriculum, even though lessons would use tasks to encourage and invoke meaningful communicative interaction, just as might be found in stronger forms of TBLT. However, the tasks may act as "self-contained activities, without a close relationship to the other pedagogic procedures used in the programme" (Bygate, 2016, p. 387). This form of TBLT might be labelled task-*supported* language teaching, or TSLT.

At its weakest, TSLT arguably replicates the classic Presentation-Practice-Production (PPP) model, and could certainly be used in the PPP-oriented classroom, with tasks contributing to the production stage. Indeed, Ellis (e.g., 2017, 2019) has suggested that TSLT *is* realised through a PPP pattern. In this case, the tasks used in the final (production) stage may require the utilisation of the grammar that has been introduced in the first (presentation) stage (but may also provide greater scope for genuine communication than more traditional forms of PPP). This, however, might make some realisations of TSLT effectively no different from weak CLT and brings with it the risk that TSLT will suffer from the essential weakness of weak CLT – limitations in developing fluency and automaticity in language use.

The pedagogical complexity in the above scenarios is that the enactment of TBLT is likely to see a blurring of the lines between learner-centred and experiential, and teacher-led and expository. This blurring of the lines has led, for example, to Hall's (2018) conclusion, which I noted at the start of Chapter 1, that it can be difficult to pin down exactly what TBLT is, because the approach has been interpreted and enacted in different contexts in significantly different ways. Hall went on to raise several important practical questions for TBLT, for example, whether it is possible to teach solely though tasks, or whether task-relevant language should be pre-taught or not.

At what point, then, does task-*based* become task-*supported*? This is a crucial question with regard to defining the limits or boundaries of TBLT, and is one to which I will return later in this chapter, and also in the final chapter of this book. At this stage, this question can perhaps be addressed in large part by considering what influences the programme that is being adopted. That is, as Bygate (2016) illustrated, stronger forms of TBLT would be informed by a programme that is fully *task*-centred. In these forms of TBLT, the task is really all that matters. Weaker forms of TBLT may be represented in a programme that provides an initial selection of language priorities. In these forms of TBLT, tasks are still important, but they may be utilised alongside non-task-like activities.

Furthermore, the cases of task implementation that I presented at the start of this chapter illustrate that what is usually driving the programme is some form of syllabus. A new kind of syllabus influences the programme, and underpins the motivation to explore task-based ideas as a way of guiding what might happen in the classroom. The syllabus thereby becomes, as Widdowson (1990) early claimed, "an instrument of educational policy" whereby its goals are "formulated not only in reference to [perceived] pedagogic effectiveness but also in accordance with ideological positions concerning the nature of education in general" (p. 127). The syllabus represents what those who have designed it believe to be important in the context.

Regardless of the approach to L2 teaching being taken, or the elements that are emphasised as a consequence of the underlying theory of learning, the syllabus is arguably a crucial component. If the goal of an L2 programme is to implement TBLT in some form, it makes sense to look at the syllabus that underlies the programme and reflect on the extent to which it promotes that goal.

The Importance of the Syllabus

Essentially, the purpose of the syllabus (however conceptualised and constructed) is to describe for teachers in a systematic way what is going to be taught. It provides the overall framework and direction for working with students over the course of a year, or several years, or several (progressive) levels, and therefore sets the pedagogic agenda. Below, I present three different approaches to syllabus design and construction:

1. the synthetic (Type A) syllabus, or, "teach the grammar in careful sequences, and let the learners synthesise the parts"
2. the analytic (Type B) syllabus, or, "present the language holistically, and let the learners analyse it for themselves"
3. the hybrid (multi-dimensional) syllabus, or, "combine the elements into a single framework."

It is important to recognise that the above syllabus types represent broad brush-stroke classifications that do not necessarily map neatly or exclusively onto the theories of learning I have emphasised in this book. Furthermore, as Long and Crookes (1992) suggested, synthetic and analytic should not necessarily be viewed in mutually exclusive, dichotomous terms, but, rather, as two points on a continuum. However, the three classifications do provide a convenient means of considering the foundational principles that inform how a syllabus may be constructed.

The Synthetic (Type A) Syllabus

Johnson (2009) noted that, until the 1970s, the dominant syllabus that informed L2 teaching and learning programmes was essentially *structural*, and organised around the grammar to be taught. This kind of grammatical syllabus attempts to categorise and order the teaching and learning in terms of a hierarchy of grammatical structures – a list and sequence of the rules, possibly with an associated list of vocabulary items. These syllabi are essentially top-down – that is, constructed *a priori* and effectively imposed on teachers as the blueprints (or descriptions) to be followed with regard to course or programme delivery (i.e., the curriculum).

Structure-based syllabi reflect what we might refer to as a "synthetic" approach to language teaching and learning whereby the different language items are to be taught in a step-by-step hierarchical way, and language acquisition is viewed as the gradual accumulation of individual parts to eventually make a more complete whole. Synthetic syllabi thus segment the target language into distinct items, propose that different elements of the language should be taught separately, and place the student into the role of *synthesising* the language, that is, combining the elements into a whole. These Type A syllabi focus on *what* should be learned. They are therefore product-oriented and determine a series of discrete objectives, with learners exposed sequentially to deliberately restricted samples of language.

Structural syllabi informed and underpinned behaviourist-influenced teaching approaches such as grammar-translation and audio-lingualism. However, developments to language pedagogy that occurred around the 1970s brought with them challenges to the traditional structural syllabus design, and refinements that went in several directions (Johnson, 2009). As part of the communicative agenda, Wilkins (1981) differentiated between the traditional grammatical syllabus and two other types: a *situational* syllabus (sometimes referred to as oral-situational) which orders and organises for teaching purposes the situations in which language may be used – buying food and drink, visiting the doctor, booking into a hotel, etc. – and a *notional* syllabus (sometimes referred to as notional-functional) which emphasises "the meanings expressed or the functions performed through language" (p. 83) – apologising, requesting, negotiating, disagreeing, etc. In these kinds of syllabus, grammar and vocabulary may also be prescribed.

Wilkins proposed that communicatively oriented situational or notional syllabi may be described as "analytic." He argued this on the basis that, in these syllabi, the focus is on meaning, and language is viewed more holistically. Underpinned by the aim to develop learners' communicative competence in the L2, these syllabi are ostensibly organised in terms of the students and their needs, that is, the purposes for which students are learning the L2, and therefore what they need to be able to do linguistically to fulfil communicative goals.

However, a careful look at situational or notional syllabi reveals that they are in fact also synthetic. They prescribe the situations and functions, they provide limited communicational opportunities because they are situated within certain settings, and they do not necessarily help learners to develop the interactional skills they need to transfer their knowledge to other contexts. Learning a language may be seen as being for communicative and real-world purposes, but the communicative goal is on the product (i.e., learning the language that is necessary to carry out a particular function). As Ellis (2019) argued, both *grammatically* and *communicatively* oriented syllabi were not essentially different. Whether the grammar items were prescribed (in the case of the former) or the contexts, notions and functions were presented (in the case of the latter), both were "interventionist and other-directed" in that "they sought to plot the course of learning for the learner" (p. 455). These kinds of syllabi informed the PPP approach within weak CLT (or the SOS syllabus whose efficacy was questioned by Prabhu).

The Analytic (Type B) Syllabus

Long and Crookes (1993) early provided a valuable critique of synthetic syllabi, whether grammatically or communicatively oriented: the content of such syllabi, they argued, is "ultimately based on an analysis of the language to be learned, whether this be overt, as in the case of structure, word, notion or function, or covert, as has usually been the case with situation and topic." Each teaching point or communicative function is taught in an isolated way. Long and Crookes went on to argue that, with regard to research into processes of SLA, no evidence has been presented to support a claim that these discrete synthetic units are "meaningful acquisition units," or that they are or can be "acquired separately, singly, in linear fashion" or "learned prior to and separate from language use" (pp. 26–27).

Holistic analytic syllabi arguably take account of Long and Crookes' (1993) criticism. In these kinds of process-oriented syllabi, in contrast to traditional syllabi, language foci are selected on the basis of communicative criteria. Hence, they take into account the communicative contexts in which learners might need to use language and the kinds of language students are likely to need to acquire for those contexts. Most fundamentally, they focus on the *process* of acquiring automaticity in language use, rather than the *end-product* of a particular teaching sequence. They may even emerge from a process of negotiation between teachers and students about what should be important foci for learning. In this regard, they may be considered as bottom-up in terms of design, and may be referred to as Type B – syllabi that are concerned with *how* the language is learned and how this language can be integrated with learners' experiences.

Purely task-based syllabi are analytic and Type B. Long (2015), for example, discussed an approach that may be taken to designing a syllabus conceptualised in terms of tasks, with the focus placed on students' ability to perform these tasks. As I intimated in Chapter 3, Long's approach was to plan pedagogic tasks that learners would be asked to complete in class as reflections of a wide range of the real-world tasks they might need to carry out outside of class. The important issue here is on the kinds of real-world tasks that students may ultimately need to engage in. That is, there are vast numbers of activities that people take part in, whether professionally, academically or socially. Language learners will only ever undertake a sub-set of these, and that sub-set can potentially be quite distinctly defined, depending on the students and why they are learning the L2. For example, if a group of nurses is enrolled in a language course specifically to develop proficiency in relation to their chosen profession, it would make sense that classroom-based tasks would reflect dimensions of the kinds of real-world tasks that they may need to undertake in that professional context.

For Long, therefore, an important component of task selection for a Type B syllabus is needs analysis. This analysis provides the opportunity for teachers, perhaps in collaboration with students, to explore the particular language learning and communicative needs of the class, and, on that basis, to design an appropriate syllabus based on tasks. In Long's view, a genuine task-based syllabus will be context-specific. It will not expect all students in all contexts, or even all students in the same context, to follow an identical programme.

Once a range of real-world tasks has been pinpointed through needs analysis, sample tasks with features in common may be grouped together and become a set of *target task types* from which pedagogic tasks can be derived. The syllabus thus becomes a sequence of pedagogic tasks, and, more importantly, one that has been informed by the immediate context of the learners. As learners complete this series of sequenced tasks, they are "helped to develop their language abilities gradually to meet the demands of increasingly complex tasks" (Long, 2015, p. 222). As Robinson and Gilabert (2007) argued, the aim of pedagogic task *sequences* is "to gradually approximate, in classroom settings, the full complexity of real-world *target task* demands" (p. 162), both situationally and interactionally. Hence, there is a hierarchy, but that hierarchy is determined by the relative complexity of the task (an issue I take up in Chapter 5), rather than by a pre-determined ascending order of complexity of grammatical structures or a prescribed order of communicative situations or functions.

Reflection Point

A syllabus of some kind frequently provides the blueprint for how teachers should plan and organise what happens in the L2 classroom.

1. What kinds of syllabus are you familiar with? How were they organised? Could you identify the syllabus as Type A or Type B?
2. How helpful do you think the syllabus is when planning for teaching?
3. When it comes to support with implementing TBLT, what elements would you like to see in a syllabus? What elements would you regard as unhelpful?

Different Syllabi for Different Purposes

It should be clear from the above that a strongly task-*based* pedagogical approach will be informed by a holistic, process-oriented, analytic Type B syllabus. In this kind of learner-centred syllabus, the focus is on meaning and communication and meeting students' communicative needs. It may be non-interventionist on the part of the teacher, but does not preclude reactive feedback on learners' task performances in order to enhance SLA. Additionally, in contrast to a hierarchical step-by-step model (Type A), this kind of syllabus arguably "allows for a great deal of naturalistic recycling ... [and] grammatical and functional items will reappear numerous times in a diverse range of contexts" (Nunan, 2004, p. 30).

This, in Nunan's view, makes it "consistent with an 'organic' view of acquisition in which numerous items are acquired simultaneously, albeit imperfectly" (p. 30). By contrast, a task-*supported* approach sits better within, and is arguably only operationalised on the basis of, a traditional, product-oriented, synthetic Type A syllabus. This kind of syllabus is prescriptive and hierarchical, and tasks become the vehicles to practise, in communicative contexts, the language, situations or notions prescribed in, and pre-taught in accordance with, the syllabus.

The distinction between Type B and Type A also suggests a clear demarcation between TBLT and TSLT. Certainly, some theorists (e.g., Ellis, 2017, 2019) make that distinction, suggesting an incompatibility. As I have already made clear, however, the real-world reality is that TBLT in practice is subject to a range of operationalisations. If we view TBLT enactment on an interactionist continuum between learner-centred and teacher-led, this is inevitable. It does, however, blur the discrepancies between the two syllabus types and also the distinction between TBLT and TSLT. This inevitability is exacerbated when we consider that teachers are pivotal in the enactment of syllabi. I will come to the teacher's role in all of this towards the end of this chapter. At this point, however, it would be useful to consider the argument for a hybrid syllabus.

A Hybrid Syllabus

What I have presented so far has, as Johnson (2009) put it, considered syllabi "as if they were, and had to be, mutually exclusive." In other words, a syllabus or course designer chooses "one parameter (the structure, the situation, the task, the function etc.) as the unit of organisation for a course, to the exclusion of all others" (p. 330). Johnson went on to assert that this does not have to be the case. One example of combining different elements for purposes of TBLT is Ellis's (2019, 2020) proposal for a "modular" syllabus. This kind of syllabus, he suggested, allows for discrete work on tasks, complemented by discrete work on structure.

As I previously noted, Ellis (2019) drew a clear distinction between TBLT, as operationalised through a Type B (task-based) syllabus which leans considerably towards the experiential end of the interactionist continuum, and TSLT, put into operation through a Type A (structurally oriented) syllabus which is essentially more teacher-dominated. He thus argued for a clear demarcation between TBLT and TSLT because they draw on different theories of learning and teaching, and, consequently, different syllabus types.

The essential difference between Type A and Type B lay in what Ellis described as the analysis component of the teaching and learning sequence. Thus, both approaches allow for attention to grammar (or form), but this attention differs with regard to whether it is, as Ellis (2020, p. 186) put it, "pre-planned and emergent" (Type A) or "just emergent" (Type B). He argued, however, that curricula or teaching plans derived from the two different approaches can involve identical instructional components even though these may be presented in a different order. Ellis has also asserted (2019) that, in his view, both TBLT and TSLT are needed, especially in instructed contexts. In this regard, he built on an early argument by Brumfit (1984) that learners ideally required an integrated curriculum that would enable a variable focus on fluency and accuracy in accordance with the developmental stage of the learners.

For Ellis (2019), the key question thus became "how to combine product- and process-based approaches" (p. 459). Ellis's modular syllabus proposal provides one means of doing this. Operationally, the modules, by his argument, should be kept distinct (albeit occurring, as necessary, in the same lesson, and not precluding opportunities to integrate accuracy and fluency through certain activities).

One of the models Ellis (2019) proposed was a model that "reverses the traditional sequence of instruction" (p. 464). That is, unlike a traditional PPP sequence, an inverted approach begins with a task or tasks, but goes on to introduce the structural component at a later stage, continuing this stage for as long as it is perceived that learners need it. Nevertheless, the emphasis is on the process, and it is proposed that the task-based component should be more dominant.

In Ellis's proposed modular approach, the structure-based component could be viewed as being "remedial" rather than prescriptive or hierarchical. The structural module would therefore not be used as a basis for pre-planning and sequencing (as with Type A). Rather, its purpose would be to note items that might present problems as a checklist against which teachers might determine the kinds of issues that require attention as emerging from learners' task performance. Furthermore, Ellis proposed that, at the beginner level, the focus might be exclusively on tasks. As learners progress in their proficiency, more room might be allowed for the structure-based component (even though, throughout, the task-based component would dominate). In contrast to a purely task-based (Type B) syllabus model, in a modular model "there is a structural component to address residual problems with specific grammatical features once basic L2 proficiency has been developed" (Ellis, 2019, p. 465). Thus, Ellis's modular proposal becomes a syllabus in which "the unit of organisation shifts at different points in the course" (Johnson, 2009, p. 331).

Ellis was careful not to present his model as "integrated." However, despite the proposed segregation of the two elements, in practice this is likely to become a combination (indeed, Ellis himself [2017] described the notion as hybrid). From this perspective, it becomes difficult to maintain a distinction between TBLT and TSLT. In turn, it may be suggested that the distinction is unhelpful, and returns us to the argument that TBLT may be enacted in a range of ways on the continuum from learner-centred and experiential to teacher-led and expository – although, for TBLT to be TBLT, learner-centred, experiential tasks must be central components.

The Teacher's Role in Enacting the Syllabus

The above presentation of different syllabus types suggests incompatibility, both theoretically and operationally, at the level of prescription and practice (Type A versus Type B). Ellis's (2019, 2020) modular model is an attempt to reconcile the incompatibility for the purposes of TBLT. The practical reality is that, just as different emphases within TBLT should be seen on a continuum, many teachers who wish to implement TBLT ideas will adopt a mixed or hybrid approach, and will place emphasis on stronger or weaker forms depending on a range of factors. These factors may influence syllabus *choice*, but they will also have an influence on syllabus *enactment*. In the final part of this chapter, I turn to the teacher's role in putting the syllabus into action.

Earlier in this chapter, I explained that the cases of task implementation I presented illustrate that some form of syllabus has supported the impetus to implement task-based ideas. It was also apparent from these cases that teachers did not blindly and uncritically follow and implement the syllabus. Teachers, it seems, mediated the requirements of the syllabus in response to what was happening in their own contexts (I will consider this reality more fully in Part III).

We can see elements of the clash between syllabus and action in the cases of Bangalore and Hong Kong. In the former context, a reaction against the structural syllabus that was then in play led to experimentation with tasks. In the latter case, a top-down syllabus to promote TBLT in classrooms was mediated by teachers who may have tried to hold on to more traditional teacher-led practices. In both cases, the clash between syllabus and enactment is precipitated by what is perceived to be effective practice in the context. Both cases illustrate that, regardless of the syllabus, TBLT in action can move in several directions – which may include embracing more task-based ideas in the face of a more structural syllabus, or conserving levels of traditional practice in the face of attempts at innovation. In both cases, the teacher is pivotal. Consequently, when it comes to putting TBLT into practice in classrooms, the syllabus, however conceptualised, may provide the *blueprint* for what is anticipated, but individual teachers will interpret the blueprint – hence a potential clash between what a *syllabus* proposes and what teachers *actually do*.

Nunan (2004), for example, conceptualised the interface between syllabus and classroom by differentiating between what he called curriculum as *plan* – presented in the syllabus, but also textbooks and other resources, alongside assessment instruments – and curriculum as *action* – operationalised by the moment-by-moment actions teachers take in response to what is going on in their classrooms as they seek to act on the plan.

According to Nunan's (2004) definition (p. 6), the *plan* (or *syllabus*) will do three things. It will:

1. propose the content to be delivered, or, "here is what you need to teach"
2. suggest how it is to be sequenced, or, "here is how you should teach it"
3. present rationales for its proposals, or, "here is why you need to teach it like this."

The *action* (or *methodology*) will also do three things. It will influence:

1. the precise content that is chosen for the classroom, or, "here is what I am actually going to teach"

2. how that precise content is sequenced, or, "here is how I am going to teach it"
3. how it is justified, or, "here is why I am going to teach it like this."

A clash can arise when there is a possible mismatch between what a syllabus proposes and what teachers consider to be effective. What, then, does this mean for practice?

Irrespective of the kind of syllabus in operation in their working contexts, teachers will still make choices about how and in what ways to implement it, perhaps selecting certain elements or emphasising particular components. In these ways, teachers exercise a significant level of control over what goes on in their classrooms. Thus, just as a task can operate at two levels – task-as-workplan (the planned action) and task-as-process (as interpreted and enacted by learners) (see Chapter 3) – syllabi can operate in the hands of teachers in a similar way.

The potential downside of the crucial mediating role of the teacher is that, even when presented with a Type B task-based syllabus, task-based ideas and principles may end up not being adopted at the level of the classroom. This is a significant challenge for TBLT which I take up in some detail in Part III. However, from the perspective of encouraging the effective implementation of TBLT in classrooms (which is what Part II of this book is all about), there is potential for TBLT ideas to be realised in classrooms, irrespective of the underlying syllabus.

Where the syllabus is in line with teachers' attempts to implement TBLT ideas (e.g., Type B), this can only be a strength. Where the syllabus works against TBLT (Type A), teachers may nonetheless circumvent the blueprint. They may, for example, introduce learner-centred tasks into their repertoires of practice even when faced with a prescriptive hierarchical syllabus.

Reflection Point

Ellis et al. (2019) asserted that the syllabus "should not function to *dictate* the procedures used in the classroom, but ... [rather] should provide teachers with *resources and freedom* to address the needs of learners differing in motivation and aptitudes as well as fluctuations in classroom dynamics" (p. 207, my emphases).

1. What do you think of this assertion?
2. How is the assertion helpful for the implementation of TBLT, whatever the context?
3. In what ways have you deviated from a prescribed syllabus in your teaching of an L2?

Conclusion

In this chapter, I have considered the TBLT bigger picture, including its diverse applications in a range of contexts and the underlying syllabi that inform these. I went on to suggest that the ultimate applications of TBLT, and the ultimate practical implementations of the syllabi, are in the hands of teachers themselves.

In contexts where teachers are open to TBLT ideas and genuinely wish to explore TBLT in practice, the curriculum in action will be influenced by three key steps that teachers might take, irrespective of the curriculum as plan, as they see for themselves what happens:

1. forward-planning, or, "I would like to try this new idea out"
2. moment-by-moment classroom decision-making, or, "how are my students responding to this new idea?" and "how should I respond to their responses?"
3. retrospective reflection, or, "what did we achieve in this lesson?" – leading to further forward-planning in light of how things went, or, "now I would like to try *this* out."

In the above light, and in particular in light of Steps 1 and 2 (planning and implementing something new), Chapters 5 and 6 return to the central task construct. However, the exploration now turns to how tasks fit into the broader context of teaching and learning sequences and how they can be put into practice in a range of ways. Consideration of the broader context respects both the crucial mediating role of teachers and the reality that an interactionist perspective on learning will be subject to (and allows for) different emphases in practice.

Suggested Further Reading

Bygate, M. (2016). Sources, developments and directions of task-based language teaching. *The Language Learning Journal, 44*(4), 381–400.

Long, M. (2015). Task-based syllabus design. In *Second language acquisition and task-based language teaching* (pp. 205–247). Wiley-Blackwell.

References

Brumfit, C. (1984). *Communicative methodology in language teaching: The roles of fluency and accuracy*. Cambridge University Press.

Bygate, M. (2016). Sources, developments and directions of task-based language teaching. *The Language Learning Journal, 44*(4), 381–400.

Carless, D. (2003). Factors in the implementation of task-based teaching in primary schools. *System, 31*(4), 485–500.

Carless, D. (2007). The suitability of task-based approaches for secondary schools: Perspectives from Hong Kong. *System, 35*(4), 595–608.

Carless, D. (2009). Revisiting the TBLT versus P-P-P debate: Voices from Hong Kong. *Asian Journal of English Language Teaching*, 19, 49–66.

Carless, D. (2012). TBLT in EFL settings: Looking back and moving forward. In A. Shehadeh & C. Coombe (Eds.), *Task-based language teaching in foreign language contexts: Research and implementation* (pp. 345–358). John Benjamins.

Chan, J. Y. H. (2019). Four decades of ELT development in Hong Kong: Impact of global theories on the changing curricula and textbooks. *Language Teaching Research* [online first], 1–25. doi:10.1177/1362168819865563.

Chinese Ministry of Education. (2001). *National English Curriculum Standards*. Beijing Normal University Press.

Chinese Ministry of Education (2007). *College English curriculum requirements*. Beijing Foreign Language Teaching and Research Press.

Chinese Ministry of Education (2011). *National English curriculum standards* (revised edition). Beijing Normal University Press.

Curriculum Development Council. (1997). *Syllabuses for primary schools: English language primary 1–6*. Government Printer.

Curriculum Development Council. (1999). *Syllabuses for secondary schools: English language (secondary 1–5)*. Government Printer.

Curriculum Development Council. (2002). *English language education key learning area: Curriculum guide (primary 1–secondary 3)*. Government Printer.

Curriculum Development Council. (2007). *English language education key learning area: English language curriculum and assessment guide (secondary 4–6)*. Government Printer.

East, M. (2012). *Task-based language teaching from the teachers' perspective: Insights from New Zealand*. John Benjamins.

Ellis, R. (2017). Task-based language teaching. In S. Loewen & M. Sato (Eds.), *The Routledge handbook of instructed second language acquisition* (pp. 108–125). Routledge.

Ellis, R. (2019). Towards a modular language curriculum for using tasks. *Language Teaching Research*, 23(4), 454–475.

Ellis, R. (2020). In defence of a modular curriculum for tasks. *ELT Journal*, 74(2), 185–194.

Ellis, R., Skehan, P., Li, S., Shintani, N., & Lambert, C. (2019). *Task-based language teaching: Theory and practice*. Cambridge University Press.

Hall, G. (2018). *Exploring English language teaching: Language in action* (2nd ed.). Routledge.

Howatt, A. P. R. (1984). *A history of English language teaching*. Oxford University Press.

Ji, Y., & Pham, T. (2020). Implementing task-based language teaching (TBLT) to teach grammar in English classes in China: Using design-based research to explore challenges and strategies. *Innovation in Language Learning and Teaching*, 14(2), 164–177.

Johnson, K. (2009). Foreign language syllabus design. In K. Knapp & B. Seidlhofer (Eds.), *Handbook of foreign language communication and learning* (pp. 309–340). De Gruyter.

Long, M. (1985). A role for instruction in second language acquisition: Task-based language teaching. In K. Hylstenstam & M. Pienemann (Eds.), *Modelling and assessing second language acquisition* (pp. 77–99). Multilingual Matters.

Long, M. (2015). Task-based syllabus design. In *Second language acquisition and task-based language teaching* (pp. 205–247). John Wiley & Sons.

Long, M., & Crookes, G. (1992). Three approaches to task-based syllabus design. *TESOL Quarterly*, 26, 27–56.

Long, M., & Crookes, G. (1993). Units of analysis in syllabus design – the case for task. In G. Crookes & S. Gass (Eds.), *Tasks in a pedagogical context: Inegrating theory and practice* (pp. 9–54). Multilingual Matters.

New Zealand Ministry of Education (2007). *The New Zealand curriculum*. Learning Media.

New Zealand Ministry of Education (2011). Genuine social interactions. http://seniorse condary.tki.org.nz/Learning-languages/Pedagogy/Social-interactions.

New Zealand Ministry of Education. (2017). Principles and actions that underpin effective teaching in languages. http://seniorsecondary.tki.org.nz/Learning-languages/Pedagogy/Principles-and-actions.

Norris, J. (2015). Thinking and acting programmatically in task-based language teaching: Essential roles for programme evaluation. In M. Bygate (Ed.), *Domains and directions in the development of TBLT: A decade of plenaries from the international conference* (pp. 27–57). John Benjamins.

Nunan, D. (2004). *Task-based language teaching*. Cambridge University Press.

Prabhu, N. (1987). *Second language pedagogy*. Oxford University Press.

Robinson, P., & Gilabert, R. (2007). Task complexity, the cognition hypothesis and second language learning and performance. *International Review of Applied Linguistics in Language Teaching*, 45, 161–176.

Skehan, P. (1996). A framework for the implementation of task-based instruction. *Applied Linguistics*, 17(1), 38–61.

Skehan, P., & Luo, S. (2020). Developing a task-based approach to assessment in an Asian context. *System*, 90, 1–15.

Van den Branden, K. (2006). Introduction: Task-based language teaching in a nutshell. In K. Van den Branden (Ed.), *Task-based language education: From theory to practice* (pp. 1–16). Cambridge University Press.

Van den Branden, K. (2009). Mediating between predetermined order and chaos: The role of the teacher in task-based language education. *International Journal of Applied Linguistics*, 19(3), 264–285.

Van den Branden, K., Van Gorp, K., & Verhelst, M. (Eds.). (2007). *Tasks in action: Task-based language education from a classroom-based perspective*. Cambridge Scholars Publishing.

Wang, Q. (2009). Primary English in China: Policy, curriculum and implementation. In M. Nikolov (Ed.), *The age factor and early language learning* (pp. 277–309). De Gruyter.

Widdowson, H. G. (1990). *Aspects of language teaching*. Oxford University Press.

Wilkins, D. A. (1981). Notional syllabuses revisited. *Applied Linguistics*, 2(1), 83–89.

Xiongyong, C., & Samuel, M. (2011). Perceptions and implementation of task-based language teaching among secondary school EFL teachers in China. *International Journal of Business and Social Science*, 2(24), 292–302.

Zheng, X., & Borg, S. (2014). Task-based learning and teaching in China: Secondary school teachers' beliefs and practices. *Language Teaching Research*, 18(2), 205–221.

5

EVALUATING, SEQUENCING AND SCAFFOLDING TASKS

Introduction

The main focus of Chapter 4 was on the bigger picture of TBLT implementation. Originally proposed as an interactionist-informed but essentially learner-centred and experiential remedy to strongly teacher-dominated approaches, TBLT in practice has been subject to discrepancies in operation and is influenced by where on the interactionist continuum its proponents sit. TBLT may be practised in a range of ways between the predominantly learner-centred and experiential, where the task is everything (TBLT in stronger forms), and the more prominently teacher-led and expository that sees an important role for tasks, but that admits (and expects) more central roles for direct teaching (TBLT in weaker forms).

In the last chapter, I also considered the underlying syllabi (the blueprints for teaching) that inform different pedagogical approaches and I raised the distinction that has sometimes been made between task-*based* (strong TBLT) and task-*supported* (TSLT, or weak TBLT) as potentially incompatible realisations of different syllabus types and different theories of learning. I intimated nonetheless that, in light of a continuum of practice, the distinction is not straightforward and the line between task-based and task-supported can be blurry.

The existence of different emphases within TBLT brings us back to the task as TBLT's distinguishing hallmark. In this regard, Samuda and Bygate (2008) raised a pertinent argument: a segregation between TBLT and TSLT would suggest a two-tiered approach, with TSLT being seen as an inferior form of TBLT or "TBLT 'lite'." However, this perception, in their view, "devalues any use of tasks that falls outside the purview of [strong] TBLT, and one that risks obscuring 'task' as a peda-gogical construct in its own right" (p. 219). In task-oriented classrooms, then, the unifying feature, or the "starting point, primary mechanism, and final goal of educational activity" (Van den Branden et al., 2009, p. 6), and the locus of TBLT's learner-centred and experiential claims, is the task. Whatever else may happen in the task-oriented classroom, the task is crucial. A primary focus on the task is therefore also crucial. If we can get the task right, and have a level of confidence in the task's fit against the theory, we are at least half way towards putting a communicative approach into practice that is "task-based."

In Chapter 3, I presented a variety of task types emerging from the theorising, research and practices of a range of authors. Building on the task considerations I explored there, this chapter moves the discussion forward by returning to the central task construct and focusing on putting tasks into action in classrooms, irrespective of how a task-based approach may be conceptualised. This means that, in what follows, I am not presuming or basing my discussion on a particular *form* of TBLT – strong, weak or somewhere in between – although inevitably I will explore how different emphases within TBLT impact on key aspects of task use. I aim, however, to present what I see as foundational issues for *tasks*, regardless of the pedagogical emphasis within which these tasks sit. Drawing on both theory and practice, I explore three key areas:

1. task evaluation, or, "to what extent is this really a task?"
2. task sequencing, or, "how can tasks be ordered according to their level of challenge?"
3. task scaffolding, or, "how can learners be supported to get the best out of tasks?"

Task Evaluation

The variety of tasks types I presented in Chapter 3 can be quite confusing for those who are considering using tasks in their classrooms. If teachers are to try out TBLT ideas and attempt to make the best use of tasks in classrooms, they need some means of evaluating a range of tasks for their fit with appropriate theoretical frameworks.

What makes one activity a task and another activity not a task? A useful place to start is with evaluating an activity that is very familiar to teachers and learners in a range of contexts, including communicative contexts, especially those who are influenced by structural (Type A) syllabi – the grammar practice exercise. In such exercises, students are asked to display their knowledge of a grammar principle, usually in a discrete "right or wrong" way. Typical exercises include: underlining key words (e.g., identifying grammatical errors in a sentence and perhaps also providing the correct form); transformation exercises (re-writing sentences from one grammatical form to another, e.g., present tense to past tense; active to passive); fill-in-the-gap exercises (requiring demonstration of knowledge of the target feature such as relative or personal pronouns); re-ordering exercises (learners re-arrange the words in a sentence to make the order grammatically correct); and matching exercises (learners match one part of a sentence to another part to make a grammatically accurate sentence). These exercises may arguably have some value in consolidating (and measuring) learners' explicit knowledge of grammatical forms (and I will return to this towards the end of this chapter). At this stage, one thing is unequivocal. These are not tasks.

If we were to evaluate typical grammar practice exercises against the essential characteristics of a task (real-world relationship; focus on meaning; gap; outcome), it is very clear that these exercises do not meet these criteria. There is no real-world relationship: a grammar practice exercise does not relate to how language is used authentically in real-world contexts beyond the classroom, whether situationally or interactionally; there may be a focus on meaning, but this focus is *semantic* (at the sentence level) rather than *pragmatic* (more broadly contextual) – which is a requirement for tasks; there is arguably a gap, but this is not a gap in communication (something that has to be determined through interaction); there is also an outcome (completing the exercises), but this outcome is purely linguistic (and certainly not communicative), leading to a display of technical knowledge. In essence, a grammar practice exercise, in and of itself, serves no communicative function. This makes it not a task for the purposes of TBLT.

Task evaluation becomes a little bit murkier when we start to consider the kinds of language practice activities that are often utilised in the more structurally oriented communicative classroom. The typical role-play scenario comes to mind. Role-plays are activities where students are given particular roles and, in those roles, are required to improvise a scene or carry out some kind of interaction based on specific information or suggestions. In a role-play, the "stock-in-trade" of many Presentation-Practice-Production (PPP)-oriented Communicative Language Teaching (CLT) classrooms, language learners work together, usually in pairs, to undertake the roles. A situationally authentic scenario is created. For example:

> You are in a café and you wish to order something to eat and something to drink from the person serving behind the counter. Using the menu the server has passed to you, order the items you would like and pay for your items.

Typically, this interaction may be practised with one partner being first the customer and then, in a second run through, the server, and vice versa. Also, the menu may well be one that is characteristically used in a café in the target country (i.e., it is authentic), rather than having been created by the teacher.

If we were to evaluate a café role-play against the essential criteria of a task, it seems to tick several boxes. There is a clear relationship to a communicative scenario in the real world beyond the classroom – people order food and drink in cafés all over the world; there is (arguably) a focus on meaning – you need to use language to get your message across; there is (arguably) a gap – you want something to eat and drink and you currently do not have it; and there is (arguably) an outcome (it is anticipated that, in the real-world scenario replicated in the role-play, the customer would receive the items requested, although in the classroom context this outcome may need to be imagined or improvised). This activity is, however, also not a task for the purposes of TBLT.

What makes the café role-play not a task? Its essential problem is that, typically, such role-plays are set up to give students opportunities to utilise formulaic language and grammar structures to which they may have been exposed in the first (presentation) stage of the lesson, and practised in the second (practice) stage. Although they could (perhaps) complete the role-play using any language, their linguistic production (final stage) is, theoretically at least, dependent on producing the anticipated targeted language and structures correctly using the language they had been taught (i.e., accuracy is an important criterion for success). Furthermore, although there is some kind of gap in that the "customer" needs to locate and communicate two items (any items) on the menu, what is basically required is to read the items from the menu card ("I would like A; I would like B"). Essentially, the two students undertaking the role-play already know (or at least have had opportunities to become familiar with) all the vocabulary and phrases they need to complete the activity successfully. Also, basically, there is no (tangible) outcome – other than a linguistic one that is determined by how well (i.e., how accurately) the partners have used the pre-learned language.

Perhaps in evaluating this activity as a task we need to go a little deeper. What if we considered this activity against Ellis and Shintani's more elaborated definitions of task characteristics (see Chapter 3 and Ellis and Shintani, 2014, pp. 135–136)?

1. Meaning focus: learners should principally be focused on processing input and creating output, rather than on grammatical form. However, in the café role-play, as currently presented, input-processing and output-creation are effectively reliant on pre-learned language.

2. Gap: there is a requirement to express information, give an opinion or deduce meaning. In the role-play case, some level of information needs to be conveyed, but it is purely formulaic. No meanings need to be deduced and no opinions expressed.

3. Own resources: learners are not specifically taught or directed to the language they need to complete the task (i.e., they are free to use any language they wish to complete the task, although they may be able to take some language directly from any provided input to help them complete it). In this case, the interlocutors are taught the language they need. They are not just borrowing; they are essentially replicating.

4. Outcome: the language is the means to reach the outcome, but not an end in itself (i.e., learners undertaking the task are not primarily focused on having to use language correctly but, rather, on reaching the goal anticipated in the task). In this case, there is a greater focus on accuracy. The goal of the activity, as previously stated, is linguistic.

This somewhat deeper analysis would indicate that the café role-play, as evaluated above, is not a task. As with a grammar practice exercise, this does not mean that it has no value in the task-oriented classroom, but we need to consider its potential learning value separately from its value as a task.

In East (2016, p. 38), I suggested one way in which the conventional café role-play could be enhanced to make it more like a task. I proposed the following task scenario:

> Work with a partner. You and your partner are in a French café on the last day of your school exchange trip and you wish to order a drink and something to eat. Between you, you are down to your last 20 euros. Goal: come to a consensus on the items you can afford to buy.

The authentic menu card may still be available as a resource. The interactional instructions may also set specified conditions that would influence individual choices (e.g., lactose intolerant; gluten free; avoids caffeine). I went on to explain:

> The task requires the partners to express an opinion about what they would like to eat and drink, but they also have to solve a problem. The partners are therefore required to go beyond their own opinions to reach an outcome (i.e., consensus on the order, given the opinions expressed). The primary goal is the outcome (rather than the language used to get there). Participants make their own choices about the language they wish to use to achieve the outcome (i.e., suitable language and grammatical structures are not pre-determined or imposed – even though particular language and grammatical structures may be anticipated in the responses).
>
> *(East, 2016, p. 38)*

The simple transactional role-play has been enhanced to become, in effect, both an opinion gap and a reasoning gap task. As I noted in East (2016), the task is now moving towards becoming what Richards (2006) called a "fluency task" in contrast to an "accuracy task." That is, in this adapted scenario the roles, in Richards' words, may still be "heavily constrained by the specified situation and characters" (p. 15). However, the language to be used may be "entirely improvised by the students" (p. 15) and the goal becomes "getting meanings across using any available communicative resources" (p. 16). Clearly, a role-play that is embellished in this way is going to be more challenging and cognitively taxing for students to complete, and this will depend on the elements involved (indeed, the relative challenge of different tasks in an issue I will look at later in this chapter). The task requires negotiation of meaning and navigating through to an outcome that is not determined. However, the embellished role-play can be considered more comfortably to be a task in line with several of the frameworks I presented in Chapter 3.

Nevertheless, referring to this role-play as more comfortably a task raises an important issue for TBLT. Occasionally it is possible to determine that a particular activity is not a task. However, often it is not simply a question of one activity being a task and another not being a task. Tasks arguably need to be evaluated on a continuum with "not task-like" at one end and "fully task-like" at the other. The evaluative question to be asked is not so much an either/or question – is this a task? Rather, the important question becomes: how task-like is it?

Indeed, Willis and Willis's (2007) six questions (see Chapter 3) are arguably a useful and practical means of evaluating the *relative* task-likeness of given tasks. Willis and Willis did not see tasks in absolute terms. Rather, they suggested that their questions represented one means of determining where on a continuum a task might lie, concluding, "[t]he more confidently we can answer *yes* to each of these questions the more task-like the activity" (p. 13). In this regard, Ellis and Shintani (2014) provided, as a footnote, what is in fact an important distinction to make – "the distinction between a 'task' and an 'exercise' [such as a communicative activity] can be seen as *continuous* rather than *dichotomous*. That is, some activities may satisfy *some* of the criteria of a 'task' but not all" (p. 159, my emphases). They went on to elaborate what they meant in a way that can be directly related to role-play examples:

> For example, cued card activities that specify the specific functions that learners must perform in order to construct a dialogue, do not have any outcome other than simply "practice" but do have a gap and do require, to some extent at least, that learners use their own linguistic resources.
>
> *(Ellis and Shintani, 2014, p. 159)*

It may be a bit disquieting to have to live with ambiguity at times, and teachers' professional judgment will play an important role. However, when considering a particular activity as a task, the central concern is to evaluate the proposed activity against a set of evaluative criteria (e.g., the Willis and Willis six questions, and/or other frameworks as presented in Chapter 3). The more the proposed activity matches up to the criteria, the greater confidence teachers can have that the proposed activity is a task.

Reflection Point

Nunan (2004) commented that there are "as many different task types as there are people who have written on task-based language teaching" (p. 56).

1. In what ways do you think Nunan's comment may be helpful for teachers who wish to introduce tasks into their repertoires of practice?
2. In what ways do you think it may be problematic?
3. What do you think of the six Willis and Willis (2007) questions as means of evaluating task-likeness? What other means could be used?

Task Sequencing

It is one thing to establish the task-likeness of a task or set of tasks. It is another to determine how tasks fit into broader sequences of teaching and learning in the instructed context. A potential problem with putting a task-based programme into action is that the programme may comprise "a seemingly random collection of tasks with nothing to tie them together" (Nunan, 2004, p. 25). Having established that a proposed activity is sufficiently task-like for it to be utilised as a task (as opposed to an exercise or communicative activity), a second level of evaluation is to determine how challenging a task might be for learners and, as a consequence, how to sequence tasks. As Baralt, Harmath-de Lemos and Werfelli (2016) put it, "[s]tarting students out with simple tasks, and facilitating their successful performance of more complex tasks where they encounter – and overcome – cognitive and linguistic challenges, is a fundamental tenet of task-based language teaching" (p. 180). Where several tasks may be used in succession, it makes sense that these tasks will be sequenced in a deliberate way, and that this sequence will run from easiest to hardest. Nunan referred to this issue as "task difficulty," arguing that the issue is of vital importance to all those who have a stake in the TBLT endeavour, whether from a theoretical, a research or a practical perspective. He concluded that, in the absence of some means of establishing task difficulty, "sequencing and integrating tasks becomes a matter of intuition" (p. 85).

Determining how challenging a task is likely to be is thus a significant concern for TBLT. Teachers need to make decisions around the kinds of tasks they think are appropriate for learners at different levels of proficiency, as well as the kinds of tasks that will effectively enhance different aspects of L2 learning (Tavakoli, 2011). If a task is too easy for learners, it will likely not inspire interest and will be demotivating. It will also not provide any opportunity for learners to develop their linguistic proficiency. If, on the contrary, a task is too difficult for learners, it will also likely lead to demotivation because learners will simply not be able to complete it. Thus, both cognitive and affective factors play a part in determining the challenge of a task. Also, teachers often feel uncomfortable about giving learners a task that is likely to be beyond their current level of proficiency and may be inclined to give them more limiting language practice through falling back on, for example, grammar practice exercises and communicative activities (see, e.g., Van den Branden, 2006).

In contexts where practitioners have TBLT-supportive syllabi, resources or text-books to guide them in their curricular and lesson planning, issues of task sequencing and task challenge may be easier to manage because, all being well, proposed tasks will already have been graded and sequenced. In contexts where practitioners are designing their own tasks, and also for purposes of evaluating the relative difficulty of any prescribed tasks teachers are aiming to use, what principles can they draw on to help them with this evaluation?

At the *operational* level, Prabhu (1987), for example, suggested that, when sequencing the three types of task he had proposed, learners might move from information gap to reasoning gap to opinion gap as they progressed in their language proficiency. He went on to suggest that genuine opinion gap tasks might only be possible at the highest levels of proficiency. In reality, the sequencing of tasks in the Bangalore project was effectively intuitive, with later tasks building on earlier ones, but perhaps involving greater amounts of information or extending the reasoning required to complete the task.

Brown et al. (1984) maintained that what they termed "static" tasks where the elements remained fixed (e.g., describe a diagram) were easier than "dynamic" tasks where components were unfixed and changeable (e.g., narrate a story). Furthermore, "abstract" tasks where the elements were variable and potentially unpredictable (e.g., give an opinion) were the most challenging. Willis's (1996) taxonomy of task types (see Chapter 3) provides another means of potentially determining task difficulty.

One early theoretical perspective (Brindley, 1987) identified three interconnected variables that influenced the challenge of a task: learner variables (the influence of individual learner differences on task completion); task variables (the influence of different task demands); and text or input variables (the influence of different kinds of source material). Indeed, several hypotheses emerged in the 1990s to inform thinking around how to sequence tasks according to their level of challenge. These included the skills hypothesis (Johnson, 1996), the limited capacity hypothesis (Skehan, 1998) and the cognition hypothesis (Robinson, 1995), each reflecting differential theoretical orientations with regard to second language acquisition (SLA) and task sequencing decisions. In this chapter, there is not the space to consider each of these. In what follows, I look at the cognition hypothesis with regard to its influence on task sequencing decisions.

The Cognition Hypothesis

Robinson (2001) suggested that there are three sets of variables to take into consideration when designing and sequencing tasks, which he referred to as the triadic componential framework. Within the framework, a range of questions might be asked (some examples are given below):

1. complexity – e.g., how many steps are involved in completing the task? How high are the reasoning demands placed on the learners?
2. difficulty – e.g., how able or proficient are the learners undertaking the task? How do they perceive the task? How do they feel about doing the task?
3. conditions – e.g., is this a one-way or two-way task? How do the learners undertake the task? Individually? In pairs? In groups?

The framework thus distinguishes between complexity and difficulty. Task *complexity* is related to the cognitive demands of the task and their influence on task performance. This will be variable. Task *difficulty* is related to what the learners bring to the task, including, for example, ability, aptitude and motivation. This will also be variable. The relative challenge of a task arises as a consequence of the interaction between complexity and difficulty variables. Furthermore, task *conditions* will have different levels of impact on both complexity and difficulty.

Of the three components in the framework, Robinson (2003) went on to suggest that *complexity* decisions should be the major drivers of proactive task sequencing when planning a task-based programme. Thus, for Robinson, a primary consideration in grading and sequencing tasks is related to the cognitive demands that tasks place on learners.

Essentially, and as I have previously stated, for language learners to develop their proficiency and move towards automaticity, the tasks they are asked to undertake need to be sequenced from straightforward to more complex. Nevertheless, tasks should be challenging for learners, requiring them, in addition to drawing on what they already know, to encounter difficulties and pay closer attention. These challenges will enable learners to move above their current proficiency level, ultimately achieving automaticity with regard to the task at hand. Where, for example, a sequence of pedagogic tasks is being used to approximate the demands of a subsequent real-world task, this sequence should be utilised in ways that progressively increase the cognitive demands of the task, gradually replicating the full complexity of the target real-world task.

The cognition hypothesis (CH) distinguishes two dimensions of task complexity – *resource-directing* and *resource-dispersing* (Robinson, 2003; Robinson & Gilabert, 2007). The resource-directing dimension is related to the linguistic concepts that need to be expressed or understood in performing the task. That is, during task completion learners may be "directed" to aspects of the language system, and thereby pushed towards greater accuracy and complexity of L2 production. For example, a less complex task may ask learners to refer to events in the present taking place in the location where the task is being undertaken (what is currently going on in the classroom); a more complex task may require learners to refer to events in the past at a different location (what happened elsewhere). Similarly, a less complex task may ask learners to state facts about a particular context (e.g., what they know about how to keep fit); a more complex task may require learners to give reasons for particular beliefs (e.g., what they believe about the effect of smoking on health and fitness, and why they believe this).

The resource-dispersing dimension does not direct learners to any specific aspect of the linguistic system. Rather, it makes differential performative or procedural demands on learners' attention and memory, thereby "dispersing" learners' attentional resources. These dimensions may include, for example, giving or limiting planning time; providing or not providing relevant background knowledge; requiring the learners to complete one or several steps; or having a fixed sequence of steps or no required sequence.

Task complexity and sequencing considerations will also be influenced by task modality (Kormos, 2014). As I noted in Chapter 3, although interactive speaking tasks feature prominently in the task-based classroom, TBLT is not limited to speaking tasks and in fact provides the flexibility for language learners to engage in tasks in several modalities. With regard to complexity and sequencing, a listing task based on listening input is arguably more straightforward than a writing task requiring an opinion, and might therefore come earlier in a sequence. In particular, the productive skills of speaking and writing draw on distinct cognitive processes and can have differential impacts on the quality and quantity of L2 learners' output (Zalbidea,

2017). A large number of empirical studies have tested the CH, in particular with regard to complexity, accuracy and fluency (CAF) in L2 production, whether spoken or written (see, e.g., Jackson and Suethanapornkul, 2013, for an overview). However, studies that have investigated the differential impact of productive task modality on CAF have led to contrasting findings (e.g., Granfeldt, 2008; Kormos & Trebits, 2012; Kuiken & Vedder, 2011; Tavakoli, 2014).

One thing is clear. Empirical studies have thus far not led to conclusive answers about task sequencing at the practical level of the classroom (Révész & Gurzynski-Weiss, 2016), and we still have no wide agreement on a model or set of criteria that can guide the process of grading and sequencing tasks (Baralt, Gilabert, & Robinson, 2016; Baralt, Harmath-de Lemos, & Werfelli, 2016). At the practical level, the question of what makes one task easier or more difficult than another is, therefore, easier posed than answered.

Révész and Gurzynski-Weiss (2016) suggested an alternative standpoint – that teachers' perspectives on how difficult a task may be for learners may provide useful data for evaluative purposes. Following Skehan (1998), the researchers interpreted task difficulty as perceived differences in overall task demands – linguistic (e.g., range and sophistication of language required in the response), cognitive (e.g., the relative clarity of the demands the learners have to process) and conditional (e.g., time limitations imposed).

Taking a bottom-up approach, Révész and Gurzynski-Weiss (2016) asked 16 ESL teachers to evaluate the linguistic ability learners would require to complete four pedagogic tasks taken from a textbook, and also to consider how they might adapt the tasks to better match the abilities of learners at lower and higher levels of proficiency (i.e., how they might make the tasks less or more complex). It was found that teachers' primary concern when evaluating task difficulty was with linguistic factors (such as the complexity of the language being used, including grammatical and lexical features). It was also found that teachers perceived that task difficulty could be increased by increasing the conceptual demands of the task (e.g., asking learners to provide justifications for stated perspectives or decisions). Conversely, decreasing both conceptual and linguistic demands would arguably decrease the difficulty of the task. In these respects, the teachers' perspectives mirrored aspects of Robinson's CH.

Baralt, Harmath-de Lemos and Werfelli (2016) provided another valuable practitioner-oriented study. They investigated two teachers' actions during an in-service professional development workshop where the focus was on sequencing tasks based on their complexity level. Both participants were practising teachers of L2 in a languages department at a large public university in the United States. One taught Italian and the other taught Spanish, and both spoke these languages as L1. The findings indicated that the teachers' consideration of task complexity was influenced by their beliefs about effective pedagogy (neither teacher was experienced with TBLT, but both valued a communicative orientation to language teaching). It was also found that both teachers took the task complexity principles of the CH into account in much the same way in their design of a task and lesson plan. They demonstrated an ability to adapt a pre-existing task to fit better with the principles of the CH to which they were introduced and both were able to sequence the adjusted task appropriately into a lesson plan. The findings suggested that the CH principles presented a valuable way of helping teachers to sequence tasks.

Where do the above arguments leave practitioners? As with task evaluation, it may be a bit unsettling to have to live with uncertainty with regard to how to sequence tasks to best pedagogical effect. Furthermore, and as I previously stated, Nunan (2004) appeared to be of the view that teachers needed to move beyond intuition and find more objective means of determining challenge and sequencing. However, studies by Baralt, Harmath-de Lemos and Werfelli (2016) and by Révész and Gur-zynski-Weiss (2016) indicate that teachers can, to a large extent, exercise judgments that are meaningful and convincingly aligned to theory. As Ellis (2017) noted, when it comes to practical decision-making about task complexity, "intuition is needed and probably always will be" (p. 514). Teachers' professional judgments will play a central role in decision-making. The more practical orientations to task selection early suggested by Prabhu (1987), Brown et al. (1984) and Willis (1996) (see earlier in this chapter) may provide useful starting points.

Task Scaffolding – The Pre-task Phase

Teachers need to made decisions about the tasks they will include in a task-based lesson or series of lessons. These decisions will include evaluating tasks for their task-likeness and considering complexity, sequencing and modality. However, making decisions about the tasks themselves is only one step in the process. That is, there would arguably be no benefit in simply throwing a task or series of tasks at learners and hoping for the best, unless the strongest form of TBLT is being advocated – and in Chapter 4 I provided a caution against this realisation of TBLT. Beyond the tasks themselves, attention needs to be given to how learners are *scaffolded* to perform tasks successfully. Scaffolding also has implications for the complexity of tasks in practice. Scaffolding considerations will nonetheless differ according to the particular "flavour" of TBLT under consideration (i.e., where on the interactionist continuum teachers are placing themselves).

Essentially, a commonly advocated model for task scaffolding may be expressed as "pre-task / task / post-task," a structure that has been proposed or advocated by several exponents of TBLT. The pre-task phase provides the space in which teachers and learners *prepare* for task performance. This phase is important because learners need to be adequately supported to carry out the task or tasks.

The pre-task phase can serve a number of purposes. Fundamentally, it provides the opportunity for teachers to specify the topic of the forthcoming task or tasks, and the outcomes that are anticipated from the tasks, so that the learners know what they are aiming at and see a purpose for what they are about to do. It builds up expectations and facilitates both task completion and language learning. However, when task sequencing and task complexity are matters of concern, a major consideration in the pre-task phase is on what Ellis (2003) referred to as non-task preparation activities that "centre on reducing the cognitive or the linguistic demands placed on the learner" (p. 246). In other words, the purpose of the pre-task phase is to "reduce cognitive complexity" so as to "ease the processing load that learners will encounter when actually doing a task, releasing more attention for the actual language that is used" (Skehan, 1996, p. 54).

At the more teacher-led end of the learning continuum, learner preparation in the pre-task phase may, at its simplest, involve the direct pre-teaching of necessary vocabulary and formulaic expressions to begin to complete the task. This is what Skehan (1996) would refer to as "focused instruction" (p. 39) or "some form of pre-teaching" (p. 54) that would set up language relevant to task completion. This pre-task preparatory work "can aim to teach, or mobilize, or make salient language which will be relevant to task performance" (p. 53). In this regard, Newton (2001) argued, "[i]f the task contains important words for the learners, then any time spent in pre-teaching them is well spent, having its payoff in more productive word use in task performance" (p. 31). I suggested in East (2012) that this explicit approach may be particularly helpful for beginner or lower level learners who are being prepared to undertake tasks focusing on a new topic.

An explicit preparatory approach may seem to be not essentially different to a PPP proposal. Indeed, Skehan (1996) argued that weak TBLT is in several respects similar to weak CLT, and could be put into practice through a PPP sequence where the final P draws on tasks (in other words, task-supported language teaching as presented by Ellis – see Chapter 4). However, a key variance to a traditional PPP sequence is that the focus here is on task-relevant language rather than on grammar – exploration of the language the learners might need rather than explanation of the rules underpinning the language. This does not preclude a level of pre-task focus on grammar where structural knowledge may be of benefit in completing the subsequent task successfully (see, e.g., Ellis et al., 2019, pp. 217–219), although a differentiating feature of TBLT is arguably its post-task grammar focus (an issue I explore in more detail in Chapter 6).

Skehan (1996) also indicated that a pre-emptive focus on language required for task completion may be made more implicit, moving what happens in the pre-task phase along the continuum to take more account of the learners' role in processing language. More implicit ways of setting learners up to do the task which still focus on language may include teacher and learners working together to predict the kind of language that may be needed to complete the task (brainstorming a list of words that may be of relevance to the task or topic), learners undertaking a co-operative dictionary search (learners working on different items in groups), or matching words to definitions (Newton, 2001).

Beyond a pure or direct focus on lexis, teacher and learners might work together to activate learners' prior knowledge of the topic. Nunan (2004) referred to this as "schema building." In addition to introducing learners to the topic and context for the task, this may serve to introduce key words and formulaic language. Learners may, for example, do some work with a sample of language input and thereby identify key words and phrases. This is commensurate with Willis's (1996) proposal that a teacher in the pre-task phase "explores the topic with the class, highlights useful words and phrases, helps students understand task instructions and prepare" (p. 38).

Among the other more implicit ways suggested by Skehan (1996) to scaffold learners into the task at hand might be watching a video that demonstrates a similar task being undertaken (this may provide opportunities to watch L1 speakers engaging in the task that will later become the focus), or listening to or reading transcripts of similar tasks.

The above suggestions for pre-task mobilisation of background knowledge and lexis exemplify the range of possibilities that are available for teachers who wish to set learners up to perform a task or series of tasks successfully. Before leaving this overview of what might happen in the pre-task phase, it is worth drawing attention to a consideration raised by Révész and Gurzynski-Weiss (2016). One finding that emerged from their study into perceived task difficulty was a recurring teacher comment that teachers might introduce relevant lexis in the pre-task phase so that subsequent task demands are lessened. The researchers referred to Newton's (2001) suggestions in support of this viewpoint. They also presented a contrary perspective from Ellis (2003) that pre-teaching of vocabulary might cause learners to view the subsequent task as simply a vehicle for practising this pre-rehearsed vocabulary, rather than as an opportunity for a focus on meaning in which they would rely on their own resources. This, in turn, would arguably make the task more aligned with a communicative practice activity (such as a structured role-play). However, direct pre-teaching may seem to be the most straightforward proposal, and one that is favoured by practitioners. We therefore need to be clearer (and, as Révész and Gurzynski-Weiss asserted, more research-informed) about the impact of pre-teaching on subsequent task performance, SLA and automaticity.

As a final consideration, the pre-task preparation phase does not necessarily have to occur at the start of the lesson. This phase could be included in the previous lesson. This would enable the upcoming lesson to focus on the task itself. Alternatively (or additionally), pre-task preparation could take place outside of the classroom and before the lesson takes place. In East (2018), I suggested a *flipped classroom* model as "[o]ne means of enabling learners to process [outside of class] the key material required for effective interactions … whilst also allowing ample classroom time for meaningful interactions to take place" (p. 113). In this learner-centred model, the learners are required to take ownership of aspects of their own learning, preparing the background work beforehand that they will need to draw on in the task in class. In this way, the classroom becomes the site for learners to collaborate interactively with each other, utilising the material that they have prepared before the class.

Reflection Point

Task complexity and task sequencing are important concerns for TBLT. Theory and research have aimed to clarify what makes one task more challenging than another. However, from a practical perspective, teachers may need to rely on their own professional judgments and intuition when it comes to sequencing tasks.

In your view:

1. What factors might make one task more challenging than another?
2. What aspects of task design might lessen or increase the challenge in a particular task?
3. What aspects of pre-task work might help learners to carry out a task more successfully?

Task Scaffolding – Moving into the Task Phase

At the point in a given teaching sequence where learners are about to embark on the task or tasks (that is, at the intersection between the pre-task and during-task phases of a lesson), three other practical considerations should be borne in mind: task planning, task resourcing and task repetition. These *resource dispersing* dimensions also have implications for the cognitive demands posed by tasks and, therefore, for task complexity (see, e.g., Ellis, 2017; Skehan, 1996). They are also relevant not only for preparation (the pre-task phase) but also while the task is being carried out (the during-task phase).

Planning time is an important consideration for both task preparation and task execution. As Ellis (2005) put it, planning may occur both pre-task (*strategic*) and during-task (*on-line*). Furthermore, as part of planning, teachers may advise learners about what and how to plan (*guided*) or learners may be left to their own devices, whether individually or working in pairs or groups (*unguided*). Practical issues involve: how much (or how little) planning time is allocated; whether this planning time will include (or not include) teacher guidance; and structures of participation for planning purposes (individual, paired, grouped). Furthermore, where the learners share an L1, it is possible that some negotiation during the planning phase will take place in the L1, rather than in the target language. I consider the issue of L1 use in Chapter 6. At this stage, let it suffice to say that, if the L1 is a tool that helps to scaffold learners into the task and reduce the cognitive load of the task, it may have a place.

Support resources represent another important issue. The key questions are whether, and what, support resources will be made available to learners as they prepare for (and complete) the task. These resources can include target language input of some form (e.g., a newspaper article, a description, a presentation, a video source), and/or other support resources (e.g., a dictionary, a word list, resource books and textbooks, access to the Internet). Different support resources will have different impacts on task complexity and task completion. Nevertheless, they often represent authentic sources that language users draw on in the real world to support them as they make sense of and try to convey meaning.

A third issue for consideration is task repetition. Arguments have been made for repetition to be viewed as a component of planning, whether labelled as *rehearsal* (Ellis, 2005) – the opportunity to rehearse a task in preparation for a subsequent task – or *integrative* (Bygate & Samuda, 2005) – allowing for the integration of different aspects of performance on the basis that "the *initial* enactment of a task is seen as a form of *planning* of processing and of content" (p. 45, my emphases). Considerations for task repetition include: whether learners should repeat the same task or a different version of the task; when the repetition should occur – same lesson, next lesson, several lessons apart; and whether or not there should be opportunities for teacher feedback between the two versions of the task.

Planning, resourcing and repetition represent and include a range of task implementation variables that will have an impact on the cognitive load of the task and differential effects on CAF.

Drawing on the findings of several studies, McDonough (2015) argued that planning time may enhance CAF. It may also lead to greater willingness to take risks with language, and increasing the amount and type of "language related episodes" that take place during task interaction – defined by Swain (1998) as "dialogue in which students talk about the language they are producing, question their language use, or other- or self-correct" (p. 70).

East (2012) viewed support resources as contributors to the scaffolding that would enable learners to operate within their ZPDs, and argued (2008) that dictionary use can contribute to making up for gaps in knowledge and enhancing rhetorical effect through increased lexical sophistication. Although dictionary use may arguably be most appropriate for individual writing tasks, learners may draw on dictionary/glossary resources collaboratively whilst they deal with the lexical demands of any productive task, whether pre-task or during-task (Newton, 2001).

Ellis (2019) suggested that task repetition can improve fluency and complexity, and may contribute to greater accuracy when a focus on grammar occurs between the repetitions. Ahmadian (2012) noted several acquisitional benefits of repeating the same or similar tasks. Task repetition may enable learners to "'buy time' not only to do mental work on what they are about to communicate but also to access and (re)formulate words and grammatical structures more efficiently, effectively, and accurately" (p. 380).

Task Scaffolding – An Example in Practice

At several points in this chapter, I have suggested that teachers' professional judgments play a crucial role in determining the tasks they will use and how these tasks may be sequenced and scaffolded. Placing the responsibility on teachers can create challenges. As this chapter draws to a close, I introduce one illustrative example of how task sequencing and scaffolding might occur in practice, provided in the *Adult ESL Curriculum Framework* published to support teachers in Alberta, Canada (ATESL, 2011a).

In a framework that represents a weaker approach to TBLT, a document dedicated to task sequencing proposes that a range of tasks and activities should be drawn on (which, it is suggested, could conceivably include grammar practice exercises and structured role-plays – thereby admitting a place for these activities alongside tasks, at least in the particular formulation of task sequencing being proposed in the document). This proposal is designed to encourage learners to "shift their attention, as necessary, among a variety of different focuses (meaning, accuracy, fluency, skills, strategies, etc.), in order to build proficiency for real-world communication" (ATESL, 2011b, p. 10). From this perspective, the framework suggests that task *modality* might progress from the receptive to the productive, thereby moving learners towards increasingly autonomous language use, and sequenced in a way that deliberately builds on learners' skills, knowledge and experience.

Furthermore, so-called *enabling* activities (including, for example, more structured role-plays) would allow productive sequences to begin with controlled practice. These activities may lack a level of authenticity and may involve greater scaffolding than, for example, a real-world task, but they "prepare learners for the freer, less scaffolded, and more authentic meaning-focused communicative tasks" (ATESL, 2011b, p. 11). Thus, the scaffolding is slowly taken away, and learners move "from dependence on the instructor to increasing independence or autonomy" (p. 14). The framework document provides useful exemplars of how these steps might work out in practice in a lesson (e.g., pp. 15–16: greet customers, take their orders and suggest drinks).

Reflection Point

As learners undertake a task or a series of tasks, several scaffolding and enhancing mechanisms may be employed with a view to supporting L2 users to succeed with completing the tasks.

In your view:

1. In what different ways might planning time and resourcing be built into the during-task phase of a lesson?
2. In what different ways might task repetition be utilised?
3. What place, if any, do you see for more traditional grammar practice exercises and structured role-plays in the task-based classroom?

Conclusion

As I noted towards the start of this chapter, regardless of the *form* of TBLT in question, in TBLT the task is both the starting point and final goal of classroom activity, and the primary mechanism through which communicative proficiency and automaticity are developed in L2 learners (Van den Branden et al., 2009). Tasks are also the locus of TBLT's learner-centred and experiential dimensions. With so much riding on tasks in TBLT, teachers need to pay careful attention to the tasks they ask learners to do and how those tasks are put together. This chapter has considered several important practical dimensions of task implementation.

Of first importance is the extent of fit of the task or tasks being considered to theoretical definitions (task evaluation). A second important dimension is how series of tasks can be put together to enable learners to develop their communicative competence (task sequencing). A third consideration, which will influence what happens in both the pre-task and during-task phases of a lesson, is how learners are supported to complete the task or tasks (task scaffolding). Each of these dimensions – evaluation, sequencing and scaffolding – has implications for task complexity, an issue which Robinson (2003) suggested should be paramount when planning a task-based programme.

In this chapter, I have focused again on the task construct, alongside important implementation issues at the pre-task and during-task stages. In Chapter 6, I continue to explore what else may need to happen in the task-oriented classroom, with particular emphasis on the place and role of grammar in the during-task and post-task phases of a lesson.

Suggested Further Reading

Ellis, R. (2019). Task preparedness. In Z. Wen & M. Ahmadian (Eds.), *Researching second language task performance and pedagogy: Essays in honor of Peter Skehan* (pp. 15–38). John Benjamins.

Lambert, C. (2020). Frameworks for using tasks in second language instruction. In C. Lambert & R. Oliver (Eds.), *Using tasks in second language teaching: Practice in diverse contexts* (pp. 13–32). Multilingual Matters.

References

Ahmadian, M. J. (2012). Task repetition in ELT. *ELT Journal, 66*(3), 380–382.

ATESL. (2011a). *Adult ESL Curriculum Framework.* https://www.atesl.ca/resources/atesl-adult-esl-curriculum-framework/.

ATESL. (2011b). *Sequencing tasks.* https://www.atesl.ca/resources/atesl-adult-esl-curriculum-framework/.

Baralt, M., Gilabert, R., & Robinson, P. (2016). An introduction to theory and research in task sequencing and instructed second language learning. In M. Baralt, R. Gilabert, & P. Robinson (Eds.), *Task sequencing and instructed second language learning* (pp. 1–34). Bloomsbury.

Baralt, M., Harmath-de Lemos, S., & Werfelli, S. (2016). Teachers' applications of the Cognition Hypothesis when lesson planning: A case study. In M. Baralt, R. Gilabert, & P. Robinson (Eds.), *Task sequencing and instructed second language learning* (pp. 179–206). Bloomsbury.

Brindley, G. (1987). Factors affecting task difficulty. In D. Nunan (Ed.), *Guidelines for the development of curriculum resources* (pp. 45–56). National Curriculum Resource Centre.

Brown, G., Anderson, A., Shillcock, R., & Yule, G. (1984). *Teaching talk: Strategies for production and assessment.* Cambridge University Press.

Bygate, M., & Samuda, V. (2005). Integrative planning through the use of task repetition. In R. Ellis (Ed.), *Planning and task performance in a second language* (pp. 37–74). John Benjamins.

East, M. (2008). *Dictionary use in foreign language writing exams: Impact and implications.* John Benjamins.

East, M. (2012). *Task-based language teaching from the teachers' perspective: Insights from New Zealand.* John Benjamins.

East, M. (2016). *Assessing foreign language students' spoken proficiency: Stakeholder perspectives on assessment innovation.* Springer.

East, M. (2018). Learning in the classroom. In A. Burns & J. C. Richards (Eds.), *The Cambridge guide to learning English as a second language* (pp. 110–117). Cambridge University Press.

Ellis, R. (2003). *Task-based language teaching and learning.* Oxford University Press.

Ellis, R. (2005). Planning and task-based performance: Theory and research. In R. Ellis (Ed.), *Planning and task performance in a second language* (pp. 3–34). John Benjamins.

Ellis, R. (2017). Position paper: Moving task-based language teaching forward. *Language Teaching, 50*(4), 507–526.

Ellis, R. (2019). Task preparedness. In Z. Wen & M. J. Ahmadian (Eds.), *Researching L2 task performance and pedagogy: In honour of Peter Skehan* (pp. 15–38). John Benjamins.

Ellis, R., & Shintani, N. (2014). *Exploring language pedagogy through second language acquisition research.* Routledge.

Ellis, R., Skehan, P., Li, S., Shintani, N., & Lambert, C. (2019). *Task-based language teaching: Theory and practice.* Cambridge University Press.

Granfeldt, J. (2008). Speaking and writing in L2 French: Exploring effects on fluency, complexity and accuracy. In S. Van Daele, A. Housen, F. Kuiken, M. Pierrard, & I. Vedder (Eds.), *Complexity, accuracy and fluency in second language use, learning and teaching* (pp. 87–98). KVAB, Universa Press.

Jackson, D., & Suethanapornkul, S. (2013). The Cognition Hypothesis: A synthesis and meta-analysis of research on second language task complexity. *Language Learning, 63*(2), 330–367.

Johnson, K. (1996). *Language teaching and skill learning.* Wiley-Blackwell.

Kormos, J. (2014). Differences across modalities of performance: An investigation of linguistic and discourse complexity in narrative tasks. In H. Byrnes & R. M. Manchón (Eds.), *Task-based language learning – Insights from and for L2 writing* (pp. 193–216). John Benjamins.

Kormos, J., & Trebits, A. (2012). The role of task complexity, modality, and aptitude in narrative task performance. *Language Learning, 62*(2), 439–472.

Kuiken, F., & Vedder, I. (2011). Task complexity and linguistic performance in L2 writing and speaking. In P. Robinson (Ed.), *Second language task complexity: Researching the Cognition Hypothesis of language learning and performance* (pp. 91–104). John Benjamins.

McDonough, K. (2015). Perceived benefits and challenges with the use of collaborative tasks in EFL contexts. In M. Bygate (Ed.), *Domains and directions in the development of TBLT: A decade of plenaries from the international conference* (pp. 225–245). John Benjamins.

Newton, J. (2001). Options for vocabulary learning through communication tasks. *ELT Journal, 55*(1), 30–37.

Nunan, D. (2004). *Task-based language teaching.* Cambridge University Press.

Prabhu, N. (1987). *Second language pedagogy.* Oxford University Press.

Révész, A., & Gurzynski-Weiss, L. (2016). Teachers' perspectives on second language task difficulty: Insights from think-alouds and eye tracking. *Annual Review of Applied Linguistics, 36,* 182–204.

Richards, J. C. (2006). *Communicative language teaching today.* Cambridge University Press.

Robinson, P. (1995). Task complexity and second language narrative discourse. *Language Learning, 45*(1), 99–140.

Robinson, P. (2001). Task complexity, cognitive resources, and syllabus design: A triadic framework for examining task influences on SLA. In P. Robinson (Ed.), *Cognition and second language instruction* (pp. 287–318). Cambridge University Press.

Robinson, P. (2003). The cognitive hypothesis of adult, task-based language learning. *Second Language Studies, 21*(2), 45–107.

Robinson, P., & Gilabert, R. (2007). Task complexity, the cognition hypothesis and second language learning and performance. *International Review of Applied Linguistics in Language Teaching, 45,* 161–176.

Samuda, V., & Bygate, M. (2008). *Tasks in second language learning.* Palgrave Macmillan.

Skehan, P. (1996). A framework for the implementation of task-based instruction. *Applied Linguistics, 17*(1), 38–61.

Skehan, P. (1998). *A cognitive approach to language learning.* Oxford University Press.

Swain, M. (1998). Focus on form through conscious reflection. In C. Doughty & J. Williams (Eds.), *Focus on form in classroom second language acquisition* (pp. 64–81). Cambridge University Press.

Tavakoli, P. (2011). Researching task difficulty: Towards understanding L2 proficiency. In A. G. Benati (Ed.), *Issues in second language proficiency* (pp. 216–232). Bloomsbury Publishing.

Tavakoli, P. (2014). Storyline complexity and syntactic complexity in writing and speaking tasks. In H. Byrnes & R. M. Manchón (Eds.), *Task-based language learning: Insights from and for L2 writing* (pp. 217–236). John Benjamins.

Van den Branden, K. (Ed.). (2006). *Task-based language education: From theory to practice.* Cambridge University Press.

Van den Branden, K., Bygate, M., & Norris, J. (2009). Task-based language teaching: Introducing the reader. In K. Van den Branden, M. Bygate, & J. Norris (Eds.), *Task-based language teaching: A reader* (pp. 1–13). John Benjamins.

Willis, J. (1996). *A framework for task-based learning.* Longman Pearson Education.

Willis, D., & Willis, J. (2007). *Doing task-based teaching.* Oxford University Press.

Zalbidea, J. (2017). "One task fits all"? The roles of task complexity, modality, and working memory capacity in L2 performance. *The Modern Language Journal, 101*(2), 335–352.

6

ATTENDING TO GRAMMAR IN TBLT

Introduction

Part II of this book focuses on putting TBLT into practice. I have made clear at several points that the task is central to TBLT and that, if we can get the *task* right, we are at least half way towards enacting TBLT. However, it should have become apparent by now that TBLT enactment is not a straightforward enterprise. In Chapter 4, I considered several conceptualisations of TBLT which can be put down to different understandings about both effective learning and effective second language acquisition (SLA). These differences in conceptualisation influence TBLT in practice. In particular, what *surrounds* the task in learners' classroom experiences will take different forms, and how learners are scaffolded into the task may differ depending on where teachers place themselves on the interactionist continuum.

In this chapter, I discuss the different ways in which attention may be paid to grammar in TBLT, with specific focus on the during-task and post-task phases of a lesson. In particular, I consider the kinds of feedback that may be made available to learners as they complete a task and the kinds of work that may subsequently need to happen, contingent on how learners have used language in the during-task phase. Grammatical (or formal) competence has long been recognised as an important pillar on which communicative competence needs to be built (e.g., Canale, 1983; Canale & Swain, 1980). It is important, however, to state at the outset that what happens in TBLT with regard to helping learners to develop this competence will, as with scaffolding, take different forms, once more depending on teachers' positionings on the interactionist continuum.

More broadly, how to attend to grammar in the instructed L2 context is a matter of considerable debate. It brings to the fore the stark contrasts between, and the historical influence of, the two early theories of learning I introduced in Chapter 1, behaviourism and innatism. It also highlights how theorists informed by interactionist perspectives have differentially conceptualised approaches to grammar, especially regarding the roles of the teacher and the learners. I start by presenting two complementary sets of theoretical positions.

Long's Triadic Model

With a view to articulating the ways in which a grammar focus may occur in the L2 classroom, Long (e.g., 1991, 2000) presented three theoretical stances:

1. focus on forms, or, "teach the learners what they need to know"
2. focus on meaning, or, "let the learners work it out for themselves"
3. focus on form, or, "work with what the learners notice."

Focus on Forms

Focus on forms (FonFs) may be described as a traditional way of attending to grammar teaching, common within grammar-translation, and mapped historically onto a behaviourist theory of learning. In FonFs, there is, as the label suggests, a specific focus on the forms or rules of the language. These are generally prescribed in hierarchical terms, as in a synthetic Type A syllabus (see Chapter 4), and taught in an overt and systematic way. FonFs will involve the teacher in carefully explaining grammatical features and rules (and this may occur in the learners' L1 where this is feasible). These are then practised by various grammar activities such as gap-fills and transformation exercises.

As I explained in Chapter 1, so-called weak Communicative Language Teaching (CLT) is essentially predicated on procedures that reflect the FonFs approach, realised through a Presentation-Practice-Production (PPP) sequence. The first (presentation) stage of the lesson provides the space for FonFs, and the second (practice) stage is where students might practise the forms systematically through grammar exercises. The taught grammar would then form the basis of communication in the final (production) stage, operationalised, for example, through a structured role-play. As a consequence, and with a focus on the *forms* of the language, genuine and spontaneous communication may be constrained.

Focus on Meaning

To borrow Long's (2000) words, a "typical response to frustration" with FonFs was "a radical pendulum swing: a shift of allegiance … and an equally single-minded *focus on meaning*" (p. 182). In meaning-focused contexts, learners are required to process whole or complete comprehensible samples of language input in contexts where they can effectively be immersed in the language. Hence focus on meaning (FonM) can be mapped historically onto an innatist theory of learning, finding expression, for example, in the Natural Approach (see Chapter 1), and also apparent in so-called strong CLT. It may be reflected in an analytic Type B syllabus. Long explained that, in this approach, it becomes the learners' responsibility to analyse the language and work out the grammar rules for themselves simply by being exposed to the input (a process that may happen subconsciously). From the FonM perspective, the grammar focus is thus implicit, and potentially the only way to process and learn complex grammatical constructions.

Long (2000) accepted that considerable progress with the L2 is evidently achievable in FonM-oriented classrooms, and that incidental learning does occur. Nevertheless, he noted evidence to suggest that, with regard to accuracy, learners emerging from naturalistic immersion classrooms often lacked sufficient competence. Long concluded that learners will benefit in terms of their speed of, and progress with, acquisition if they receive instruction directed at the rules. To achieve this in a way that does not see a return to FonFs, Long put forward the notion of focus on form or FonF.

Focus on Form

Long (2000) defined FonF as a procedure that entails "briefly drawing students' attention to linguistic elements (words, collocations, grammatical structures, pragmatic patterns, etc.) in *context*, as they arise incidentally in lessons whose overriding focus is on meaning, or communication" (p. 185). These brief moments where learners shift their focus of attention are prompted by occasions when learners come up against a comprehension or production problem during interaction. The shift in attention is designed to stimulate "noticing" (Schmidt, 1990, 1993, 2001), thereby raising students' awareness of particular forms and their uses (see Chapter 2).

The learner may already partially understand the meaning or function of the new form in the input but may not yet have full control of the grammar behind it. FonF is built on the premise that, when learners begin to notice forms and patterns in the input, they are developmentally ready to acquire those forms. In the context of task completion, FonF might be enacted through some form of corrective feedback that draws learners' attention to an error, or by the teacher getting the learners to step back from what they are doing (whether during-task or post-task) and to interrogate an inaccurate language sample, thinking through why it may be wrong and how it might be put right. FonF provides systematic provision for attending to language as object, although no pre-determined hierarchy of rules is imposed.

In FonF, provision is made for the learner's active processing ability in tandem with teacher direction. This interactionist approach would seem to make FonF a good fit with TBLT. However, before moving on to consider how FonF might be put into operation within TBLT, it would be useful also to point out a complementary understanding of approaches to grammar.

A Complementary Triadic Model

The interface position is a triadic SLA conceptualisation that describes the different theoretical relationships that might exist for L2 learners between explicit and implicit grammatical knowledge:

1. non-interface, or, "explicit and implicit are completely independent"
2. interface, or "explicit becomes implicit through practice"
3. weak interface, or "explicit facilitates implicit through 'noticing'."

The non-interface position, influenced by Krashen's (e.g., 1981) acquisition-learning hypothesis, sees explicit and implicit knowledge as distinct – what is learned explicitly cannot be acquired implicitly (see Chapter 2). This leads to an innatist "zero grammar" approach (or FonM) (see, e.g., Ellis, 2005).

The interface (or strong interface) position, by contrast, suggests that explicit knowledge becomes implicit knowledge if learners have plenty of opportunities for communicative practice. This may be realised through a deductive approach to the exploration of grammar, where the initial focus is on consciously knowing the rules, and learners work from the rule in question to the rule in use. This position reflects aspects of FonFs procedures, but leaves greater room for genuine communicative interaction. It finds some expression in traditional realisations of PPP. More particularly, it is aligned with Skill Acquisition Theory and with so-called task-*supported* language teaching.

The weak interface position (e.g., Ellis, 2005) suggests that explicit knowledge helps with noticing and thereby acquiring the forms implicitly. Direct focus on the rules can therefore be minimal if there is opportunity for learners to notice the rules and thereby acquire them. This may be realised through an inductive approach to grammar exploration, where the emphasis is on the development of unconsciously applying the rules in communication, and learners work from the rule in use to the rule in question. This approach reflects aspects of FonF, and also usage-based approaches to SLA, and leaves room for explicit attention to form.

Attending to Form in TBLT

The complementary theoretical positions presented above demonstrate that there is no single straightforward answer to the question of how a focus on grammar should occur in instructed L2 contexts. However, in light of the central importance of grammar to communicative competence, both the acquisition of grammatical competence and the role of instruction in this acquisition have been strong foci of SLA research, with research concerns considering both accuracy and fluency in this regard (see, e.g., Loewen, 2020).

One area of broad agreement is that, when it comes to developing communicative proficiency that is both accurate and fluent, *meaning*-embedded or *communicatively linked* grammar instruction is seen as more effective than decontextualised grammar instruction (represented, for example, in FonFs as realised in grammar-translation). This perspective is supported by the findings of a range of studies, whether laboratory- or classroom-based (Sato & Oyanedel, 2019).

There remains disagreement, however, about the place, timing and extent of an explicit grammar focus. In an attempt to reconcile different perspectives, Loewen (2018) suggested, firstly, that FonFs and FonF may be subsumed under the broader category of "form-focused instruction" (FFI), which may be defined as *"any* pedagogical effort which is used to draw the learners' attention to form either implicitly or explicitly … within meaning-based approaches to L2 instruction" (Spada, 1997, p. 73, my emphasis). Importantly in FFI, the classroom approach being adopted is *communicative*, and the purpose of the grammar focus is to enhance effective communication. However, learners can be directed to pay attention to grammatical rules in operation either reactively (so-called integrated FFI) or discretely (so-called isolated FFI). Loewen suggested that, consequently, FonFs and FonF "represent two ends of a continuum which differ in the primary goal of instruction, whether communication or attention to language features," and also that "various types of instruction fall along the continuum" (p. 2).

As with FonF, FFI would appear to be a good fit with TBLT because it seems to be an approach that could be adopted, with different emphases, in stronger or weaker variants of TBLT. It is important here to note a clear difference between Long and Ellis with regard to FFI.

Long (e.g., 2015) essentially dismissed the *planned* explicit instruction that may be a component of FFI. For Long, FonF can refer *only* to activities that arise *incidentally* in communicative interaction and that are not scheduled. Furthermore, FonF is initiated *reactively*, that is, in *response* to a communication problem (i.e., it is integrated). The during-task phase presents opportunities for both learners and teachers to focus on grammatical aspects of task performance through different feedback mechanisms, which do not have to exclude the presentation of an explicit grammar rule in response to a breakdown in communication. Being reactive, however, the grammar focus will also occur in the *post*-task phase where noticed errors can receive more overt attention.

Importantly, in Long's (2015) view, FonF is typically initiated by the learner, and optimum FonF will occur "in tandem with the learner's internal syllabus" (p. 28) and "in harmony with the learner's developmental readiness" (p. 321). In other words, there is no point in paying overt attention to forms that learners are not ready to acquire, hence a focus on *reacting* to what learners notice for themselves.

In the broader context of acknowledging the complexities involved in developing grammatical competence, Ellis (e.g., 2009a) argued that attention to form in TBLT does not have to occur exclusively through FonF as articulated by Long. Ellis also saw FonF as moving *beyond* occasions where a problem in communication necessitates negotiation of meaning. Consequently, from Ellis's perspective a grammar focus can occur in a broader range of ways, making this focus more commensurate with FFI as articulated by Spada. Ellis thus conceded a potentially greater role for direct (or isolated) teaching of grammatical rules in the task-oriented classroom (see also his argument for a modular approach to syllabus design – Chapter 4).

Differences in perspective between Long and Ellis also frame considerations about where in the task cycle attention to grammar should occur and how it should occur. Crucially, there are those who have suggested that a direct or explicit form focus *might* occur in the *pre*-task phase of a lesson. Kim (2013), for example, noted that the inclusion of some kind of form focus in the pre-task phase would essentially be "to raise learners' awareness of these forms during planning time as well as during task performance" (p. 10). Indeed, Ellis et al. (2019), who presented the first study to investigate how pre-task grammar instruction might influence task performance and learning, went so far as to suggest that explicit *pre*-teaching of the target structure may have some value in encouraging the use of that structure in a subsequent task.

Nonetheless, and essentially following Long, Samuda and Bygate (2008) made the argument that a "key criterial element" in TBLT is the timing of the grammar focus, "*arising* from task performance and not *preceding* it" (p. 208, my emphases). I will return to this argument towards the end of this chapter.

Reflection Point

The triadic frameworks of *forms/meaning/form* and *non-interface/interface/weak interface* represent complementary ways of theorising approaches to grammar in the L2 classroom.

In your experiences of learning an L2:

1. How was grammar attended to? What kinds of things were helpful and not helpful in getting you to use the grammar correctly?
2. Which theoretical framework(s) underpinned the approach(es) you have experienced?

When teaching an L2 from a TBLT perspective:

1. What approaches to grammar do you think would be the most helpful for learners?

Taking the above theoretical perspectives into account, the realisation of FonF/FFI (hereafter form focus) in TBLT classrooms is going to have different emphases in accordance with different points on the interactionist continuum. I turn now to a consideration of how a form focus may occur in practice, in particular in the during-task and post-task phases of a task-based lesson.

Form Focus – The During-task Phase

Structures of Participation

As I indicated in Chapter 5, there are several ways in which learners can be organised to undertake tasks. Below I discuss a range of configurations and task modalities and present the possibilities for during-task form focus to occur, whether peer-to-peer or teacher–learner. Importantly, these configurations may be adopted within a single lesson, or over a series of lessons where the tasks bear a relationship to the theme or topic the teacher and learners are exploring. (I take it as a given that tasks will have been differentiated from, say, communicative activities by virtue of their [relative] fit to theoretical definitions of the task construct, as I outlined in Chapter 5.)

With regard to spoken interactive tasks, both pair work and group work provide opportunities for the negotiation of meaning that has been theorised, from a cognitive-interactionist perspective, to be critical for SLA to occur. That is, peer-to-peer interaction facilitates spaces for comprehensible input, feedback and output, thereby promoting language learning. Viewed from a sociocultural-interactionist perspective, peer-to-peer interactions provide opportunities for scaffolding, facilitating co-construction and attention to grammar without the teacher's intervention. (See, e.g., Philp et al., 2014, and Oliver & Philp, 2014, for more detailed considerations of the potential of peer interaction.)

For learners to derive the most peer-to-peer benefit from speaking tasks, including opportunities for meaningful feedback on language use, it is important for decisions to be made regarding who works with whom, that is, to take into consideration so-called interlocutor effects (O'Sullivan, 2002). These include, for example, the age and gender of the learners, cultural or L1 background, personality, or how well the partners in a pair or group know each other and get on with each other. Each of these variables may influence how much and how successfully each interactant can negotiate meaning and therefore profit from the interaction in terms of SLA.

The decision about working partnerships could be made by the learners, and there may well be affective advantages in friendship groups. For teachers, considerations beyond friendship will influence pair/group decisions. One important consideration is proficiency. Pairing or grouping two or more learners of comparable linguistic ability may be advantageous in that the pair or group may feel more comfortable working together as equals, but this may have drawbacks in terms of successful negotiation of meaning. Grouping two or more learners of different ability may be useful in that the more highly proficient learner(s) may be able to support the lower proficiency learner(s) in line with a sociocultural theory of language acquisition. However, this may not work to the advantage of the more proficient learner(s).

In scenarios where a sequence of tasks is undertaken (whether in a single lesson or a series of lessons), re-arranging the pairs or groups will help ensure that differences in proficiency (or indeed other learner variables) are, to some extent, levelled out as different combinations of learners, under the organisation of the teacher, complete the tasks. Similarly, where several speaking tasks are sequenced to follow one another, it may be possible, or advantageous, to vary the interactional patterns (e.g., starting with pairs, moving to groups), depending on the proposed outcomes. A third option is to repeat the task, either as the same task (perhaps with different interlocutors) or a modified version of the task.

Learners undertaking speaking tasks could also be required to complete some kind of co-constructed written response. This could, for example, take the form of summarising or reporting in written form on the outcomes of the spoken task. This enables learners to pay attention to different components of language use. García-Mayo and Imaz Agirre (2019), for example, have pointed out that some studies have indicated that tasks that elicit speaking cause learners to pay more attention to meaning, whereas tasks that include a written element present learners with more opportunities to focus on accuracy and grammatical form. In comparison with speaking tasks alone, collaborative tasks that include a written component will likely elicit more language related episodes (LREs) which (as I pointed out in Chapter 5) constitute learners' discussions on and modifications of the language they are producing (Swain, 1998), with potential learning benefits in terms of accuracy. However, opportunities for collaborative (pair or group) writing do not necessarily need to have been preceded by a speaking task (i.e., a task could involve input processing, e.g., reading a newspaper article or watching a televised news report on a topical theme and then co-constructing a written position piece on its content that presents one or several perspectives).

Tasks that require some kind of written output also lend themselves to individual work, where learners may have more time to process output and focus on accuracy, and can be integrated with other skills. This may include, for example, reading and responding (replying to an email or letter; opinion piece; book review), or listening/watching and responding (listing key information from a phone message; summarising key points from a podcast or lecture; film review). Individual writing tasks may be conducted as part of whole class work (e.g., the class listens to or reads the same input and provides some kind of individual written response). This could lead to pair, group or whole class work where outcomes are shared (and feedback opportunities provided), and could be developed into a monologic speaking task in the form of individual presentations. Such tasks could also be completed, in whole or in part, outside class.

A key issue that underpins drawing on different task types and modalities, alongside different structures of participation, is that they enable learners to pay attention to different dimensions of the L2 and also to recycle language. They also enable learner difference variables to be managed in ways that will ideally cater to the needs and learning styles of all learners in the class.

Consciousness-raising Tasks

The above discussion makes it clear that certain kinds of tasks are likely to elicit more direct attention to form than others. In Chapter 3, I drew attention to the concept of focused tasks that would encourage specific use of a target language structure. So-called consciousness-raising (C-R) tasks (Ellis, 2003) represent a kind of focused task designed to promote collaborative opportunities to pay more direct attention to form. Their purpose, as explained by Ellis, is to develop learners' "awareness at the level of 'understanding' rather than awareness at the level of 'noticing'" (pp. 162–163).

The anticipated outcome of a C-R task is recognition of how a particular linguistic structure works. In these tasks, the rule in operation is the important component of the input, and explicit knowledge of the rule in practice is seen to lead to implicit knowledge. Such tasks therefore invoke learners' own processing abilities as they seek to discover the rules by solving a problem. Learners may, for example, be presented with an explicit rule alongside input that illustrates the rule in practice, or they may be encouraged to think through for themselves how the rule works in the input and thereby come up with the rule themselves.

Of several examples of C-R tasks cited by Fotos (1994), the following is described as an information gap task which targets relative clause use. The task concerned making sentences using *who, whom, which* and *that*, and also asking questions using *who* or *whom*. There were four task cards. The task instructions were essentially as follows:

> Individual students in a group of four each receive a task card which gives a rule, alongside correct and incorrect sentences demonstrating the rule. Students take turns to read the rule and the sentences, and make their own sentence to illustrate the rule. Students then note down all the rules and take turns to create sentences.

Does this task sufficiently meet the criteria for being a task (real-world relationship; focus on meaning; gap; and outcome)? A *situationally* authentic real-world relationship is tenuous, although *interactionally* the task is more authentic; the focus is *primarily* on meaning in that learners are required to create language and may use whatever language they wish (within the constraints of the target structure); there is a gap – learners have to identify appropriate use of the rule for themselves and also apply it appropriately; there is an outcome – ultimately creating sentences to illustrate the rules, leading (all being well) to learners' awareness of how the structure works.

Ellis (2003) added two useful caveats. First, he suggested that C-R tasks might not be appropriate for younger learners who might see language as a vehicle for communicating something rather than as an object to be studied. Second, learners may find the discussion more difficult if they do not have sufficient metalanguage (i.e., the language they can use to analyse and describe language samples – noun, verb, clause, etc.). Nevertheless, within a broader repertoire of task types, C-R tasks arguably have value at stages in learning the L2 and, as Fotos (1994) noted, enable attention to explicit knowledge which is processed in a learner-centred and meaning-focused way.

The Role of the Teacher

I have so far highlighted how *learners* can be encouraged to collaborate and provide feedback to their peers where the focus can be on accuracy. However, the *teacher* is also a significant support resource during task execution. As Van den Branden (2009) explained it, teacher support is initiated when the teacher takes the role of motivator (launching students into action through constructing or co-constructing what needs to be done); organiser (ensuring that students are clear about what they need to do, and determining how long the task will take and how students will work together); and partner and supporter (supporting students as they undertake the task, in whatever ways seem necessary for successful task completion). The attention Van den Branden drew to the teacher brings to the fore the important place of *teacher* feedback on task performance, in particular in relation to grammatical form. Indeed, as Spada (1997) pointed out with regard to FFI, pedagogical attention to grammar can be mediated, in part, by responding to the errors that learners make in the form of corrective feedback. As the previous discussion of task type and modality indicated, feedback in one form or another can already be mediated by the partners in peer-to-peer interactions. The teacher's role is pivotal, however, because the teacher represents "the more proficient, knowledgeable interlocutor" (Van den Branden, 2009, p. 284). The scaffolding role of the teacher through feedback is a critical component in enhancing SLA, seen from both cognitive-interactionist and sociocultural-interactionist perspectives.

The important role of feedback for SLA has been raised in the seminal work of Lyster and Ranta (1997) with regard to oral corrective feedback (CF) and Truscott (1996) with regard to written corrective feedback (WCF). Both oral and written feedback have become agendas for research in their own right and form distinct areas of investigation through a wide range of studies (see, e.g., Li & Vuono, 2019, for an overview). In general, research into feedback has been carried out by those who are concerned more broadly with SLA. WCF in particular has not been a major focus of attention by those who might align themselves with mainstream TBLT research. Notable exceptions include Ellis (e.g., Ellis, 2010; Sheen & Ellis, 2011), Li (e.g., Fu & Li, 2019; Li, 2010; Li & Roshan, 2019), and Kim (e.g., Kim et al., 2020). Nevertheless, both forms of feedback have relevance for, and are important in, the context of enhancing learners' grammatical competence through task completion.

Oral Corrective Feedback

So-called CF, or feedback this is offered in the context of spoken interaction, may, at its simplest, be defined as "responses to learner utterances containing an error" (Ellis, 2006, p. 28). Kartchava (2019, p. 4) neatly summarised the potential benefits:

> CF not only provides learners with information about what is incorrect or impossible (i.e., negative evidence) in the L2, and does it at the time when

this information is necessary (generally, during meaning-focused interactions) or in reaction to a linguistic difficulty the learner is experiencing, but also helps them to notice the gaps, and possibly holes, in their interlanguage.

As Lyster et al. (2013) argued, CF plays "a pivotal role in the kind of scaffolding that teachers need to provide to individual learners to promote continuing L2 growth" (p. 1). From a cognitive-interactionist perspective, CF presents opportunities for learners to notice target features in the input during interaction. From a sociocultural-interactionist standpoint, CF is a scaffolding mechanism that moves learners from what they can do only with support to what they can do independently and unaided (see, e.g., Sato & Ballinger, 2012).

Teachers' responses to errors during task execution can be referred to as "online CF." Citing Long (2007), Li (2014) argued that online CF provides opportunities for "a brief timeout from the ongoing interaction for learners" and "an immediate juxtaposition of the wrong and correct forms," thereby providing "an ideal form-focusing device" (p. 197).

Lyster and Ranta (1997) identified six types of CF strategy. Li (2014, p. 196) illustrated how these categorisations might work in practice in several responses to the incorrect utterance "He has dog," where the indefinite article ("a") is missing:

1. Recast – a reformulation with the correct utterance: "a dog."
2. Explicit correction – signalling the error to the learner and then presenting the correct form: "No, you should say '*a* dog'."
3. Clarification request: "Sorry?"
4. Metalinguistic feedback: "You need an indefinite article."
5. Elicitation – prompting for the correct form: "He has …?"
6. Repetition: repeating the incorrect sentence as a question: "He has dog?"

Ranta and Lyster (2007) subsequently placed their earlier six categorisations into two broader CF categories: reformulations and prompts. The first two feedback types (reformulations) provide the correct form and do not therefore promote a response (or "uptake") from the learner, whereas the final four (prompts) do not make the correct form immediately apparent and are therefore more likely to lead to learner uptake. Sheen and Ellis (2011) proposed a similar taxonomy to Lyster and Ranta (1997), distinguishing between two categories – CF that provides the correct form (recasts and explicit correction, including or excluding metalinguistic explanation) and CF that does not provide the correct form (metalinguistic feedback and elicitation).

There is debate about the relative efficacy of different feedback types. Lyster et al. (2013) argued that learners are more likely to notice more explicit CF (e.g., explicit correction or metalinguistic feedback) over more implicit CF (e.g., recasting the language with the error corrected), and prompts (e.g., clarification requests or elicitation) over recasts. They further suggested that explicit CF might be more effective in the shorter term.

However, recasts may be particularly valuable in the context of completing an interactional task because, as Lyster et al. (2013) put it, they "create ideal opportunities for learners to notice the difference between their interlanguage forms and target-like reformulations while preserving their intended meaning" (p. 10). Also, in their view, recasts do not interrupt the flow of communication, enable interactants to continue to focus on meaning, and scaffold learners in ways that push them to perform above their current levels of knowledge. Several task-based studies have investigated the role of recasts as one dimension of enhancing SLA (e.g., Baralt, 2013; Kourtali & Révész, 2020; Révész, 2009; Révész et al., 2014).

In contrast to recasts, explicit correction and prompts may be less effective due to their potential interruption of interactional processes (Long, 2007). Prompts place a greater demand on learners to produce modified output. However, being pushed to self-repair is important and promotes learner autonomy. Self-correction can be successful, provided that the learner has a basic knowledge of the linguistic form in question. From this perspective, implicit feedback (prompts) might be encouraged, at least initially, over explicit feedback (Lyster, 2004).

CF does not have to be solely down to the teacher. There is (as I have already noted) a role for peer CF. Studies that have investigated peer interaction in comparison to interaction between learners and teachers or L1 speakers have indicated that peer interaction fosters SLA because learners will work more on breakdowns in communication (i.e., negotiate meaning) when they are working with each other. This has positive implications for learning. As Lyster et al. (2013) explained, research findings suggest that peer interaction enables L2 learners to work collaboratively with regard to CF and provides comfortable or safe places for learners to test their linguistic hypotheses. It seems, however, that peer CF is likely to focus less often on highlighting grammatical errors than teacher–learner CF. Important too is that learners do need to have noticed their interlocutor's errors.

Bearing in mind on-going arguments about the relative effectiveness of different feedback types, alongside evidence that learners would prefer to receive *some* kind of CF rather than no attention being paid to the errors they are making, what can we conclude for classroom practice?

Variables that will impact on the effectiveness of CF include the context, the learners' proficiency levels, their age, and the extent of their current metalinguistic and explicit grammar knowledge. It is advisable for teachers to draw on the whole range of CF strategies, because this is likely to prove more effective than consistently adhering to only one type (Lyster & Ranta, 1997; Lyster et al., 2013). Additionally, constant error correction can be demotivating and may hinder learners' efforts to engage in interaction. For these reasons, focused CF may be a better strategy (see, e.g., Lasagabaster & Sierra, 2005). In this connection, Lightbown (2008) argued, "[w]hen feedback is focused on a limited number of objects or available in some classroom activities but not others, learners can take greater responsibility for creating and monitoring their own output" (p. 41).

> **Reflection Point**
>
> Lyster and Ranta (1997) suggested six oral feedback strategies, which included direct (reformulating) feedback and indirect (prompting) feedback. In your experiences of either learning or teaching an L2:
>
> 1. What feedback strategies have you encountered or used?
> 2. What strategies did you think were particularly helpful?
> 3. What strategies did you think were unhelpful?

Form Focus – The Post-task Phase

Written Corrective Feedback

When WCF is offered, this is likely to occur as a component of post-task feedback. The essential focus of WCF, which is a response to errors in written language, is (as with CF) to enhance grammatical competence and accuracy. WCF may be done explicitly (direct error correction) or implicitly (indicating that there is an error through direct reference, such as underlining, or indirect reference in the margin, including metalinguistic feedback, e.g., "article error") – see Ellis (2009b).

Truscott's (1996) seminal paper actually made the case against WCF. He proposed the argument that "grammar correction has no place in writing courses and should be abandoned" (p. 328). Truscott added an important caveat, namely, that both grammatical accuracy and feedback as a teaching method, in and of themselves, have value. What Truscott questioned was "correction of grammatical errors for the purpose of improving a student's ability to write accurately" (p. 329). Since that time, a considerable amount of research has concluded that such feedback does have a place in L2 instructional contexts – see, e.g., the work of some of the main researchers in this field – although none of these would claim an affiliation to TBLT research (Bitchener & Ferris, 2012; Bitchener & Knoch, 2010; Bitchener & Storch, 2016; Hyland, 2010; Storch, 2010).

Lee (2019) distinguished between *comprehensive* written corrective feedback (CWCF) and *focused* written corrective feedback (FWCF), and argued that the latter (which involves responding to errors in a selective and focused way) should be more emphasised. Two of Lee's arguments against CWCF are that, first, it sends a message to writers that an important (or possibly main) priority for students is "to aim at producing grammatically perfect writing that is free of errors in every attempt." Another message is that "students are incapable of identifying any of their own errors and so teachers have to work very hard to underline or circle them all for students" (p. 525). These messages also make CWCF an essentially teacher-dominated practice whereby learners become passive recipients and the focus is on error elimination. By contrast, as Lee explained, one of the goals of a teacher's use of WCF should be to support learners to become independent writers who are proficient in their own self-editing.

With regard to TBLT, it might be suggested that focused feedback should be targeted at a particular grammar structure that teachers may have been aiming to encourage in the task, or on the structures that appear to have caused the most issues for learners as they engaged in written task completion. FWCF arguably aligns well with interactionist perspectives that inform TBLT.

From a cognitive perspective, learners receiving FWCF can draw on teacher feedback to enhance their overall proficiency in writing rather than focus primarily on grammatical accuracy, with the corollary that learners would be more inclined to take risks – that is, experiment with new language to express their intended meaning rather than keep to expressions they know to be correct, thereby building their fluency and confidence (Lee, 2019).

FWCF also helps learners to notice, and therefore be more aware of and understand, their errors (Bitchener & Storch, 2016), because a smaller number of grammatical items has been selected for learners' attention. Lee (2019) also argued that, from a sociocultural perspective, FWCF might be better for learning because it helps learners to progress gradually within their ZPDs.

Explicit Grammar Focus

The above presentation of task modalities and feedback practices reveals a range of ways of enacting a form focus in the task-oriented classroom. In summary, at the more learner-centred end of the continuum, this focus might place stronger emphasis on learners' active processing ability and, therefore, on learners' noticing of form as they become conscious of breakdowns in communication while negotiating for meaning. This may be described as incidental FonF (Ellis, 2001), and aligns most clearly with Long's perspective. The teacher's role here will likely be one of bringing learners' attention to form in indirect or prompting ways.

Alternatively or additionally (and moving along the continuum), the form focus might place stronger emphasis on bringing learners' attention to form in more direct or reformulating ways. This may still be contingent on learners' first noticing that there is a problem in communication during meaning negotiation, but there will be "teachable moments" which the teacher will exploit as opportunities for direct teaching (see, e.g., East, 2017). C-R tasks or focused tasks may also be utilised to encourage knowledge or use of a targeted structure. At the more teacher-led end of the continuum, there is greater room for explicit teaching that may well arise from a context where sequences of grammatical structures have been determined in advance, so-called planned FonF (Ellis, 2001).

A final concern for this chapter is the place of specific instruction in the target language feature. As Spada (1997) noted, as far as FFI is concerned, pedagogical efforts to draw learners' attention to form will include, in addition to feedback, direct teaching of grammatical rules. Lyster et al. (2013) suggested that CF and instruction should be seen as complementary pedagogical processes. It is important to note evidence in favour of CF *and* explicit attention to grammar found in a large number of research studies (see DeKeyser, 2017, for a brief summary).

The post-task phase of the lesson may provide the space where teachers, having observed errors in practice or having aimed to elicit students' noticing of a particular form during task performance, turn their attention to a more direct focus on the form(s) in question. Where choices are made to provide explicit instruction, several crucial issues come to mind.

One important consideration is whether form-focused teacher input and direction (either during-task or post-task), or completion of, for example, C-R tasks, should occur in the L2 or in students' L1. Certainly, in contexts where students do not share a common L1, the form focus will necessarily continue in the L2. In homogeneous contexts where the L1 is shared, L1 use arguably has value at different stages in the task cycle. As Philp and Tognini (2009) put it, where students have the L1 in common, interaction is "often characterized by code-switching between L1 and L2" (p. 260). Students' shared L1 use potentially provides a level of support that enables them to work at a higher level than would have been possible if they were only using the target language (Alegría de la Colina & García Mayo, 2009; Lightbown & Spada, 2020). In this respect, Swain and Lapkin (2000) argued, "[t]o insist that no use be made of the L1 in carrying out tasks that are both linguistically and cognitively complex is to deny the use of an important cognitive tool" (p. 269).

When it comes to L1 use in L2 classrooms, an important caveat is in order. Turnbull and Dailey-O'Cain (2009) presented a worthwhile collection of studies that explored this issue. They maintained, however, that it was important to recognise that the overarching goal of the L2 classroom is "the learning of the target language" such that "practices that undermine this ultimate goal must be avoided" (p. 2). Regardless of the important arguments that can be offered around the social and cognitive supports that L1 use can bring, the goal of communicative competence in the L2 should not be unduly hindered.

Furthermore, it is imperative that grammar does not become decontextualised from the communicative goals of the tasks. This is a genuine risk. Larsen-Freeman (2015) noted that, regardless of the setting, grammar instruction does not appear to have been influenced that greatly by the findings of research. Rather, grammar instruction "remains traditional for the most part, with grammar teaching centered on accuracy of form and rule learning, and with mechanical exercises seen as the way to bring about the learning of grammar" (p. 263). Furthermore, as Sato and Oyanedel (2019) made clear, there are contexts (in particular in Asia) where a tendency persists to approach grammar instruction in a more traditional top-down way (which, as I noted in Chapter 4, has influenced the realisation of TBLT in Asian contexts).

In light of the persistence of teacher-dominant grammar practices, it would be counter-productive to initiate a return to what was essentially a behaviourist-informed weak CLT model in which the first P of PPP becomes a teacher-led grammar focus, and the final P becomes the opportunity to practise a selected rule in some kind of "communicative" guise. This (despite its limitations) has certainly proved to be popular – but it would not be TBLT as understood by many of its advocates. Additionally, concern has been raised that a pre-task form focus might cause learners to overly pay attention to the target structure in subsequent task performance, thereby compromising a focus on spontaneous communicative interaction and making the task essentially a grammar practice exercise (see e.g., Willis, 1996). I repeat Samuda and Bygate's (2008) argument that a "key criterial element" of TBLT is that the language focus is positioned as a *post*-task activity arising from task performance. From this perspective, the use of pre-task direct instruction raises important issues for TBLT for which Ellis et al. (2019) suggested that more research is needed.

Nevertheless, it is important to find the appropriate balance between, and sequencing of, form focus and meaning focus, and we have not yet arrived at a clear position on that. Long (2015, p. 26) argued:

> [t]he jury is still out on optimal uses and timing of various kinds and combinations of instruction (explicit, implicit, focus on form, focus on forms, etc.), as well as how best to match type of instruction to students' language aptitude profiles.

Balance between meaning and form may well vary from class to class, and from student to student. Furthermore, studies into teachers' and learners' beliefs and preferences (e.g., Sato & Oyanedel, 2019; Valeo & Spada, 2016) have demonstrated that teachers see value in a communicatively linked form focus, but also tend to incorporate more traditional teacher-led practices into their repertoires. As with several dimensions of practice I presented in Chapter 5, teacher professional judgment will play a role in the decision-making.

Reflection Point

Valeo and Spada (2016) argued, "L2 teachers would be advised to incorporate both integrated and isolated FFI into their instructional practice with the knowledge that each is valuable for L2 learning" (p. 333).

1. What do you think of this assertion?
2. Do you see this assertion as compatible or incompatible with FonF as advocated by Long?
3. In light of everything I have presented in this book so far, including the learner-centred and experiential nature of tasks, what do you think about the place and role of a pre-task grammar focus in TBLT?

Conclusion

In Part II of this book, I have covered a great deal with regard to the practical implementation of TBLT. Aspects of what I have presented demonstrate the complexity of enacting TBLT. I have moved well beyond the central task construct to consider a range of important issues. The task, however, remains pivotal.

Ellis (2009a) attempted to reconcile, on the one hand, the centrality of tasks and, on the other hand, broader pedagogical considerations. He argued that teachers do need to make decisions about the types of tasks they will include in a course and how to sequence these tasks to promote learning. Methodologically, they need to decide how to structure a task-based lesson, taking into account several of the issues I raised in Chapter 5. Ellis concluded, however, that although a task-based lesson might involve three phases (pre-task/task/post-task), "only one of these (the main task phase) is obligatory" (p. 224). Commenting on Ellis's perspective, I noted in East (2012) that structures of participation can justifiably include students working individually, in pairs or groups, or as a whole class, enabling space for teacher-input and utilising both productive and receptive skills. I emphasised nonetheless that the distinguishing component of TBLT is "not that only one participatory structure can be utilised, but rather how the task is – or can be – set up" (p. 83). In Part III, I turn from the practical implementation of TBLT to the evaluation of its effectiveness.

Suggested Further Reading

Long, M. (2000). Focus on form in task-based language teaching. In R. D. Lambert & E. Shohamy (Eds.), *Language policy and pedagogy: Essays in honor of A. Ronald Walton* (pp. 179–192). John Benjamins.

Keck, C., & Kim, Y. (2014). Instructed L2 grammar acquisition: Six key theory-practice links. In *Pedagogical grammar* (pp. 145–169). John Benjamins.

References

Alegría de la Colina, A., & García Mayo, M. P. (2009). Oral interaction in task-based EFL learning: The use of the L1 as a cognitive tool. *International Review of Applied Linguistics in Language Teaching*, 47(3/4), 325–345.

Baralt, M. (2013). The impact of cognitive complexity on feedback efficacy during online versus face-to-face interactive tasks. *Studies in Second Language Acquisition*, 35(4), 689–725.

Bitchener, J., & Ferris, D. R. (2012). *Written corrective feedback in second language acquisition and writing*. Routledge.

Bitchener, J., & Knoch, U. (2010). The contribution of written corrective feedback to language development: A ten-month investigation. *Applied Linguistics*, 31(2), 193–214.

Bitchener, J., & Storch, N. (2016). *Written corrective feedback for L2 development*. Multilingual Matters.

Canale, M. (1983). On some dimensions of language proficiency. In J. W. J. Oller (Ed.), *Issues in language testing research* (pp. 333–342). Newbury House.

Canale, M., & Swain, M. (1980). Theoretical bases of communicative approaches to second language teaching and testing. *Applied Linguistics*, 1(1), 1–47.

DeKeyser, R. (2017). Knowledge and skill in ISLA. In S. Loewen & M. Sato (Eds.), *The Routledge handbook of instructed second language acquisition* (pp. 15–32). Routledge.

East, M. (2012). *Task-based language teaching from the teachers' perspective: Insights from New Zealand*. John Benjamins.

East, M. (2017). "If it is all about tasks, will they learn anything?" Teachers' perspectives on grammar instruction in the task-oriented classroom. In M. J. Ahmadian & M. P. García Mayo (Eds.), *Recent perspectives on task-based language learning and teaching* (pp. 217–231). De Gruyter Mouton.

Ellis, R. (2001). Introduction: Investigating form-focused instruction. *Language Learning*, 51 (S1), 1–46.

Ellis, R. (2003). *Task-based language teaching and learning*. Oxford University Press.

Ellis, R. (2005). Principles of instructed language learning. *System*, 33(2), 209–224.

Ellis, R. (2006). Researching the effects of form-focussed instruction on L2 acquisition. *AILA Review*, 19, 18–41.

Ellis, R. (2009a). Task-based language teaching: Sorting out the misunderstandings. *International Journal of Applied Linguistics*, 19(3), 221–246.

Ellis, R. (2009b). A typology of written corrective feedback types. *ELT Journal*, 63(2), 97–107.

Ellis, R. (2010). A framework for investigating oral and written corrective feedback. *Studies in Second Language Acquisition*, 32(2), 335–349.

Ellis, R., Li, S., & Zhu, Y. (2019). The effects of pre-task explicit instruction on the performance of a focused task. *System*, 80, 38–47.

Fotos, S. (1994). Integrating grammar instruction and communicative language use through grammar consciousness-raising tasks. *TESOL Quarterly*, 28(2), 323–351.

Fu, M., & Li, S. (2019). The associations between individual differences in working memory and the effectiveness of immediate and delayed corrective feedback. *Journal of Second Language Studies*, 2(2), 233–257.

García Mayo, M. P., & Imaz Agirre, A. (2019). Task modality and pair formation method: Their impact on patterns of interaction and LREs among EFL primary school children. *System*, 80, 165–175.

Hyland, F. (2010). Future directions in feedback on second language writing: Overview and research agenda. *International Journal of English Studies*, 10(2), 171–182.

Kartchava, E. (2019). *Noticing oral corrective feedback in the second language classroom: Background and evidence*. Lexington Books.

Kim, Y. (2013). Effects of pre-task modelling on attention to form and question development. *TESOL Quarterly*, 47, 8–35.

Kim, Y., Choi, B., Kang, S., Yun, H., & Kim, B. (2020). Comparing the effects of direct and indirect synchronous written corrective feedback: Learning outcomes and students' perceptions. *Foreign Language Annals*, 53(1), 176–199.

Kourtali, N.-E., & Révész, A. (2020). The roles of recasts, task complexity, and aptitude in child second language development. *Language Learning*, 70(1), 179–218.

Krashen, S. (1981). *Second language acquisition and second language learning*. Pergamon Press.

Larsen-Freeman, D. (2015). Research into practice: Grammar learning and teaching. *Language Teaching*, 48(2), 263–280.

Lasagabaster, D., & Sierra, J. M. (2005). Error correction: Students' versus teachers' perceptions. *Language Awareness*, 14(2/3), 112–127.

Lee, I. (2019). Teacher written corrective feedback: Less is more. *Language Teaching*, 52(4), 524–536.

Li, S. (2010). The effectiveness of corrective feedback in SLA: A meta-analysis. *Language Learning*, 60(2), 309–365.

Li, S. (2014). Oral corrective feedback. *ELT Journal*, 68(2), 196–198.

Li, S., & Roshan, S. (2019). The associations between working memory and the effects of four different types of written corrective feedback. *Journal of Second Language Writing*, 45, 1–15.

Li, S., & Vuono, A. (2019). Twenty-five years of research on oral and written corrective feedback in System. *System*, 84, 93–109.

Lightbown, P. (2008). Transfer appropriate processing as a model for class second language acquisition. In Z. Han (Ed.), *Understanding second language process* (pp. 27–44). Multilingual Matters.

Lightbown, P., & Spada, N. (2020). Teaching and learning L2 in the classroom: It's about time. *Language Teaching*, 53(4), 422–432.

Loewen, S. (2018). Focus on form versus focus on forms. In J. I. Liontas (Ed.), *The TESOL encyclopedia of English language teaching* (pp. 1–6). John Wiley & Sons.

Loewen, S. (2020). *Introduction to instructed second language acquisition* (2nd ed.). Routledge.

Long, M. (1991). Focus on form: A design feature in language teaching methodology. In K. de Bot, R. Ginsberg, & C. Kramsch (Eds.), *Foreign language research in cross-cultural perspective* (pp. 39–52). John Benjamins.

Long, M. (2000). Focus on form in task-based language teaching. In R. D. Lambert & E. Shohamy (Eds.), *Language policy and pedagogy: Essays in honor of A. Ronald Walton* (pp. 179–192). John Benjamins.

Long, M. (2007). *Problems in SLA*. Lawrence Erlbaum.

Long, M. (2015). *Second language acquisition and task-based language teaching*. Wiley-Blackwell.

Lyster, R. (2004). Differential effects of prompts and recasts in form-focused instruction. *Studies in Second Language Acquisition*, 26(3), 399–432.

Lyster, R., & Ranta, L. (1997). Corrective feedback and learner uptake: Negotiation of form in communicative classrooms. *Studies in Second Language Acquisition*, 19(1), 37–66.

Lyster, R., Saito, K., & Sato, M. (2013). Oral corrective feedback in second language classrooms. *Language Teaching*, 46(1), 1–40.

O'Sullivan, B. (2002). Learner acquaintanceship and oral proficiency test pair-task performance. *Language Testing*, 19(3), 277–295.

Oliver, R., & Philp, J. (2014). *Focus on oral interaction: Research-led guide exploring the role of oral interaction for second language learning*. Oxford University Press.

Philp, J., Adams, R., & Iwashita, N. (2014). *Peer interaction and second language learning*. Routledge.

Philp, J., & Tognini, R. (2009). Language acquisition in foreign language contexts and the differential benefits of interaction. *International Review of Applied Linguistics in Language Teaching*, 47(3/4), 245–266.

Ranta, L., & Lyster, R. (2007). A cognitive approach to improving immersion students' oral language abilities: The awareness-practice-feedback sequence. In R. DeKeyser (Ed.), *Practice in a second language: Perspectives from applied linguistics and cognitive psychology* (pp. 141–160). Cambridge University Press.

Révész, A. (2009). Task complexity, focus on form, and second language development. *Studies in Second Language Acquisition*, 31(3), 437–470.

Révész, A., Sachs, R., & Hama, M. (2014). The effects of task complexity and input frequency on the acquisition of the past counterfactual construction through recasts. *Language Learning*, 64(3), 615–650.

Samuda, V., & Bygate, M. (2008). *Tasks in second language learning.* Palgrave Macmillan.

Sato, M., & Ballinger, S. (2012). Raising language awareness in peer interaction: A cross-context, cross-method examination. *Language Awareness,* 21(1–2),157–179.

Sato, M., & Oyanedel, J. C. (2019). "I think that is a better way to teach but …": EFL teachers' conflicting beliefs about grammar teaching. *System,* 84, 110–122.

Schmidt, R. (1990). The role of consciousness in second language learning. *Applied Linguistics,* 11(1), 17–46.

Schmidt, R. (1993). Consciousness, learning and interlanguage pragmatics. In G. Kasper & S. Blum-Kulka (Eds.), *Interlanguage pragmatics* (pp. 21–42). Oxford University Press.

Schmidt, R. (2001). Attention. In P. Robinson (Ed.), *Cognition and second language instruction* (pp. 3–32). Cambridge University Press.

Sheen, Y., & Ellis, R. (2011). Corrective feedback in language teaching. In E. Hinkel (Ed.), *Handbook of research in second language teaching and learning* (vol. 2, pp. 593–610). Routledge.

Spada, N. (1997). Form-focused instruction and second language acquisition: A review of classroom and laboratory research. *Language Teaching,* 30(2), 73–87.

Storch, N. (2010). Critical feedback on written corrective feedback research. *International Journal of English Studies,* 10(2), 29–46.

Swain, M. (1998). Focus on form through conscious reflection. In C. Doughty & J. Williams (Eds.), *Focus on form in classroom second language acquisition* (pp. 64–81). Cambridge University Press.

Swain, M., & Lapkin, S. (2000). Task-based second language learning: The uses of the first language. *Language Teaching Research,* 4(3), 251–274.

Truscott, J. (1996). The case against grammar correction in L2 writing classes. *Language Learning,* 46(2), 327–369.

Turnbull, M., & Dailey-O'Cain, J. (2009). Introduction. In M. Turnbull & J. Dailey-O'Cain (Eds.), *First language use in second and foreign language learning* (pp. 1–14). Multilingual Matters.

Valeo, A., & Spada, N. (2016). Is there a better time to focus on form? Teacher and learner views. *TESOL Quarterly,* 50(2), 314–339.

Van den Branden, K. (2009). Mediating between predetermined order and chaos: The role of the teacher in task-based language education. *International Journal of Applied Linguistics,* 19(3), 264–285.

Willis, J. (1996). *A framework for task-based learning.* Longman Pearson Education.

PART III

Evaluating TBLT

7
USING TASKS FOR CLASSROOM ASSESSMENT PURPOSES

Introduction

In Part I of this book, I aimed to provide a useful theoretical basis for TBLT by outlining several key foundational principles for teaching and learning, relating them to a task-based perspective. Essentially, due to TBLT's learner-centred and experiential approach to L2 pedagogy, learners have a crucial role to play in their own second language acquisition (SLA). TBLT is nonetheless informed by interactionist perspectives which allow room for what the teacher does alongside what the learners do. However, the balance between these two roles will be different depending on where teachers position themselves on the interactionist continuum from learner-centred to teacher-led.

The focus of Part II was on putting TBLT into practice. I made it clear that, despite different emphases that have emerged in light of different theoretical orientations, and as teachers have grappled with the relative balances between teachers' and learners' roles, the task is central to TBLT. The task is therefore the focal point for experiential learning, and I proposed that, if we can get the task right, we are well on the road towards putting into practice an approach to L2 pedagogy based on tasks. Building on the crucial task construct, I presented ways in which TBLT may be practised in a wide range of contexts, depending on where on the interactionist continuum its proponents place themselves.

A final fundamental consideration for TBLT is to address how well TBLT is going in practice. More broadly, this consideration needs to take into account not only successes with regard to TBLT, but also challenges. This will include teachers' reflections on their own practices in light of theory and research, and thinking about what aspects of practice might need to change if TBLT is to achieve its potential as an effective learner-centred and experiential pedagogy. Put another way, it is important now to consider components of Step 3 of the three-step process I introduced at the end of Chapter 4, that is, retrospective reflection, or a consideration what has been achieved. Part III turns to the important matter of evaluation and explores how TBLT and its effectiveness for learners might be evaluated in a range of ways. The chapters in Part III discuss the collection of evaluative evidence and consider the implications of this evidence for TBLT as a viable educational endeavour.

The focus of Chapter 7 is on the use of tasks for purposes of assessment. Consequently, the chapter turns from one set of theoretical bases and literature (SLA and learning theories) to a different set (language testing and assessment). With this in mind, Chapter 7 parallels Chapter 1. After presenting a brief introduction to the assessment of students' learning in the task-based classroom, the chapter takes an historical look at developments, but this time in the field of language assessment. The chapter goes on to focus predominantly on the classroom-based use of communicative tasks for assessment purposes in local contexts. It then considers the use of different kinds of assessment instruments to gather a range of evidence on students' learning outcomes. It concludes with a brief discussion of how the practice of TBLT in classrooms may be influenced by so-called *high-stakes* assessment systems.

Assessing Students' Learning

In Chapter 4, I presented Nunan's (2004) conceptualisation of TBLT in practice as having two components – the curriculum as plan and the curriculum as action. The curriculum as plan, enacted through documents such as syllabi, textbooks and other resources, may be regarded as the basis for teaching and learning programmes and is concerned with what we wish students to learn in the programme. The curriculum as action represents the moment-by-moment realisation of the planned curriculum – what teachers do with the plan. Nunan included assessment instruments as part of the plan. Furthermore, he presented a third component of the curriculum – the curriculum as *outcome*, or what students actually learn as a result of the instructional process. Evaluation of the effectiveness of TBLT is aligned not only with Step 3 of *enacting* the curriculum, but also, more broadly, with the *outcomes* of the curriculum.

Articulating the relationship between plan, action and outcome in the language classroom, Bachman and Damböck (2018) noted, "[t]he primary purpose of language teaching and of language teaching/learning tasks is to *improve students' language learning*." The purpose of assessment from this perspective is "to collect *information* about your students' *language ability* – *what* and *how much* they have learned" (p. 9, my emphases). In essence, the curriculum as outcome may be realised through assessment opportunities that have been included as part of the plan – in other words, assessment information may provide evidence of learning gains.

What Is Assessment?

For many people, the very first thing that comes to mind when they think about the word "assessment" is tests, and often the notions of "test" and "being tested" connote negative reactions. Shohamy (2007), for example, put it like this: thinking back to her days at school, she described the contradiction between "the enjoyment and fun of learning" and the act of being tested, which she saw as "a hurdle, an *unpleasant* experience." She went on to describe her experiences with tests in a series of negative words – pain, tension, unfairness, anger, frustration, pressure, competition, humiliation. She concluded, "[i]f learning is so meaningful, rewarding, and personal, why is it that it needs to be accompanied by the unpleasant events of *being tested!*" (p. 142).

Shohamy (2007) was referring to a time in history when assessments were narrowly viewed as purely instruments of measurement, operationalised in controlled (i.e., timed test) conditions, and when marks and grades were often the only feedback to test takers and were frequently the basis of major decisions about large groups of students. Assessment does not need to be so painful. Bachman and Damböck (2018), for example, drew attention to significant developments in thinking around assessment whereby, in many respects, assessment is now concerned with beneficial consequences for learners, including providing information that might improve teaching and learning.

As I explain in more detail below, the momentum for alternative forms of assessment, including a stronger focus on classroom-based assessment opportunities, has been growing over a good number of years. Task-based language assessment (TBLA), where communicative tasks are used to gather evidence for evaluative purposes, is one realisation of that momentum. This does not mean that tests and examinations in controlled conditions no longer have roles to play in the assessment of language proficiency (indeed, they still remain in operation in many contexts). It does mean that there is considerable scope for teachers to use communicative tasks for assessment purposes.

Before considering what TBLA might look like in the language classroom, in what follows I present a brief history of key milestones in the language assessment journey to complement the historical overview of language teaching and learning I presented in Chapter 1. Its two purposes are to uncover the implications of developments in thinking in and for the task-oriented communicative classroom, and also, later in the chapter, to consider the range of evidence that may help teachers to determine whether and to what extent tasks are working as instruments to promote SLA.

Collecting Evidence of Linguistic Proficiency

In Chapter 1, I began the historical journey into language teaching methodology with an outline of grammar-translation, an approach to language pedagogy stretching back into the 1800s. In this behaviourist-informed approach, students' linguistic proficiency was assessed in largely positivist (right/wrong) discrete ways, based on students' knowledge of isolated vocabulary items and grammatical structures. A central means of assessment was through the translation of texts, primarily from the target language into students' L1 (translation), and secondarily from L1 into the target language (prose composition). Performances were rated as correct or incorrect (section by section) relative to the accuracy of the translated items and the ways in which students demonstrated command of the underlying vocabulary and grammatical principles. There was no emphasis on assessing communicative proficiency.

In the 1940s, and in an attempt to bring more authentic language use into classrooms, linguists at the University of Michigan began to develop what came to be known as the audio-lingual method for language learning. As I outlined in Chapter 1, its emphases were on the listening and speaking elements of language that were perceived to be neglected in grammar-translation. During the 1950s and 1960s, the method grew in popularity, particularly in North America.

Subsequent to the emergence of Michigan's audio-lingual initiative was the publication of what came to be a classic and influential text in the field of assessment – Robert Lado's *Language Testing* (Lado, 1961). In his role as Director of Testing in the English Language Institute of the University of Michigan (a position he took up towards the end of the 1940s), Lado was instrumental in creating English language tests to assess the linguistic proficiency of the increasing numbers of L2 speakers of English coming into the university, and contributed to the development of the Michigan English Language Assessment Battery (MELAB). This was essentially a test to determine L2 students' ability to pursue university-level study in an English-medium context. The MELAB was used for this purpose up to as recently as 2018, after which time it was superseded by the considerably broader assessment known as the Michigan English Test or MET, first introduced in 2008 (Michigan Assessment, n.d.).

Influenced not only by the behaviourist-informed audio-lingual approach, but also by structural linguistics, Lado precipitated what might be described as the psychometric-structuralist era of language testing (Spolsky, 1977). Lado (1961) argued, "language is a system of habits of communication ... [which] involve matters of form, meaning, and distribution at several levels of structure, namely those of the sentence, clause, phrase, word, morpheme, and phoneme" (p. 22). From this perspective, measuring linguistic proficiency continued elements of the grammar-translation model where items were tested discretely in a positivist right/wrong way, although test items did not involve translation, an assessment technique of which Lado was critical (see, e.g., Lado, 1964). This *discrete item* or *discrete point* testing drew on such test items as fill-in-the-blank and multiple choice. Lado regarded these question formats as objective (and therefore reliable) indicators of proficiency, whereas, in his view, performances of writing and speaking were open to subjective evaluation (i.e., difficulty in pinning down exactly what level a student had reached), making them "not easy to score" (Lado, 1961, p. 31).

As Communicative Language Teaching (CLT) began to emerge in the late 1960s as a response to calls for greater emphasis on authentic communication in L2 classrooms, a primary criticism of discrete point tests was that language cannot just be regarded as an objective structural system. Structural elements do not operate in isolation or in a vacuum. Rather, the structures constitute ways of expressing meaning, and their use makes fuller sense in meaningful contexts. As Underhill (1982) maintained, "there is no real-life situation in which we go around asking or answering multiple choice questions" (p. 18). This is arguably an over-reactionary assertion – there are of course real-life contexts (such as marketing or evaluative surveys) in which multiple choice questions are used and which require understanding and processing of language input. The argument was nonetheless that discrete point tests could not hope to replicate (or measure) real-world language use. Furthermore, students could achieve high scores in discrete point tests, but might not be able to use the language for any functional or communicative purpose. As with translation, the scores therefore provided no evidence of *communicative* proficiency.

An early move towards a more holistic view of language assessment was found, for example, in the work of Lado's contemporary, the American psychologist John B. Carroll. Carroll (1961) acknowledged the high level of reliability that could be achieved through discrete point tests. He argued nonetheless that we needed not only to collect, for assessment purposes, samples of language that replicated language as used in real-world contexts beyond the assessment, but also to score these samples of language in a way that would differentiate between different levels of test taker performance. Thus, measurement of the ability to undertake spoken interactions or compose whole texts in writing came to the fore, and, particularly as CLT began to exert greater influence, so-called *integrative* tests of speaking and writing grew in prominence.

Integrative tests of the productive skills appeared to offer a significant way forward from a communicative perspective. However, such tests proved to be expensive and time-consuming, and (as Lado had fore-shadowed) challenging to score reliably. John Oller, at that time recent founder of the Department of Linguistics at the University of New Mexico, supported Carroll's argument that tests should aim to integrate structures and language in actual use, and early proposed integrative tests (Oller, 1979). However, he proposed forms of testing which he claimed would measure the same kinds of skills as those measured in open-ended speaking and writing assessments, only more efficiently.

Two test items that emerged from Oller's work were the cloze procedure (a reading comprehension activity) and the dictation (a listening/writing activity). A cloze activity might present test candidates with a meaningful text in which certain lexical items have been removed. This fill-in-the-blank test became a means for candidates to demonstrate their understanding of appropriate words in context. The candidates might be given a separate list of the words that could be used. If the input was sufficient in length, it would be possible for a range of grammatical and lexical features to be required and tested. Test takers would need to make use of the contextual clues and could not merely process the text word by word or phrase by phrase. A dictation activity would follow a standard dictation procedure: the teacher (as test administrator) would read the whole text;

then the text would be read in segments (one or a few times); finally, the whole text would be read again. The segments would be long enough to challenge the test takers' short-term memory capacity, and success would require the test takers to understand the text's meaning.

Despite the greater apparent integration of structure and language in use that was ostensibly achieved in Oller's integrative test proposals, both cloze and dictation were problematic from a communicative perspective. They were artificial and were found to remain fundamentally measures of language knowledge (that is, assessing the same kinds of things as discrete point tests). Furthermore, they were primarily receptive. Once more, the tests were inadequate measures of communicative proficiency.

Towards Communicative Language Testing

As I explained in Chapter 1, as theorists began to wrestle with the question of "what it means to know a language and to be able to put that knowledge to use in communicating with people in a variety of settings and situations" (Hedge, 2000, p. 45), theoretical frameworks of communicative competence began to emerge. An early influential model was proposed by Canale and Swain (Canale, 1983; Canale & Swain, 1980). Later models were developed by others, such as Bachman (1990) and Bachman and Palmer (1996). (See the introductory chapter in Walker et al., 2018).

Alongside the emergence of CLT, communicative language testing became the dominant paradigm for language tests. This represented what Spolsky (1977) called the psycholinguistic-sociolinguistic period, and marked, in Bachman's words (2000), the beginning of a movement away from the "narrow conception of language ability as an isolated 'trait'" that could be measured reliably through discrete point or integrative (but still knowledge-oriented) tests. Rather, language in actual use began to be perceived as "the creation of discourse, or the situated negotiation of meaning," and language ability came to be regarded as "multicomponential and dynamic" (p. 3). That is, *communicative* language use is context-specific and context-driven. It requires language users to create language, often in real time, as they negotiate meaning and, in that process, integrate several skills. For Bachman, the implications for assessment were clear: assessments of language proficiency needed to "take into consideration the discoursal and sociolinguistic aspects of language use, as well as the context in which it takes place" (p. 3). In other words:

> [T]he kinds of linguistic knowledge that could arguably be established (and measured) via the tests and examinations associated with grammar-translation, or the mimicking of words and phrases that had been common to audio-lingualism, were no longer sufficient. Rather, it was necessary to view proficiency more holistically in terms of carrying out genuine communication in a range of contexts.
>
> *(East, 2016, pp. 5–6)*

Thus, from the perspective of the communicative agenda, Lado had been painted as the antithesis, and Oller had not solved the dilemma of measuring communicative proficiency. The scene had been set for the use of communicative tasks for assessment purposes.

Reflection Point

Bachman and Damböck (2018) spoke of "an entirely new way of looking at the way you assess your students ... by first asking yourself what beneficial consequences you want to help bring about by using an assessment" (p. 2).

1. What different kinds of assessment have you encountered as a learner of an L2?
2. What kinds of assessment have you preferred, and why?
3. In your view, what kinds of assessment are likely to give the most useful information (lead to the most beneficial consequences) for teachers and students from a TBLT perspective?

Broader Considerations with Regard to Assessment

It is important, at this juncture, to acknowledge significant shifts that were occurring more universally in the field of testing and assessment as behaviourism as the dominant psychological model gave way to different understandings of human learning, and as the psychometric tradition in language testing, with its focus on objectivity and test scores, broadened out to embrace alternative approaches.

Gipps (1994) spoke of a "paradigm shift" in educational assessment that began to challenge the accepted orthodoxy that tests and examinations should be central and that embraced a broader model. This model would offer a range of assessment instruments (including classroom-based assessments, practical and oral assessments, and coursework and portfolios) alongside a variety of approaches (including more formative and performance-based uses of assessment tasks). This shift in thinking was built on the argument that "the major traditional model underpinning assessment theory, the psychometric model, is no longer adequate, hence the paradigm shift" (p. 1).

Furthermore, Gipps and Murphy (1994) asserted that assessment needed to fulfil one of two goals: a "managerial and accountability" goal (a summative assessment model whose purpose is to measure, at the end of a course or a series of lessons, what students have learned in relation to the goals of the programme) and a "professional and learning" goal (a formative assessment model situated within the teaching and learning process that provides opportunities for feedback and feedforward with a view to improving learning). A broadening to embrace a professional/learning model that includes classroom-based assessment, the main purpose of which is to help teachers to improve their teaching and students to improve their learning, has led to what Bachman and Damböck (2018, p. 3) described as "dramatic and exciting developments" over the last several decades.

Towards Task-based Language Assessment (TBLA)

Gipps (1994) had spoken broadly of a paradigm shift in educational assessment. Focusing on the L2 classroom, Antón (2015) more recently argued that placing greater focus on authentic and classroom-based assessments would lead to "empowering roles for teachers and learners" and would "hold potential for a paradigm shift in second language assessment" (p. 74). One such paradigm shift is TBLA, described succinctly by Shehadeh (2018) as "a framework for language testing/assessment that takes the task as the fundamental unit for assessment and testing." He went on to say that TBLA is "based on the same underlying principles as TBLT, but extends them from the learning-and-teaching domain to the testing domain" (p. 157). If, in the task-based classroom, the communicative task is the central focus point and the construct of interest, it makes sense that evidence of learning should primarily be gathered from performances on tasks. Shehadeh spoke of TBLA as being essentially formative and classroom-based in nature. This approach aligns with Antón's view that teachers "naturally integrate assessment into their teaching, whether formally or informally, with the goal of collecting evidence on student learning to inform subsequent instruction" (p. 74).

At its most informal, classroom-based TBLA is (ideally) happening all the time as teachers monitor students' engagement with and performances on tasks, make decisions about during-task and post-task feedback, and consider next steps in the learning process (see Chapter 6 for the kinds and nature of feedback that may have value for learning). This kind of *formative* or *diagnostic* assessment may also be more *formally* put into operation through the specific use of communicative tasks chosen for assessment purposes. The tasks may in fact be no different from the kinds of tasks that teachers might regularly use in the TBLT-oriented classroom. Their purpose, however, moves beyond language in use to the more deliberate collection of diagnostic evidence.

As with informal classroom-based evidence, using tasks for more dedicated assessment purposes will enable teachers to provide feedback to learners on their strengths and weaknesses in performance, and will help learners (and teachers) to identify the next steps in the learning process. These kinds of formative assessment opportunities may be described as low-stakes in the sense that the outcomes of the assessment do not have any particular consequences for learners beyond the purpose of improving teaching and learning in the classroom. Teachers could also use TBLA at the end of a series of lessons or programme of study. The purpose here would be to collect summative evidence that learning has taken place.

What kinds of evidence of learning gains might teachers collect? At its simplest, teachers could observe how students perform a task and they could draw conclusions from that. Here, the primary evidence becomes whether or not the students are able to complete the task and, in particular, reach the stated outcome. In this respect, and for assessment and evidence purposes, the main goal of TBLA, as Long and Norris (2000) put it, "is not to measure the display of linguistic knowledge, nor to assign learners to broadly defined levels of language ability, but to ascertain whether students can use the L2 to accomplish target tasks." That is, "the construct of interest is performance of the task itself" (p. 600).

In some circumstances, successful task completion may give us sufficient evidence of learning gains. In Chapter 4, I noted the example of nurses enrolled in a language course to help them develop their proficiency in relation to their chosen profession. Thus, the goal of a particular English for Specific Purposes (ESP) course may be to prepare nurses for successful interactions with patients in clinical settings. In this situation, we would be interested primarily in whether nurses *can* interact successfully with patients, and the tasks we ask them to complete will be aligned with that goal. It may be argued that successful achievement of the outcome of a given task may be regarded as sufficient evidence of performance (and, therefore, of learning).

Task outcome evidence is limited, however. Successful completion of one task does not provide evidence that learners can complete other tasks equally successfully (whether these tasks are essentially the same, or similar, or quite different). Collecting outcome evidence over time and over a series of different tasks may be a more robust source of evidence of having reached the required level in the required skill or skills. In this connection, Long (2016) provided a useful example, using filling out application forms as the target task domain. This domain may be practised, for example, through completing various forms for a wide range of real-life applications (e.g., driver's licence, job application, bank account). Long went on to suggest that arising from these learning opportunities are two "testable predictions" (p. 7), that is, performance outcomes on which we can gather evidence: students' ability to complete two of the application forms successfully may be sufficient not only to *represent* what they can do with forms in other contexts, but also to *predict* their ability to complete other application forms they have not necessarily come across.

Thus, in Long's view, we can arguably generalise from performance on one or two pedagogic tasks to broader performance on the real-world target tasks, on the basis of learners reaching the outcome. This does have some predictive value. However, task outcome evidence (if measured simply in terms of successful completion of the task or tasks) does not tell us very much about the more general underlying skills that underpin successful task performance. For example, a successful interaction between a nurse and a patient assumes a level of general language proficiency on which the interlocutor can draw and that the interlocutor can apply in other (or different) situations. Task outcome evidence, particularly if it is determined in a dichotomous "yes/no," "completed/not completed," "pass/fail" way, does not tell us anything about individual students' language proficiency, and how their levels of ability differ from other students. Nor does it necessarily tell us very much about learning gains.

More detailed and fine-grained analyses of performances will therefore provide greater evidence of learning gains than a simple reliance on achieving the outcome. Particularly when tasks are being used summatively for assessment purposes, teachers may find it helpful or necessary, instead of or in addition to diagnostic feedback, to assign a mark or grade to students' performances. This requires articulation of what a specific mark or grade actually means, particularly when these are used to make decisions about individual students – such as classifying students into different groups, or moving students from one class level to another. Depending on the importance of the decisions that might be taken, the stakes for students may be relatively low (an in-class grade at the end of a series of lesson), or somewhat higher (being moved into a different class or group). They may perhaps be even higher when score interpretation and use may have important consequences for students (such as being or not being able to proceed to the next level in a language programme, or being certified to have reached a sufficient level of language proficiency for a professional context). Particularly when the stakes are high, it is important to ensure that the scores, as representations of students' language proficiency, are as meaningful and accurate as possible.

More Fine-grained Evidence of Proficiency

Green (2021) asserted that language assessment "involves obtaining evidence to inform inferences about a person's *language-related* knowledge, skills or abilities" (p. 5, my emphasis). Weaver (2012) argued that TBLA "involves evaluating the *degree* to which language learners can use their L2 to accomplish given tasks" (p. 287, my emphasis). These arguments reflect the reality that linguistic competence is relative and not absolute. Weaver went on to propose that evaluating students' degrees of proficiency requires the articulation of *assessment criteria*. These criteria can be used to differentiate between different levels of performance among students, and should ideally provide opportunities for the most informative feedback to students. From this perspective, therefore, TBLA moves *beyond* performance of the task itself as the construct of interest, as Long and Norris (2000) had put it. The outcome evidence is *also* being used to measure the display of linguistic knowledge and assign students to broadly defined levels of language ability. In this sense, the assessment moves beyond *task*-based to *construct*-based.

Construct-based Assessments

Bachman and Palmer (2010) argued, "[i]f we are to make interpretations about language ability on the basis of performance on language assessments, we need to *define* this ability in sufficiently precise terms to distinguish it from other individual attributes that can affect assessment performance" (p. 43, my emphasis). This definition is the *construct* that underlies a particular assessment, that is, "the specific definition of an ability that provides the basis for a given assessment or assessment task and for interpreting scores derived from this task" (p. 43).

In the case of a construct-based assessment, the construct definition becomes the springboard or foundation from which to devise an appropriate task for assessment purposes. This means that, first of all, we need to articulate sufficiently and clearly the construct that the assessment intends to measure. This could be done by relating the proficiency in question to a general theoretical model of communicative competence (e.g., Canale, 1983; Canale & Swain, 1980) – for example, ability to use the "language code" accurately, including correct lexis and spelling, accurate formation of words and sentences, and pronunciation; and/or ability to use and understand language appropriate to a stated sociolinguistic context, and to choose suitable meanings and forms for the context. Alternatively, or additionally, the construct could be defined by stating the facets that are key components of the specific task – for example, the ability of the interlocutor to apologise, negotiate or complain.

Subsequent to a clear construct definition comes the process of ensuring that the proposed assessment task will adequately measure the construct. In the case of TBLA, an important consideration will be to design a task for assessment purposes that not only reflects the model of general language ability that underpins it, but that also fulfils the essential criteria of a task (see Part I). Articulating the underlying construct does not need to be a complex process, largely because, from a task-based perspective, the communicative constructs underpinning the task are implicit in the goals and purposes of communicative tasks. That is, communicative tasks can be mapped onto theoretical definitions of communicative competence, and it may therefore also be feasible to map a particular task for assessment purposes onto the construct definition (i.e., to identify the facets of communicative competence represented in the task).

Thus, the task for TBLA could emerge from a consideration of the construct or constructs of interest, and/or the construct(s) of interest could be identified in the task, or both. In this sense, therefore, tasks for the purposes of TBLA can be conceptualised as *both* task-based *and* construct-based, and there are situations where we arguably need both kinds of evidence – that is, evidence that the student is able to reach the outcome of the task *and* evidence that the student can demonstrate facets of the defined construct.

Going back to the example café task I presented in Chapter 5, I explained in East (2016) that, when two partners are negotiating what to buy in the café and wish to demonstrate their ability to interact successfully, we may be interested not only in whether the partners can complete the task successfully. Over and above that, we may be interested in determining the extent to which the partners can demonstrate proficiency in the different facets of the construct underlying the task. Being able to show proficiency across the different facets of the defined construct is arguably *implicit* in the partners' ability to reach the outcome of the task successfully. Completing the task successfully may well be hindered if proficiency in any one of the defined facets has been insufficiently developed.

In other words, the *task* (i.e., what we are asking students to do alongside the task-related outcomes we would like them to achieve) is important. Of equal importance is the *construct* (i.e., the underlying proficiency on which we would like to gather outcome evidence).

The importance of defining the construct (and the facets of proficiency that make up that construct) lies in enabling definitions of different levels of student performance to be articulated, which may then be linked to specific marks or grades. Thus, the next stage in the process of designing a task for assessment purposes is to make transparent what the levels of performance are. This requires the development of some kind of rating scale, the levels of which can be used as assessment criteria.

In some teaching contexts, scoring criteria for assessments may be prescribed for teachers. Additionally, several published rating scales exist, and any of these may be adopted (or adapted) by teachers to suit the purposes of the task. The Common European Framework of Reference for languages or CEFR (Council of Europe, 2001) provides one straightforward means of determining the relative achievements of learners across several skills, benchmarked against a six-point scale (A1 to C2). The scale can be further subdivided (for example, A1+). A somewhat more fine-grained articulation of proficiency is provided in the Proficiency Guidelines of the American Council for the Teaching of Foreign Languages (ACTFL, 2012). The Guidelines present 11 levels of attainment across different skills and a wide range of languages (Novice low-medium-high; Intermediate low-medium-high; Advanced low-medium-high; Superior; and Distinguished). Other scales exist for specific purposes. Examples include the six-level scale of the English Language Proficiency Requirements of the International Civil Aviation Organisation (2010), or the six-band proficiency scale of the Occupational English Test (2020).

Furthermore, specific scales exist for different skills. For example, one well-established scale that has shown itself to be popular for the assessment of writing is the ESL Composition Profile (Jacobs et al., 1981). The Profile distinguishes five facets of a writing construct (content, organisation, vocabulary, language use and mechanics) and presents short descriptors for four proficiency levels within each facet (very poor; fair to poor; good to average; excellent to very good). For some facets, a range of scores is possible within each proficiency band, allowing for more precise interpretation of levels.

Although established and published criteria may be useful, there are important arguments for teachers to draw up their own assessment criteria in the classroom-based assessment context, even if these draw on aspects of previously published criteria. First, just because a scale is popular (as is the case with the Jacobs et al. scale) does not make it ideal. Haswell (2005), for example, critiqued the Jacobs et al. profile on the basis that "the main criteria ... were derived not from L2 essays, nor from L2 teachers, nor much from teachers at all." He went on to note that the main traits of other published criteria "probably have equally troubling and mysterious histories" (p. 202). Second, teachers are essentially the experts in their own local contexts. They are the ones who can make judgments about the individual facets of constructs and the levels of measurement that will provide useful data on their students' proficiency. In cases where scoring criteria are not prescribed, there is value in teachers designing their own criteria. The key design issue is the opportunity to provide useful and meaningful information, not only to students but also to teachers, as means of evaluating learning gains.

Moreover, scales do not need to be complex or elaborate. They may operate holistically, that is, leading to the award of one individual score that essentially sums up the level of performance in a given skill against a global descriptor. They may alternatively operate analytically, that is, leading to the award of several scores that benchmark against descriptors of levels of performance in several sub-skills or sub-facets. Scoring using an analytic scale arguably provides more detailed information to teachers and students about students' relative proficiency, but holistic scales can be easier to apply.

Reflection Point

With regard to using tasks for assessment purposes, Bachman (2002) argued that a given assessment needs to be "*both* construct-based *and* task-based" because "any test design that ignores either task specification or construct definition is likely to lead to results that are not useful for their intended purpose" (p. 470, my emphasis).

1. To what extent do you agree with this viewpoint?
2. Rating scales ideally reflect facets of the construct to be measured in a given assessment. What different rating scales are you familiar with? How useful do you think rating scales are for measuring task outcomes?
3. What do you see as the benefits and drawbacks of holistic versus analytic rating scales?

Reliability and Construct Validity

The higher the stakes in the assessment, the more important it becomes to have a score-awarding process that is robust and fair, so that all stakeholders (and, above all, the students) can have confidence that the scores are meaningful and accurate representations of students' ability. Rating scales are part of that process. Considerations for construct-based assessments also raise the important issues of reliability and construct validity.

Reliability and construct validity may be described as the two essential *measurement* characteristics of tests and assessments. They have implications for the meaning and accuracy of awarded scores as measurements of the underlying construct or constructs, where the scores are indicators of the ability of interest. In high-stakes testing contexts, test setters are particularly concerned about reliability and validity.

Reliability relates to the way the scores are awarded (and thus the extent to which the process of awarding the scores is adequate). When it comes to the productive skills in particular, reliability is undoubtedly enhanced (and primarily determined) through having clearly articulated criteria for assessment aligned to different levels of student performance. Furthermore, using more than one independent marker or rater of students' performances (whose independent scores can be compared) can potentially increase reliability.

Reliability also (or alternatively) relates to whether the same task (or a different version of the task) leads to comparable results on different occasions (so-called *test–retest* and *parallel forms* reliability). That is, if a task for assessment purposes is working reliably, we would anticipate that students would perform similarly across different versions of the same kind of task. Some variation in performance across tasks is inevitable for reasons that may have nothing to do with the task itself. However, if performances across two administrations of the same or a parallel task lead to widely different scores or outcomes, this would raise concern about why this is. We would not know for sure which performance outcome gives us the more accurate information about the student's actual ability. (Going back to Long's form-filling example, if a student can fill in one form very successfully but struggles to complete a similar form, we do not have reliable evidence from which we can make inferences about this student's ability to complete forms.)

Construct validity has to do with the extent to which the scores are adequate representations of students' abilities, as defined by the construct(s), that is, "the agreement between a test score or measure and the quality it is believed to measure" (Kaplan & Saccuzzo, 2012, p. 135). Weir (2005) saw construct validity and reliability as so inter-dependent that he described reliability as "scoring validity."

In the context of classroom-based assessments, particularly when this assessment is lower in the stakes at hand, utilising two or more raters (although ideal and aspirational) is probably impractical. Most of the time, teachers will be reliant on one set of scores. However, if a scoring rubric is applied, particularly across several different tasks, a picture of students' abilities (learner profiles demonstrating a range of performances) will emerge that can provide useful information.

Bottom line: construct-based assessment tasks which are aligned with construct-relevant and differentiated scoring criteria have the potential to lead to scoring evidence that will give us some useful information about linguistic competence, and, by implication, the extent to which tasks are promoting SLA and learning gains are being made. In this sense, therefore, Lado's (1961) original concerns about assessing the productive skills are addressed.

Other Sources of Evidence of Learning Gains

When it comes to determining the learning gains that occur by virtue of task engagement and task use, Weaver (2012) proposed that teachers should draw on a range of measures and techniques for data collection so that different sources of outcome data can be compared. By collecting different types of information, we can enhance the validity and the reliability of outcome and learning gain evidence and also have a stronger basis on which to make changes to teaching and learning practices. Particularly in lower-stakes classroom-based contexts, what other data sources can teachers draw on to enhance and broaden the available evidence of students' learning gains?

It is useful here to come back to the history of language testing I presented earlier in this chapter and the range of test types that have emerged over the years. Reflecting on the on-going relevance of the historical development of language tests over time, McNamara (2000) suggested, "the testing practices associated with earlier approaches have far from disappeared." We see this, for example, in the discrete point items that still persist in contemporary contexts such as the Michigan English Test, and its predecessor, the MELAB, which included discrete point testing of vocabulary and grammar knowledge. McNamara went on to argue that this is why taking a look at earlier testing models is useful for understanding "the current rather eclectic scene in language testing" (p. 21). More recently, Bachman and Palmer (2010, p. 6) put the reality of eclecticism in a different way:

> In any [assessment] situation, there will be a number of alternatives, each with advantages and disadvantages. … If we assume that a single "best" test exists, and we attempt either to use this test itself, or to use it as a model for developing a test of our own, we are likely to end up with a test that will be inappropriate for at least some of our test takers.

Taking these arguments into account, no assessment measure will be fully fit for purpose. If we want to use assessment as a means to evaluate learning gains (and therefore the efficacy of TBLT for the learners), it makes sense to draw on a range of assessment types. Beyond the use of communicative tasks, discrete point tests and integrative (fill-in-the-blank) tests have some value in determining aspects of learners' linguistic proficiency. Furthermore, they are very practical to administer and score. They could easily be utilised in what we can refer to as a pre-test post-test model, that is, measuring learners' linguistic proficiency before completing a communicative task or series of tasks, and then after they have completed the task(s). A comparison of pre-test and post-test scores may provide some evidence that SLA has been enhanced by virtue of engagement with the tasks. This is a matter I take up in more detail in Chapter 8.

A Note on High-stakes Assessments

In concluding this chapter, I would like to add a brief discussion on high-stakes language assessments. In language learning classrooms across the world, students are often planning to take, or are being prepared to take, a set of summative examinations, the outcomes of which may be crucial to their future, including, for example, entrance to higher education or particular careers. Each of these examinations, where the outcomes will have important consequences for test takers, may therefore be described as high-stakes. For English as L2, examples include the examinations of the International English Language Testing System (IELTS) as part of the Cambridge suite of examinations available through Cambridge Assessment English, or the Test of English as a Foreign Language (TOEFL) and the Test of English for International Communication (TOEIC) available through the Educational Testing Service (ETS).

On the positive side, each of the above examinations, theoretically at least, aligns itself with a *communicative* orientation to language pedagogy. Tests of the productive skills are often open-ended and task-like. Indeed, the IELTS speaking assessment, for example, is described as being interactive and replicating real-life scenarios as closely as possible. Ellis et al. (2019) noted that, at least as far as the testing of speaking in the Cambridge suite is concerned, tasks have a prominent position.

However, none of the above assessment systems is fully aligned with theoretical frameworks that inform TBLT. As Skehan and Luo (2020) pointed out, although the Cambridge suite certainly incorporates in its speaking tests "an interactive-ability approach to testing" (p. 3), on the whole there is minimal evidence that the activities required in these high-stakes tests have been influenced by a consideration of the task-based literature. Indeed, replication of task characteristics is less in evidence in the receptive assessment activities, and some question types may include discrete point items (e.g., multiple choice, short answer, matching and sentence completion in IELTS listening and reading tests).

Bearing in mind that good performance on tests such as IELTS, TOEFL and TOEIC can be a high priority for language learners, to the extent that many of them will choose to enrol in dedicated preparation courses, there are implications for courses and programmes that wish to be task-based. That is, students will inevitably wish to do as well as possible on forthcoming high-stakes tests, and teachers will naturally want to do all they can to prepare students for the tests. As Wall (2012, p. 79) put it:

> It is now well accepted that tests can have important consequences – for students, whose future may be determined by their test results, and for their teachers, whose self-esteem, reputation and even career progression may be affected by how successful they are at preparing their students to cope with test requirements.

This leads to the phenomenon of *washback* or *backwash* – the influence of a test on the teaching and learning that is going on in classrooms, and the tailoring of classroom activities to the demands and expectations of the test. Teachers may, for example, place greater emphasis on some components of a prescribed teaching plan or syllabus, and de-emphasise other components, because they believe that specific components will be highlighted in the test (Wall, 2012).

Several authors over a number of years have addressed the specific issue of the washback of language tests. East and Scott (2011) noted, "washback can be positive, in terms of promoting good pedagogical practices and enhancing learning, or negative, in terms of influencing what happens in classrooms in ways that are not considered to be in accord with good language pedagogy" (p. 95). Messick (1996) earlier argued that washback is "not simply good or bad teaching or learning practice that might occur with or without the test, but rather *good or bad practice* that is *evidentially linked* to the introduction and use of the test" (p. 254, my emphases). In Messick's view, language assessments that are likely to lead to *positive* washback will include assessment tasks across a range of skills – both productive (speaking and writing) and receptive (listening and reading) – that offer "authentic and direct samples" of communicative behaviour (p. 241). Smallwood (1994) early suggested that *on-going* assessment is preferable to a single, high-stakes examination. With regard to speaking, for example, he noted that regular classroom-based assessment could be expected to promote more positive washback in that "this approach is likely to have a real effect on the actual teaching styles used in the classroom regarding the encouragement of oral production by the students in a wide variety of contexts" (p. 70).

For TBLT, the washback implications of high-stakes tests are clear. The greater the alignment between the teaching and the assessment, the higher the likelihood that task-based ideas can be adopted in an on-going way as central components of the language learning endeavour. At least with regard to the speaking assessments of the Cambridge suite, Ellis et al. (2019) maintained, "the washback that is likely from these tests is vital: one could not prepare for these tests by learning lists of grammar or vocabulary items" (p. 275). Conversely, where assessments (particularly summative high-stakes assessments) do not emphasise or include tasks, the uptake of task-based ideas at the level of the classroom may be impacted negatively.

Reflection Point

"Tests that have important consequences will have washback" (Alderson & Wall, 1993, p. 120).

1. What has been your experience of the washback effects of a major test/ examination, either as a learner/test taker or as a teacher?
2. What do you see as the most critical risks of washback for TBLT?
3. How might these risks be lessened?

Conclusion

The purpose of the chapters in Part III of this book is to address the question of how well TBLT is going in practice. This chapter has focused on the classroom use of communicative tasks to collect evidence of the effectiveness of TBLT. I have suggested that *outcome* evidence (whether learners achieve the goal or outcome of the task successfully) is one straightforward evaluative technique. It provides a kind of "achieved/not achieved" benchmarking which, in some contexts, may be sufficient. More fine-grained analysis of language gains can be secured by measuring task performances against scoring rubrics. This construct-based approach maps students' performances at different levels against the different facets of a communicative competence construct that are deemed to be important in the context. Greater validity and reliability of outcome evidence may be attained by using a range of different test types to collect evidence of learning gains. In Chapter 8, I look at other ways in which teachers at the classroom level can evaluate the effectiveness of TBLT and I also address programme-level evaluation.

Suggested Further Reading

Norris, J. (2016). Current uses for task-based language assessment. *Annual Review of Applied Linguistics, 36*, 230–244.
Shehadeh, A. (2018). Task-based language assessment: Components, development and implementation. In A. Burns & J. C. Richards (Eds.), *The Cambridge guide to learning English as a second language* (pp. 156–163). Cambridge University Press.

References

ACTFL. (2012). ACTFL Proficiency Guidelines 2012. http://www.actfl.org/publications/guidelines-and-manuals/actfl-proficiency-guidelines-2012.
Alderson, J. C., & Wall, D. (1993). Does washback exist? *Applied Linguistics, 14*(2), 115–129.
Antón, M. (2015). Shifting trends in the assessment of classroom interaction. In N. Markee (Ed.), *The handbook of classroom discourse and interaction* (pp. 74–89). John Wiley & Sons.
Bachman, L. (1990). *Fundamental considerations in language testing*. Oxford University Press.
Bachman, L. (2000). Modern language testing at the turn of the century: Assuring that what we count counts. *Language Testing, 17*(1), 1–42.
Bachman, L. (2002). Some reflections on task-based language performance assessment. *Language Testing, 19*(4), 453–476.
Bachman, L., & Damböck, B. (2018). *Language assessment for classroom teachers*. Oxford University Press.
Bachman, L., & Palmer, A. (1996). *Language testing in practice: Designing and developing useful language tests*. Oxford University Press.
Bachman, L., & Palmer, A. (2010). *Language assessment in practice: Developing language assessments and justifying their use in the real world*. Oxford University Press.
Canale, M. (1983). On some dimensions of language proficiency. In J. W. J. Oller (Ed.), *Issues in language testing research* (pp. 333–342). Newbury House.
Canale, M., & Swain, M. (1980). Theoretical bases of communicative approaches to second language teaching and testing. *Applied Linguistics, 1*(1), 1–47.
Carroll, J. B. (1961). Fundamental considerations in testing for English language proficiency of foreign students. In *Testing the English proficiency of foreign students* (pp. 30–40). Center for Applied Linguistics.

Council of Europe. (2001). *Common European framework of reference for languages.* Cambridge University Press.

East, M. (2016). *Assessing foreign language students' spoken proficiency: Stakeholder perspectives on assessment innovation.* Springer.

East, M., & Scott, A. (2011). Working for positive washback: The standards-curriculum alignment project for Learning Languages. *Assessment Matters, 3,* 93–115.

Ellis, R., Skehan, P., Li, S., Shintani, N., & Lambert, C. (2019). *Task-based language teaching: Theory and practice.* Cambridge University Press.

Gipps, C. (1994). *Beyond testing: Towards a theory of educational assessment.* The Falmer Press.

Gipps, C., & Murphy, P. (1994). *A fair test? Assessment, achievement and equity.* Open University Press.

Green, A. (2021). *Exploring language assessment and testing: Language in action* (2nd ed.). Routledge.

Haswell, R. (2005). Researching teacher evaluation of second language writing via prototype theory. In P. Matsuda & T. Silva (Eds.), *Second language writing research: Perspectives on the process of knowledge construction* (pp. 195–220). Routledge.

Hedge, T. (2000). *Teaching and learning in the language classroom.* Oxford University Press.

International Civil Aviation Organisation. (2010). *Manual on the implementation of ICAO language proficiency requirements* (2nd ed.). ICAO.

Jacobs, H. L., Zinkgraf, S. A., Wormuth, D. R., Hartfiel, V. F., & Hughey, J. B. (1981). *Testing ESL composition: A practical approach.* Newbury House.

Kaplan, R. M., & Saccuzzo, D. P. (2012). *Psychological testing: Principles, applications, and issues* (8th ed.). Centage.

Lado, R. (1961). *Language testing: The construction and use of foreign language tests.* McGraw-Hill.

Lado, R. (1964). *Language teaching: A scientific approach.* McGraw-Hill.

Long, M. (2016). In defense of tasks and TBLT: Nonissues and real issues. *Annual Review of Applied Linguistics, 36,* 5–33.

Long, M., & Norris, J. (2000). Task-based teaching and assessment. In M. Byram (Ed.), *Routledge encyclopedia of language teaching and learning* (pp. 597–603). Routledge.

McNamara, T. (2000). *Language testing.* Oxford University Press.

Messick, S. (1996). Validity and washback in language testing. *Language Testing, 13*(3), 241–256.

Michigan Assessment. (n.d.). *Michigan English test.* https://michiganassessment.org/michigan-tests/met/.

Nunan, D. (2004). *Task-based language teaching.* Cambridge University Press.

Occupational English Test. (2020). *Results and assessment.* https://www.occupationalenglishtest.org/test-information/results-assessment/.

Oller, J. (1979). *Language tests at school.* Longman.

Shehadeh, A. (2018). Task-based language assessment: Components, development and implementation. In A. Burns & J. C. Richards (Eds.), *The Cambridge guide to learning English as a second language* (pp. 156–163). Cambridge University Press.

Shohamy, E. (2007). Tests as power tools. Looking back, looking forward. In J. Fox, M. Wesche, D. Bayliss, L. Cheng, C. E. Turner, & C. Doe (Eds.), *Language testing reconsidered* (pp. 141–152). University of Ottawa Press.

Skehan, P., & Luo, S. (2020). Developing a task-based approach to assessment in an Asian context. *System, 90,* 1–15.

Smallwood, I. M. (1994). Oral assessment: A case for continuous assessment at HKCEE level. *New Horizons: Journal of Education, Hong Kong Teachers' Association, 35,* 68–73.

Spolsky, B. (1977). Language testing: Art or science? In G. Nickel (Ed.), *Proceedings of the Fourth International Congress of Applied Linguistics*, Volume 3 (pp. 7–28). Hochschulverlag.

Underhill, N. (1982). The great reliability validity trade-off: Problems in assessing the productive skills. In J. B. Heaton (Ed.), *Language testing* (pp. 17–23). Modern English Publications.

Walker, I., Chan, D., Nagami, M., & Bourguignon, C. (Eds.). (2018). *New perspectives on the development of communicative and related competence in foreign language education*. De Gruyter.

Wall, D. (2012). Washback. In G. Fulcher & F. Davidson (Eds.), *The Routledge handbook of language testing* (pp. 79–92). Routledge.

Weaver, C. (2012). Incorporating a formative assessment cycle into task-based language teaching in a university setting in Japan. In A. Shehadeh & C. A. Coombe (Eds.), *Task-based language teaching in foreign language contexts: Research and implementation*, (pp. 287–312). John Benjamins.

Weir, C. J. (2005). *Language testing and validation: An evidence-based approach*. Palgrave Macmillan.

8

CLASSROOM AND PROGRAMME-LEVEL EVALUATIONS OF TBLT

Introduction

In Chapter 7, I explored some ways in which students' performances on tasks might be evaluated at the classroom level, thereby helping to provide levels of evidence about learning gains. Bearing in mind that, in TBLT, the task is central to classroom endeavours, it makes sense that tasks can and should also be used as assessment instruments. Their use may be formative (providing diagnostic feedback on performances that will also feed forward into teaching and learning programmes) or summative (providing an end-of-unit or end-of-course summation of what students can do with the language as determined through task outcomes). In addition to evidence on achieving the outcomes of tasks, further and complementary evidence of learning gains can be gathered in several ways.

This chapter takes the matter of evaluation a stage further and considers more broadly how evidence can be gathered about how TBLT in practice is working. Long (2015) compared the broader evaluation of TBLT to the undertaking of research into the TBLT endeavour, making the assertion that the growing range and volume of empirical research into TBLT makes it resemble "the closest thing to a researched pedagogy that exists" (p. 343). Research findings are therefore important in helping to inform and underscore the learning potential of programmes based on tasks. Ultimately, however, the success of innovations such as TBLT is determined by whether these innovations can be shown to work, not just in theory and research, but also (and arguably more importantly) in practice. That is, we need to determine whether programmes are achieving their goals, so that we can make evidence-informed decisions about whether they should continue as they are or whether they should be modified. Long (2015, p. 341) proposed two key questions that need to be addressed:

1. Are programmes doing what they say they are doing?
2. Are students learning what they need to learn?

Furthermore, Long argued that programmes are unique and that TBLT implementation needs to be evaluated in its *particular* context. In other words, evaluating TBLT and its effectiveness is context-specific because each context will have its own vagaries and challenges.

A useful means of distinguishing between types of evaluation is to differentiate between *micro*-evaluation which looks at how teachers implement specific tasks in their own classrooms and *macro*-evaluation which investigates whole courses or programmes (Ellis, 1998, 2011). In what follows, I consider ways in which teachers might undertake their own micro-evaluations in an effective way. I conclude by presenting some examples of macro-evaluation and begin to draw implications for the TBLT endeavour.

The Micro-evaluation of TBLT Implementation

The micro-level of the individual classroom is arguably the level at which the success (or otherwise) of TBLT really takes place. Micro-evaluation will help in determining how teachers working within their own local contexts make (or do not make) TBLT work. Thus, when it comes to evaluating the potential of TBLT in actual practice, a powerful and valuable form of micro-evaluation is one that is undertaken by teachers themselves as part of their own reflective work. Its power lies in enabling teachers to take a retrospective look at their own practices and conclude for themselves what has and has not worked. This retrospection is therefore important in cases where teachers have taken steps to integrate tasks into their day-to-day work and wish to determine the extent to which this has been successful.

Evaluation as Part of a Reflective Cycle

In Chapter 4, I suggested that teachers who are open to TBLT ideas and who would like to explore TBLT in action will be guided by three foundational principles: forward-planning; moment-by-moment classroom decision-making; and retrospective reflection. I have elsewhere conceptualised this three-step cyclical process as reflection for-in-on action (e.g., East, 2014a, 2014b).

The forward-planning component that constitutes reflection-*for*-action (Killion & Todnem, 1991) is not just about planning the tasks that may be used. More broadly, it creates the space for teachers to reflect on theory and to think about what that theory might mean for classroom practice. Reflection-for-action is therefore a vital point of departure in the reflective cycle, and arguably builds a foundation for future practice as teachers "step outside of their own definitions of the world and see new perspectives" (Davis, 2005, p. 18). Essentially, this initial reflection helps practitioners to consider the theoretical implications of new ideas for their practice.

Bearing in mind that TBLT represents an innovation to practice for many teachers, the forward-planning stage requires teachers to invest time (whether individually or collectively) to plan what they are going to do in light of theoretical considerations. I have earlier asserted that simply presenting students with a task and asking them to get on with it is likely to be counter-productive (TBLT is arguably not as effective when students are left solely to their own devices to work on tasks without any mediation from the teacher). A similar argument is true for teachers implementing TBLT. It is not sufficient simply to promote TBLT as "a good idea." TBLT needs to be interpreted in light of theory and mediated in practice, and this is likely to be a lengthy and time-consuming process. The preparatory stage will likely need to involve teacher familiarisation with the theoretical frameworks that inform TBLT as explored in Part I of this book, and some form of structured professional development or teaching support may be necessary to scaffold teachers in their forward-planning endeavours. Teachers may well have to invest quite a bit of time at this initial planning stage. (This is a teacher preparation issue that I take up in Chapter 9.)

Teachers reflecting for action will also need to consider the range of lesson-related elements I presented in Part II. In contexts that are conducive to the implementation of task-based ideas, the forward-planning stage will hopefully be supported by (at the very least) a guiding syllabus of some kind (see Chapter 4), and/or resources such as task-based textbooks Teachers might also find themselves having to develop or adapt tasks presented to them in different resources to ensure their alignment both with the task construct and with the local context (textbooks can be a weak link in the chain, a challenge for teachers that I acknowledge in Chapter 9).

Once teachers have made the decision to implement some form of TBLT, have developed a level of understanding of TBLT in theory and have planned a task or series of tasks for the classroom, they will be confronted with a range of moment-by-moment decisions that arise from monitoring how each lesson is progressing. Moment-by-moment classroom decision-making constitutes what Schön (1983) called reflection-*in*-action. This is the reflection that takes place while a particular lesson is underway as teachers evaluate what is happening in their classroom and make real-time adjustments.

Crucial decisions will arise from how the task is going in practice, and will include: when (and when not) to intervene and re-direct the activity; when (and when not) to offer feedback; what kind of feedback to offer. In turn, these decisions will inform the lesson's post-task phase (which items of form to focus on).

Retrospective reflection equates to Schön's reflection-*on*-action. This is the reflection that teachers engage in *after* the lesson is over, and requires teachers to take a step back from the classroom and to consider carefully what actually happened. As a response to reflecting on what was achieved in the lesson, teachers might decide to change their practices in some way in the next lesson. However, evidence is required to help teachers to make appropriate decisions. Only in light of evidence emerging from what actually happened can meaningful forward-planning take place. An important consideration is the kind of evidence teachers can draw on to enable them to draw defensible conclusions about what has worked and what has not. More broadly, teachers may need to gather evidence over time (e.g., over a series of lessons) in order to identify the progress (or otherwise) of students' learning.

In essence, reflection that is *for* action represents what needs to happen at the beginning stages of contemplating and planning for TBLT as innovation. Through reflection *in* and *on* action, teachers respond to the real-world realities of a planned teaching sequence. This leads back to reflection *for* future action. In the course of enacting reflection for-in-on action, teachers will need to make decisions about tasks and their use. Each step raises its own challenges.

Reflection Point

Reflection for-in-on action represents a cyclical process where teachers: (1) think about and plan the implementation of something new; (2) undertake moment-by-moment evaluations of how the innovation is working in a lesson; and (3) step back from the lesson to consider what did and did not work, with a view to future planning and practice.

Think about implementing TBLT as innovation:

1.   As teachers reflect *for* action, what support do you think they might need or find helpful?
2.   As teachers reflect *in* action, what challenges for TBLT do you think might emerge in the classroom?
3.   How might reflection *on* action help to address the challenges as teachers plan further lessons?

Collecting Evidence for Evaluative Purposes

As I suggested in Chapter 7, one straightforward means of evaluating task effectiveness is for teachers simply to observe how a task works in practice and draw conclusions from what they see. In my own work with beginning teachers undertaking a pre-service course in language teaching, and in the context of encouraging the teachers I was working with to undertake reflection for-in-on action, I have required students to undertake a four-step process:

1.   design a task for use with a real class
2.   justify the task as a task against several theoretical definitions
3.   try out the task with the class
4.   reflect on how successful the task was and what adaptations might need to be made to the task if it were to be used again.

Subsequent to following this four-step process, my students were required to report back to their peers in a ten-minute presentation. In these presentations, the teachers: described the teaching context and the task (Step 1); explained why, in their view, the task was a task (Step 2); outlined how they used the task (Step 3); and presented their perceptions of its effectiveness alongside identified future changes (Step 4). In East (2018), I presented the outcomes of several of these evaluations, concluding on the basis of these outcomes that when teachers are "confronted with theory about TBLT, and are then called upon to reflect on that theory when engaged in actual practice, they are able to make logically defensible decisions about what constitutes an effective task in the local context" (p. 47). Thus, this form of micro-evaluation represents a way of undertaking a small-scale appraisal of task effectiveness that, in my experience, has led in practice to valuable reflections and learning gains for teachers as students.

Teacher-focused reflective evaluations are straightforward and manageable, and have some potential in helping teachers to identify what works and does not work in real classrooms. They are nevertheless limited by their reliance on self-reports of practice, including self-reflections on task efficacy. No evidence is provided about the extent to which students make gains in their learning and proficiency through task completion. Ellis (2011) argued that more comprehensive forms of micro-evaluation enable teachers to "go *beyond* impressionistic evaluation by examining *empirically* whether a task 'works' in the way they intended and how it can be improved for future use" (p. 230, my emphases).

With regard to the task itself, an evaluation might usefully look at the *product* of the task (i.e., the outcome the students reach) or the *process* of undertaking the task (i.e., how students actually performed the task). Ellis (2011) argued that both product and process are important foci of investigation because teachers would benefit from evidence not only that students can achieve the stated task outcome but also that students have learned something by virtue of the task completion process. The broader range of assessment opportunities I discussed in Chapter 7 provides several sources of potential evidence of students' learning through tasks.

Beyond the evidence available from a variety of assessment outcomes, Ellis (2011) outlined several student-oriented possibilities for micro-evaluation which might help to investigate both product and process. Other useful areas of investigation might look at the impact of one or more of the task implementation variables I introduced in Chapter 5, such as task pre-planning, task repetition and task complexity. In each case, a micro-evaluation will be concerned with the extent to which the task variable demonstrates "a beneficial influence on performance, outcome and learning" (Ellis, 2011, p. 224). For these evaluations, some kind of comparative evidence will be necessary. For example, student outcomes could be investigated in different conditions – pre-planning versus no pre-planning; single task versus repeated task; simple task versus more complex task. In each case, Ellis suggested that the micro-evaluation can involve the collection of different kinds of evidence:

- What do *students* think about the task? This student-focused evaluation might draw on evidence from self-report data elicited from questionnaires, interviews or focus groups.
- How did students *perform* the task? This kind of evaluation seeks to establish the extent to which the task led to the performance processes and outcomes that were anticipated. It may require observation and/or recording of students' performances as they complete the task alongside consideration of any product that emerges from task completion.
- What *learning* took place as a consequence of completing the task? This kind of evaluation would investigate the extent to which task performance has enabled learning to occur. This may require the collection of some form of pre-test post-test evidence which would help pinpoint shifts in students' ability to use the target language or target language feature. That is, pre-task, students may be measured in some way on the linguistic feature (perhaps through some kind of discrete point instrument, and/or students' use of a target feature in a task); they may be measured again post-task with a similar kind (parallel form) of measurement instrument; performances may be compared, and learning gains determined from differences in outcome.

One useful process for undertaking a student-focused task-based micro-evaluation, which essentially follows standard procedures for a small-scale empirical study, was presented by Ellis (1998, 2011). In summary, Ellis's proposal included five elements:

1. describe the task
2. plan the evaluation
3. collect the data
4. analyse the data
5. draw conclusions and consider next steps.

This five-step process is not essentially different from the four-step procedure I outlined earlier. It does, however, move *beyond* the impressionistic evidence that might arise from a teacher-centred evaluation to enable a focus on student outcomes. The key issue for the evaluation will be the choice of student focus – perceptions, performance or learning gains. Teachers will need to consider processes such as when evidence will be gathered (i.e., during or after task completion) and what instruments might be used (e.g., survey, interview, focus group, pre- and post-test). Conclusions drawn from the data will include whether changes to the task or teaching process are required.

Ellis (2011, pp. 226–230) outlined several examples of micro-evaluations that drew on the above five-step process and drew attention to the evidence for effectiveness of the tasks in question. He went on to underscore the reality that micro-evaluations that follow the above procedures, although worthwhile in terms of the evidence they may uncover, are also time-consuming and require a considerable amount of work. As Ellis noted, teachers may not be able to carry out such micro-evaluations on a frequent basis, but their occasional use may be manageable. He also conceded that some evaluations are easier to carry out than others. For example, student-based evaluations (such as asking students to fill in a short survey on their perceptions after they have completed a task) are arguably very straightforward to design, conduct and analyse. Response-based observation or recording of students as they complete the task (even when perhaps focusing on one pair or small group), and then transcribing the recording and analysing the students' interactions, are more complex evaluations with regard to design, conduct and analysis.

Reflection Point

To determine the extent to which tasks in practice are working as effective means of promoting second language acquisition (SLA), teachers need to undertake some kind of evaluation of students' learning and proficiency gains.

1. To what extent do you think that task outcome evidence alone (reaching the goal or outcome of the task) provides a useful indication of learning and proficiency gains?
2. Think about and describe a pre-test post-test evaluative design that might help with collecting useful evidence of learning gains.
3. Think about and describe a student-focused evaluative design that might do the same.

The Macro-evaluation of TBLT Implementation

There is scope for individual teachers in individual teaching contexts to undertake their own micro-evaluations of practice, and these have the potential to impact meaningfully on practice. Macro-evaluative work looks at the broader context of what is happening at the institutional, regional or national level, and may have value in informing us about the possibilities and constraints for TBLT as experienced by a wider range of teachers and learners.

In Chapter 4, I presented short accounts of a variety of contexts where the introduction of TBLT has taken different forms as TBLT's precepts have been variously interpreted and applied. The introduction of TBLT ideas into each of these contexts has also been evaluated in a range of ways that have moved beyond the level of the individual teacher. Several important issues have arisen from these macro-evaluations of TBLT in practice. In what follows, I revisit the contexts I presented in Chapter 4 and present aspects of evaluations of these contexts.

Revisiting the Contexts Where TBLT Ideas Have Been Introduced

India

As I noted earlier, the Bangalore Communicational Teaching Project in South India (1979–1984) focused on improving school-aged learners' acquisition of English as L2, based on tasks. This was very much a bottom-up process that emerged from teacher dissatisfaction with prevailing grammar-oriented practices, even though it quickly became driven by one proponent in particular: N. S. Prabhu.

The project and its impact were quite extensively documented (see, e.g. Prabhu, 1987). Prabhu also invited several applied linguists from the UK to visit. Evaluations were published in a range of journals (Beretta, 1989, 1990; Beretta & Davies, 1985; Brumfit, 1984; Roberts, 1982), with several of these drawing in large part on the detailed scrutiny provided in Beretta's doctoral thesis supervised by Davies (Beretta, 1986).

Beretta (1986) described the Bangalore project as essentially "a local response to a local problem" (p. 153). The problem was professional dissatisfaction with a structure-based approach that had become quite embedded in teachers' practices but was not leading to learning outcomes that Prabhu and several other colleagues found satisfactory. The response was the encouragement for teachers to move away from the explicit teaching of structure and to focus on SLA through the implementation of a series of tasks.

Several evaluations referenced by Beretta (1986) spoke of the initiative in positive terms. The project was something that would "arouse considerable interest" (Roberts, 1982, p. 190) as an "exciting" initiative (Brumfit, 1984, p. 240) that would arguably contribute to "the most interesting arguments of the eighties, if not beyond" (Howatt, 1984, p. 288). A particular focus of interest in the evaluation reported by Beretta and Davies (1985) was the project's underlying innatist-influenced assertion that "grammar construction can take place through a focus on meaning alone" (p. 126). Their analysis of achievement test results that compared students who had taken part in the task-based work with those who had not led the researchers to the conclusion that there was a level of support for the assertion, albeit support that needed to be treated cautiously.

Brumfit (1984, p. 235) also argued that the project could be judged a success based on three criteria: (1) a "careful grass-roots experiment" can be carried out effectively; leading to (2) "valuable evidence about a major current model for language learning"; and, as I pointed out in Chapter 3, (3) a collection of materials that might be adopted or adapted to promote learner fluency in any L2 context, whether or not the context was built on the underlying premises that informed the original project. Despite the positive perspectives which emerged from the evaluative evidence, several cautions were also raised. Crookes (1986), for example, referred to a "lack of hard information about the success of the project" (p. 25), perhaps resulting in complete absence of reference to the project by applied linguists outside the UK.

One major issue to surface from the evaluations was that pair and group interactions were noticeably absent. Classroom processes appeared to centre exclusively around teacher–student interactions. This suggested an over-reliance on the teacher in interactive scenarios, and also led on occasions to some lack of participation by some students. The avoidance of pair and group work was ostensibly due to concerns about L1 use and the fact that, thus far, group work in the context had not been normative. Concern was also raised that there was an over-reliance on reasoning gap tasks, leading to a sense of monotony, and students seemed to be exposed to a limited range of rhetorical functions.

Arguably the most challenging aspect of the project's implementation was that most of the teachers involved were not the usual or regular teachers in the schools. Rather, they were more highly qualified teachers recruited specifically for the project who may have felt a sense of obligation to follow its precepts and had a level of commitment to make it work. By contrast, there was some evidence to suggest that the regular teachers were less engaged and more likely to revert to more traditional practices. Impacting factors here may have been their comparative lack of proficiency in English, concerns to maintain discipline in large classes and demands on their time. Consequently, the regular teachers tended to revert to more familiar structure-based procedures and output-based tasks tended to become fewer as the project continued. (In this connection, Beretta [1986] noted one teacher who admitted that she provided extra coaching in grammar for the weaker students in her class.)

The teacher variable raises an issue about whether the positive findings emerging from evaluations were largely down to the specifically recruited teachers rather than the initiative itself. Beretta (1990) concluded that it would be reasonable to deduce that the project "would not be readily assimilable by typical teachers in South Indian schools (or, by extension, in other schools elsewhere where similar antecedent conditions pertain)" (p. 333).

Belgium

The extensive long-term initiative to implement TBLT for programmes for Dutch as L1 or L2 in Flanders, the Dutch-speaking region of Belgium, began in 1990, targeting learners in primary, secondary and adult education contexts, with a particular focus on adult immigrants and their children learning Dutch as L2. In contrast to India, the introduction of TBLT was essentially a top-down initiative, commissioned by the Flemish government as "a large-scale test case for the implementation of task-based language education" (Van den Branden, 2006, p. 13).

The project, overseen by a team based at the Centre for Language and Education at the University of Leuven, involved several hundred school teams, alongside educational counsellors, policy makers and educationalists. Teacher support programmes ran between 1994 and 2003. The Leuven team put in place a reflective cycle to ensure step-by-step evaluation of the project, "carefully monitoring the reactions of all the parties involved and redressing its implementation strategies when necessary" (Van den Branden, 2006, p. 14). Thus, substantial on-going work was put in to evaluate the effectiveness of the TBLT implementation exercise.

Van den Branden (2009) outlined four research-based accounts of how the initiative played out in practice. On the positive side, it seemed that teachers in schools valued a task-based approach because they could see it as a way of enhancing students' functional and academic proficiency in Dutch as L2 as well as motivating them in their school work. It appeared that TBLT operated both as an extrinsic motivator, driven by the need for the students to develop their communicative competence in Dutch, and as an intrinsic motivator in that tasks were seen to be inherently motivating.

In practice, however, the studies revealed (as with the Bangalore case) that the teacher variable led to several complexities in implementing TBLT as innovation. In particular, teachers' beliefs were influential in how they adopted TBLT ideas in their classrooms. Experienced teachers, who had been asked to implement externally developed tasks created by professional syllabus developers, tended to adapt their implementation to suit their own ends, rather than adhering strictly to the task scenarios. For example, structures of participation may have been modified (e.g., proposed group work became whole-class discussion); task modality may have changed (e.g., a reading task became a listening task); input may have been simplified or output expectations modified; certain phases of the task cycle may have been omitted or added.

Thus, on occasions, teachers revised and adapted tasks to make them align more appropriately with their own beliefs and understandings about effective pedagogy. Tasks were modified to make them: more suitable for what the teachers wanted to happen in their own classrooms; a better fit with their preferred teaching style; or better aligned with what they believed their students could do. Teachers who did not wish their classes to be perceived as out of control adapted tasks so that they would not generate too much noise as students aimed to complete the tasks. Teachers also adapted tasks to avoid running out of time in the lesson. It was also found that students were occasionally inclined to modify the task to better suit how they wished to work and better match with how they thought they could reach the outcome.

The research team reached several significant conclusions about the enactment of TBLT. Focusing on the teachers, Van den Branden (2009) concluded that, in accordance with the conditions prevailing in their own individual classrooms, teachers will "tend to modify task scenarios … in countless ways" (p. 281). More broadly, Berben et al. (2007) argued that a task cannot (and should not) be perceived as a "fixed entity." Rather, a task "appears to behave as highly flexible and kneadable material that can take on different existential guises as it passes through the minds, mouths and hands of different persons making use of it" (p. 56).

Norris (2015) drew two important conclusions from the on-going reflective cycle in which the Flanders team engaged. These conclusions underscore the vital impact (whether positive or negative) of the teacher variable. Norris noted that evaluation was crucial not only in revealing the extent to which TBLT as innovation was being implemented effectively, but also by demonstrating the impact that teachers' beliefs, practices and needs were having, thereby "stimulating improvements." Essentially, Norris concluded that, when it comes to the success of implementing TBLT as innovation, "teacher change takes time, requires individualized support that respects the teacher's agency, and must value the central mediating role played by the teacher in enabling instructional innovation in the first place" (p. 47).

Hong Kong

The initiative to introduce TBLT for the teaching of English as L2 in primary and secondary schools in Hong Kong was, as with the Belgian case, a top-down initiative, and TBLT in the schools sector became officially adopted and supported through prescribed syllabi published over a number of years (Curriculum Development Council, 1997, 1999, 2002, 2007). As Adamson and Davison (2003) explained, grammar-translation had been officially phased out in the late 1960s and 1970s and subsequently replaced by oral-structural, and then notional-functional, approaches. TBLT, formally introduced in the 1990s, became quite entrenched since the early 2000s as the "core conceptual framework for the curriculum" (p. 28).

Candlin's (2001) analysis of the Hong Kong case led him to view the available guidelines as documenting, as Carless (2012) put it, an exemplary example of what was possible. Candlin noted that the task construct had come to be seen as "a powerful element in, and to an extent a driving force for, innovation in the school curriculum for language education." In his view the Hong Kong guidelines illustrated acute awareness on the part of curriculum planners of recent theorising about effective SLA, alongside openness and readiness to embrace in the guidelines "a generally held current view of language as communication and of language learning as a process, and the classroom as an interactive site of engagement" (p. 237). From this perspective, it seemed that Hong Kong was responding positively, proactively and deeply to contemporary theorising around effective language pedagogy.

Carless has presented several aspects of evaluations of the Hong Kong case emerging from his own research (2003, 2007, 2009). This evaluative work led Carless to conclude that, despite appearances, and despite Candlin's (2001) positive view, "[t]he reality at the chalk-face revealed … different issues to the more idealized picture presented in curriculum guidelines" (Carless, 2012, p. 349).

For example, Carless's (2007) study into the secondary school sector adoption of TBLT was carried out with a view to "probing stakeholders' conceptions of task-based teaching and its suitability for state school systems" (p. 596). It drew on semi-structured interviews with both classroom teachers (n = 11) and teacher educators (n = 10), and revealed tensions in practice that mirrored some of the apprehensions noted by some teachers in the Belgium case. Teachers in Hong Kong expressed concern about the amount of time it took to organise and complete a task. They were also concerned about losing control of the class and too much noise.

Additional identified constraints for teachers included having to deal with large classes, students being off task and using too much L1 and lack of teacher expertise in TBLT. There was also top-down pressure both at the level of curriculum as *plan* (a perceived need to complete the assigned textbook and keep to the teaching schedule) and curriculum as *outcome* (a perceived need to prepare students adequately for a competitive examination system). Hence, the syllabus statements as published appeared to be at odds with other aspects of curriculum implementation (with implications for negative washback).

With regard to pedagogical approach, several teachers in Carless's (2007) study noted that they preferred a more traditional Presentation-Practice-Production (PPP) sequence. Indeed, PPP was described by one participant as "better" because, in this teacher's view, "[i]t is difficult to integrate grammar teaching and task-based teaching" (p. 601).

Carless's evaluation provides further evidence that teachers' beliefs and understandings have a significant influence on how TBLT may be put into practice in classrooms. An essential tension emerging was that the driving precepts of TBLT as understood by the teachers contradicted the more traditional, top-down, teacher-led view of learning, aligned with a Confucian Heritage Culture (CHC), to which teachers might be adhering. As a consequence, and as Carless (2007) put it, in what is effectively a Chinese cultural model, TBLT "may prove to be in conflict with traditional educational norms" (p. 596). In Adamson and Davison's (2003) words, the top-down implementation of TBLT proved to be problematic because it "challenges traditional conceptions of good teaching and learning" and "contradicts long established pedagogic practices and community attitudes" (p. 28).

Carless's evaluation of the Hong Kong case did not lead him to conclude, however, that TBLT had no place in the context. Carless (2012) highlighted the necessity to identify teaching approaches that are grounded in and suitable for local needs and contexts, thereby aligning with Norris's (2015) assertions around teacher agency and support. With this in mind, Carless (2012, p. 347) argued that primary considerations are how TBLT might need to be *adapted* to suit the immediate context, or, alternatively, "the extent to which educational traditions may need to change" so that effective learning can take place. In other words, the adaptation, by this argument, needs to go both ways – it is not just a question of TBLT modified to suit the context; it may also be a question of the context adjusting itself to TBLT. This might mean in practice that "adaptations of TBLT may involve some form of *merging* the global with localized methodologies" (my emphasis). With regard to TBLT, Carless speculated that what we need in practice are "inclusive non-doctrinaire approaches." This would arguably apply not only in the Hong Kong context, but also more broadly.

China

The Chinese National English Curriculum Standards (NECS) (e.g., Chinese Ministry of Education, 2011) have supported the use of a task-based approach in Chinese primary and secondary schools. At tertiary level, the College English Curriculum Requirements (CECR) have done similar (e.g., Chinese Ministry of Education, 2007). Furthermore, although not mandated as a pedagogical approach, recent EFL textbooks aligned with revised curricular expectations have provided a stronger focus on communication than was previously the case, alongside specific topics and more "authentic" activities, thus supporting the implementation of TBLT.

However, as I noted in Chapter 4, and as with the Hong Kong case, the CHC background of teachers and students in China has meant that students have traditionally largely been taught through a grammar-translation approach. Earlier research in the Chinese context has indicated that TBLT has been challenging to adopt due to lack of a supportive environment (Zhang, 2007). Subsequent studies have underscored the tensions for TBLT implementation in China (e.g., Luo & Xing, 2015; Xiongyong & Samuel, 2011; Zheng & Borg, 2014).

Luo and Xing's (2015) study into school teachers' perceptions of TBLT in the Chinese context, which drew on responses to a written questionnaire (n = 47) and interview data (n = 5), highlighted both positive and negative perspectives. On the positive side, it was found that teachers were very interested in innovating their teaching because they wanted to be effective teachers. Most respondents saw TBLT as potentially useful and effective due to its focus on meaningful communication in the target language and potential to motivate learners.

Nevertheless, Luo and Xing (2015) noted several challenges for the implementation of TBLT. Some teachers reported lack of their own proficiency in English as a potential inhibiting factor. Many respondents had not been to an English-speaking country and were therefore heavily reliant on authentic materials as reference points for designing tasks. However, there was a perceived lack of authentic teaching resources and teachers also stated that they had little time to prepare their own materials. In some situations, large classes also presented challenges. Furthermore, many respondents reported lack of opportunity to receive TBLT-focused teacher education as a strong contributor to problems with TBLT implementation. Some respondents were also concerned about their students' low English proficiency and resistance to participating in tasks in class.

A more traditional grammar-focused examination model was also seen as an influential impacting factor. For example, China's National Matriculation English Test, a high-stakes examination taken by secondary school students who wish to gain admission to Chinese universities and colleges, is an entirely written examination. Speaking is not included (Wang & Zhang, 2016). The College English Test, which currently looms large in China's tertiary education system and is designed to assess students' English proficiency against the teaching goals prescribed in the CECR, places strong emphasis on reading and vocabulary knowledge. A Spoken English Test, first added in 1999, is optional.

With regard to the implications of assessment at the school level, Luo and Xing (2015) noted that teachers found more teacher-fronted approaches to be "more controllable and helpful in taking the grammar-based examinations" (p. 147).

That is, where teachers' and students' lives are dominated by "the grammar and vocabulary knowledge-focused national examinations" (p. 150), which are seen as not only crucial in evaluating learners' language proficiency but also influential for their future lives, teachers may opt for more established methods to support their students with examination preparation, and teachers and students express unwillingness to participate in tasks and question the effectiveness of TBLT.

Thus, in the Chinese context it would seem that the continuance of teacher-led practices aligned to a CHC educational model is exacerbated by a traditional and grammar-oriented examination system that, as far as the implementation of TBLT is concerned, leads to negative washback. As Skehan and Luo (2020) noted with regard to the NECS, the intention may be to encourage a task-based pedagogy, but this teaching objective is not aligned to effective methods of assessment.

It seems that, despite a level of success with reform efforts from primary through to tertiary, curriculum goals that encourage TBLT continue to be hindered by factors such as teachers' lack of knowledge, lack of appropriate professional development opportunities and limitations in the current testing culture (see, e.g., Liu & Xiong, 2016; Ruan & Leung, 2012). Furthermore, and in words reminiscent of Carless's (2012) assertion regarding adaptations to TBLT to suit the context, Luo and Xing (2015) argued that, in addition to asking questions about whether it is *appropriate* to implement TBLT in China (and, if it is, what kinds of support teachers need), we must also consider as a research agenda "how to *localize and contextualize* the TBLT approach so that it accommodates teachers and benefits students' learning" (p. 150, my emphasis). More recently, Liu and Guo (2020) reached a similar conclusion, referring, as had Carless, to the need to consider "non-doctrinaire approaches" (p. 216).

Importantly, much of what teachers say about TBLT in their classrooms in both Hong Kong and mainland China, and the difficulties they have encountered, are reportedly common in several Asian countries (Butler, 2017). As Lai (2015) explained, despite the fact that many Asian governments have taken progressive steps to implement TBLT ideas by way of reforming the delivery of the English curriculum, "[i]n general, research on TBLT in Asia has identified a slow uptake of TBLT in classrooms, and has highlighted areas of incompatibility between TBLT and the particularities of the Asian contexts so far investigated" (p. 23). Adams and Newton (2009) put it like this: "large scale top-down curricular revisions may not directly impact actual language teaching practice" (p. 1), and this may be particularly so in contexts that continue to support traditional language teaching methods. The teacher variable is once more crucial for the success of the TBLT endeavour.

New Zealand

The New Zealand case I presented in Chapter 4 regarding the teaching and learning of languages additional to the language of instruction in the New

Zealand school system is an interesting one in comparison with several of the contexts I have described so far.

Essentially, teaching and learning programmes in New Zealand schools are governed by a document known as the New Zealand Curriculum or NZC (New Zealand Ministry of Education, 2007). The NZC itself is mandatory in that it represents, as a top-down document, "a statement of official policy relating to teaching and learning in English-medium New Zealand schools" and "applies to all English-medium state schools" (p. 6). However, despite its top-down nature and mandatory status, both teachers and schools are given considerable freedom to interpret its enactment. That is:

> The New Zealand Curriculum *sets the direction* for teaching and learning in English-medium New Zealand schools. But it is a framework rather than a detailed plan. This means that while every school curriculum must be clearly aligned with the *intent* of this document, schools have considerable flexibility when determining the *detail*. In doing this, they can draw on a *wide range* of ideas, resources, and models.
>
> *(New Zealand Ministry of Education, 2007, p. 37, my emphases)*

The NZC document (New Zealand Ministry of Education, 2007) specifies eight learning areas. This includes *Learning Languages*, the learning area through which, as a central goal of L2 programmes aligned to the NZC, students "learn to communicate in an additional language" (p. 17). However, how the communicative goal is realised in specific classrooms is entirely in the hands of individual teachers, who may (or may not) choose TBLT, or aspects of TBLT, as one of several means of reaching the goal.

In practice, the implementation of TBLT in the New Zealand context is not emerging in a bottom-up way as a reaction to more traditional, teacher-led, grammar-focused approaches. Nor is TBLT implementation occurring as a consequence of a top-down mandate. Rather, TBLT is *encouraged*, with the guidance that Ellis's conceptualisation of a language learning task (e.g., Ellis, 2009) is "relevant" to all teachers of languages (New Zealand Ministry of Education, 2017), but TBLT is not specified or required as a realisation of NZC expectations.

In East (2012), I provided some useful evaluative evidence of how key stakeholders were interpreting the requirements of *Learning Languages*, seen from a task-based perspective, and at an early stage in the implementation of the NZC. In this largely qualitative study, interviews were carried out with practising secondary school teachers of a range of languages – the curriculum implementers (n = 19) – alongside those who were employed to support these teachers' work in several contexts – the curriculum leaders (n = 8). The precepts of TBLT were used as lenses through which to interpret what participants had to say.

On the positive side, findings revealed that many teachers had begun to reflect on what tasks and TBLT might mean for their classroom work, and several examples were given of how teachers were trying to use tasks in their classrooms.

The curriculum leaders demonstrated good understanding of aspects of TBLT and willingness to support and encourage task-based practices in schools. The evidence suggested "opportunities for TBLT as a means of realising the aims of *Learning Languages* in New Zealand" (East, 2012, p. 191).

Inevitably, however, challenges were also apparent. These included teachers' apprehension around how students might most effectively reach the curriculum goal of communication, and negative washback ensuing from some aspects of the high-stakes assessments. Tensions thus emerged around the balance to be maintained between teacher-fronted top-down elements and learner-centred experiential opportunities, and concerns were expressed about whether the learning would be effective if the primary focus was on tasks (East, 2017).

Furthermore, and despite a range of support resources that had been put in place, teachers showed variable knowledge and understanding of TBLT, ranging from quite well developed (42%) to partially developed (32%) to virtually non-existent (26%) – as one teacher put it, "to be honest I am sometimes still confused – what's 'task-based'?" (East, 2012, p. 194). From the perspective of one curriculum leader, there was "a real need to actually promote task-based learning a lot more," alongside a need for "a lot more examples of how teachers are doing that" (p. 195).

The opportunities and challenges in the New Zealand case must be interpreted against the "complex operational context" (East, 2012, p. 202) that lies essentially in teachers' relative freedom to interpret the curriculum, and a focus on the goal of communication in language teaching, in any ways they choose. As I explained, New Zealand's Ministry of Education needed to navigate a careful pathway between offering teachers adequate guidance to support them with curriculum implementation and ensuring enough autonomy to teachers so that they could make their own pedagogical decisions. It was "as if the Ministry has put the concepts of 'task' and TBLT into the dialogue with teachers and is now standing back and waiting to see what teachers will make of them" (p. 205). I concluded that this minimally directive approach had both positive and negative consequences for TBLT. On the positive side, teachers who wished to explore TBLT were able (indeed, encouraged and supported) to do so. On the negative side, teachers who did not wish to consider TBLT ideas could bypass them quite easily. From the perspective of introducing TBLT as innovation, eclecticism in practice is the norm.

A more recent useful study into teachers' interpretations and implementation of TBLT in the New Zealand school system is provided in Erlam and Tolosa (2021). The researchers investigated the consequences of teacher participation in a dedicated professional development programme that included a focus on TBLT and opportunities to experiment with tasks in real classrooms. The study revealed on-going challenges in practice as teachers navigated their own classroom contexts and showed varying degrees of understanding of the task construct and its place in teaching and learning sequences.

Reflection Point

In this chapter, I have revisited the contexts of TBLT implementation that I presented in Chapter 4 and have outlined some of the challenges emerging from evaluations of these contexts.

1.   What seems to make TBLT in Asian contexts a particularly challenging issue?
2.   More broadly, what role do you see for teacher education and professional development in the successful implementation of TBLT?
3.   What issues do you think should be addressed in TBLT-oriented teacher education and professional development programmes?

Conclusion

Context-specific micro-evaluations enable evidence of the effectiveness of TBLT to be gathered at the local level of the individual classroom. At their simplest, micro-evaluations might collect impressionistic evidence as teachers engage in reflection for-in-on action. Student-oriented micro-evaluations can be carried out in a range of ways and can help to establish learning gains. However enacted, the bottom line for any micro-evaluation is to establish, in specific and local contexts, "whether and in what ways a 'task' works" (Ellis, 2011, p. 232). In contexts where TBLT is being implemented, it is important to evaluate more broadly the extent to which that implementation is working. Context-specific macro-evaluations of programmes can offer us insight into the opportunities for, and barriers to, success from which we can draw lessons for future practice. Each of the cases of TBLT implementation I have outlined in this chapter has in common the motivation to challenge more traditional teacher-fronted approaches to language pedagogy and to encourage the development of learners' communicative competence through tasks.

The macro-evaluations I have presented shed some light on the extent to which TBLT has or has not worked, or could be made to work better, in a specific context. They reveal one common theme that I began to articulate in Chapter 4 when I first presented the example cases of TBLT implementation and when I considered teachers' enactment of prescribed syllabi – that *teachers* are a crucial variable in the success (or otherwise) of the TBLT endeavour. Thus, regardless of the direction from which an encouragement to consider TBLT is occurring (bottom-up or top-down), it seems that teachers hold a critical role. In Chapter 9, I consider, in light of the crucial teacher variable, some of the broader issues facing tasks and TBLT if they are to be shown to work longer term.

Suggested Further Reading

Bryfonski, L., & McKay, T. (2019). TBLT implementation and evaluation: A meta-analysis. *Language Teaching Research, 23*(5), 603–632.

Ellis, R., Skehan, P., Li, S., Shintani, N., & Lambert, C. (2019). Evaluating task-based language teaching. In *Task-based language teaching: Theory and practice* (pp. 303–330). Cambridge University Press.

References

Adams, R., & Newton, J. (2009). TBLT in Asia: Constraints and opportunities. *Asian Journal of English Language Teaching*, 19, 1–17.

Adamson, B., & Davison, C. (2003). Innovation in English language teaching in Hong Kong primary schools: One step forward, two steps sideways? *Prospect*, 18(1), 27–41.

Berben, M., Van den Branden, K., & Van Gorp, K. (2007). 'We'll see what happens': Tasks on paper and tasks in a multilingual classroom. In K. Van den Branden, K. Van Gorp, & M. Verhelst (Eds.), *Tasks in action: Task-based language education from a classroom-based perspective* (pp. 32–67). Cambridge Scholars Publishing.

Beretta, A. (1986). Evaluation of a language teaching project in South India. [Doctoral dissertation, University of Edinburgh]. Edinburgh Research Archive. https://era.ed.ac.uk/handle/1842/18718.

Beretta, A. (1989). Attention to form or meaning? Error treatment in the Bangalore Project. *TESOL Quarterly*, 23(2), 283–303.

Beretta, A. (1990). Implementation of the Bangalore Project. *Applied Linguistics*, 11(4), 321–337.

Beretta, A., & Davies, A. (1985). Evaluation of the Bangalore Project. *ELT Journal*, 39(2), 121–127.

Brumfit, C. (1984). The Bangalore procedural syllabus. *ELT Journal*, 38(4), 233–241.

Butler, Y. G. (2017). Communicative and task-based language teaching in the Asia-Pacific region. In N. Van Deusen-Scholl & S. May (Eds.), *Second and foreign language education. Encyclopedia of language and education* (3rd ed., pp. 327–338). Springer.

Candlin, C. N. (2001). Afterword: Taking the curriculum to task. In M. Bygate, P. Skehan, & M. Swain (Eds.), *Researching pedagogic tasks: Second language learning, teaching and testing* (pp. 229–243). Longman.

Carless, D. (2003). Factors in the implementation of task-based teaching in primary schools. *System*, 31(4), 485–500.

Carless, D. (2007). The suitability of task-based approaches for secondary schools: Perspectives from Hong Kong. *System*, 35(4), 595–608.

Carless, D. (2009). Revisiting the TBLT versus P-P-P debate: Voices from Hong Kong. *Asian Journal of English Language Teaching*, 19, 49–66.

Carless, D. (2012). TBLT in EFL settings: Looking back and moving forward. In A. Shehadeh & C. Coombe (Eds.), *Task-based language teaching in foreign language contexts: Research and implementation* (pp. 345–358). John Benjamins.

Chinese Ministry of Education. (2007). *College English curriculum requirements*. Beijing Foreign Language Teaching and Research Press.

Chinese Ministry of Education. (2011). *National English curriculum standards* (revised edition). Beijing Normal University Press.

Crookes, G. (1986). Task classifications: A cross-disciplinary review. In *Technical report no. 4*. Center for Second Language Classroom Research, Social Science Research Institute, University of Hawaii.

Curriculum Development Council. (1997). *Syllabuses for primary schools: English language primary 1–6*. Government Printer.

Curriculum Development Council. (1999). *Syllabuses for secondary schools: English language (secondary 1–5)*. Government Printer.

Curriculum Development Council. (2002). *English language education key learning area: Curriculum guide (primary 1–secondary 3)*. Government Printer.

Curriculum Development Council. (2007). *English language education key learning area: English language curriculum and assessment guide (secondary 4–6)*. Government Printer.

Davis, S. (2005). Developing reflective practice in pre-service student teachers: What does art have to do with it? *Teacher Development*, 9(1), 9–19.

East, M. (2012). *Task-based language teaching from the teachers' perspective: Insights from New Zealand*. John Benjamins.

East, M. (2014a). Encouraging innovation in a modern foreign language initial teacher education programme: What do beginning teachers make of task-based language teaching? *The Language Learning Journal*, 42(3), 261–274.

East, M. (2014b). Mediating pedagogical innovation via reflective practice: A comparison of pre-service and in-service teachers' experiences. *Reflective Practice: International and Multidisciplinary Perspectives*, 15(5), 686–699.

East, M. (2017). "If it is all about tasks, will they learn anything?" Teachers' perspectives on grammar instruction in the task-oriented classroom. In M. J. Ahmadian & M. P. García Mayo (Eds.), *Recent perspectives on task-based language learning and teaching* (pp. 217–231). De Gruyter Mouton.

East, M. (2018). How do beginning teachers conceptualise and enact tasks in school foreign language classrooms? In V. Samuda, M. Bygate, & K. Van den Branden (Eds.), *TBLT as a researched pedagogy* (pp. 23–50). John Benjamins.

Ellis, R. (1998). The evaluation of communicative tasks. In B. Tomlinson (Ed.), *Materials development in language teaching* (pp. 217–238). Cambridge University Press.

Ellis, R. (2009). Task-based language teaching: Sorting out the misunderstandings. *International Journal of Applied Linguistics*, 19(3), 221–246.

Ellis, R. (2011). Macro-and micro-evaluations of task-based language teaching. In B. Tomlinson (Ed.), *Materials development in language teaching* (2nd ed., pp. 212–235). Cambridge University Press.

Erlam, R., & Tolosa, C. (2021). *Pedagogical realities of implementing task-based language teaching in the classroom*. John Benjamins.

Howatt, A. P. R. (1984). *A history of English language teaching*. Oxford University Press.

Killion, J., & Todnem, G. (1991). A process of personal theory building. *Educational Leadership*, 48(6), 14–16.

Lai, C. (2015). Task-based language teaching in the Asian context: Where are we now and where are we going? In M. Thomas & H. Reinders (Eds.), *Contemporary task-based language teaching in Asia* (pp. 12–29). Bloomsbury Publishing.

Liu, C., & Guo, R. (2020). A study of localization of task-based language teaching in China. *Chinese Journal of Applied Linguistics*, 43(2), 205–218.

Liu, Y., & Xiong, T. (2016). Situated task-based language teaching in Chinese colleges: Teacher education. *English Language Teaching*, 9(5), 22–32.

Long, M. (2015). *Second language acquisition and task-based language teaching*. Wiley-Blackwell.

Luo, S., & Xing, J. (2015). Teachers' perceived difficulty in implementing TBLT in China. In M. Thomas & H. Reinders (Eds.), *Contemporary task-based language teaching in Asia* (pp. 139–155). Bloomsbury Publishing.

New Zealand Ministry of Education. (2007). *The New Zealand curriculum*. Learning Media.

New Zealand Ministry of Education. (2017). Principles and actions that underpin effective teaching in languages. http://seniorsecondary.tki.org.nz/Learning-languages/Pedagogy/Principles-and-actions.

Norris, J. (2015). Thinking and acting programmatically in task-based language teaching: Essential roles for programme evaluation. In M. Bygate (Ed.), *Domains and directions in the development of TBLT: A decade of plenaries from the international conference* (pp. 27–57). John Benjamins.

Prabhu, N. (1987). *Second language pedagogy*. Oxford University Press.

Roberts, J. (1982). Recent developments in ELT – Part II. *Language Teaching*, 15(3), 174–194.

Ruan, J., & Leung, C. B. (2012). Introduction. In J. Ruan & C. B. Leung (Eds.), *Perspectives on teaching and learning English literacy in China* (pp. ix–xii). Springer.

Schön, D. A. (1983). *The reflective practitioner: How professionals think in action*. Basic Books.

Skehan, P., & Luo, S. (2020). Developing a task-based approach to assessment in an Asian context. *System*, 90 [Article 102223], 1–15.

Van den Branden, K. (Ed.). (2006). *Task-based language education: From theory to practice*. Cambridge University Press.

Van den Branden, K. (2009). Mediating between predetermined order and chaos: The role of the teacher in task-based language education. *International Journal of Applied Linguistics*, 19(3), 264–285.

Wang, D., & Zhang, X. (2016). National Matriculation English Test in China: Its past, present and future. *Journal of Applied Linguistics and Language Research*, 5(4), 183–199.

Xiongyong, C., & Samuel, M. (2011). Perceptions and implementation of task-based language teaching among secondary school EFL teachers in China. *International Journal of Business and Social Science*, 2(24), 292–302.

Zhang, Y. (2007). TBLT innovation in primary school English language teaching in mainland China. In K. Van den Branden, K. Van Gorp, & M. Verhelst (Eds.), *Tasks in action: Task based language education from a classroom-based perspective* (pp. 68–91). Cambridge Scholars Press.

Zheng, X., & Borg, S. (2014). Task-based learning and teaching in China: Secondary school teachers' beliefs and practices. *Language Teaching Research*, 18(2), 205–221.

9

THE POTENTIAL AND THE CHALLENGE OF TBLT

Arguments For and Arguments Against

Introduction

When it comes to the goal of language learners developing their communicative competence in the target language, I have argued throughout this book for the effectiveness of TBLT as a learner-centred and experiential pedagogical approach, albeit one that does not preclude teacher intervention. TBLT offers a great deal of potential as a contrast to more traditional, teacher-dominated approaches. As a consequence, a vital concern for Part III of this book has been how well TBLT is going in practice.

Over the last two chapters, I have considered how we might gather evaluative evidence of the effectiveness of TBLT. I outlined how we could undertake evaluations of TBLT and the learning potential of tasks at the level of the individual classroom. I also presented some outcomes of evaluations at the national level in a range of contexts. Macro-evaluative evidence in particular has demonstrated that teachers represent what I have described as a crucial variable for the success (or otherwise) of the TBLT endeavour.

As we come to the end of this book, and taking into consideration the issues emerging from the macro-evaluations I presented in Chapter 8, it is important to return to the educational bigger picture and to consider how arguments and counter-arguments must inform on-going debates about TBLT. In this concluding chapter, I explore some of the factors that impact teachers as they seek to implement innovation and consider ways in which those factors may be mitigated to strengthen teachers' implementation of task-based ideas in real classrooms. In doing this, I will return to several of the key concepts that I introduced in Chapter 1.

The TBLT Initiative and Its Theoretical and Pedagogical Underpinnings

The three theories of learning I considered in Chapter 1 – behaviourism, innatism and interactionism[1] – provided broad brushstroke pictures of sometimes radically different theoretical takes on what might influence effective pedagogical practice.

Grammar-translation and audio-lingualism exemplified behaviourist-informed teacher-led and expository approaches to L2 pedagogy. As Lightbown and Spada (2013) noted, it must be conceded that both methods have produced highly proficient L2 learners. Nevertheless, many students have become frustrated by these methods because, even after years of attending classes, they have found themselves unable to participate in everyday interactions with L1 speakers. In innatist-informed approaches to L2 learning, direct instruction would be seen as unnecessary. Rather, students' ability to work principles out for themselves as they are immersed in language would be crucial. Krashen and Terrell's (1983) Natural Approach represents one realisation of this viewpoint. Lightbown and Spada (2013) again provided critique, arguing that there is a lack of support for the hypothesis that second language acquisition (SLA) will be automatic if language learners just focus on meaning in comprehensible input.

An interactionist perspective on learning allows for a classroom balance between teacher-led moments and learner-centred exploration and experimentation. Interactionism recognises that each learner is unique and that the relative balances between teacher-led and learner-centred might vary according to students' perceived and actual needs.

From a broader educational perspective, the interactionist stance on teaching and learning may be labelled *constructivist*. A constructivist theory of learning owes much to the work of psychologists such as Jean Piaget and Lev Vygotsky (see Chapter 1). Constructivism is realised in approaches that emphasise students' *active construction* of their own knowledge, in contrast to sitting passively and receiving information from teachers or textbooks. From this perspective, imparting knowledge to students is not enough. Students must have opportunities to construct their own meanings as they work independently (whether individually or with others), and "raise their own questions, generate their own hypotheses and models as possibilities and test them for validity" (Fosnet, 1996, p. 29). (The extent to which the construction of knowledge is down to the individual [constructivism à la Piaget] or down to the individual in interaction with others [social constructivism à la Vygotsky] is a matter of debate.)

The constructivist label acknowledges what students need to bring to the learning situation, but recognises the supportive and facilitative roles of teachers. However, in contrast to a strongly teacher-led approach, teacher intervention is more supportive and less directive. As Weimer (2013, p. 23) explained:

> Instructors using constructivist approaches do lecture, but generally this direct transfer of information occurs after students have grappled with the issue, after they have a sense of what it is they need to know. The benefit of

waiting is that once students realize they need to know something, they listen attentively for the answers.

To support a growing argument for constructivism as a theory of learning, Weimer (2013) spoke of the increasing body of research that justified its effectiveness from a variety of perspectives. Weimer summarised a range of studies, arguing that "[t]his research offers a convincing commendation of learner-centered approaches. When they are used, the claim can be justifiably made that they promote a [comparatively] different, deeper, and better kind of learning" (p. 33). She came to the conclusion, "it is best to let the evidence speak for itself" (p. 54).

In the above light, TBLT has much to commend it as a pedagogy clearly aligned to constructivist principles. As Norris et al. (2009) expressed it, TBLT is built on an educational philosophy that sees "important roles for holism, experiential learning, and learner-centered pedagogy" aligned with interactionist theories of learning that support "the interactive roles of the social and linguistic environment in providing learning opportunities, and scaffolding learners into them" (p. 15). Furthermore, from a research perspective, Long (2015) argued that "the basic tenets of TBLT are motivated by, and broadly consistent with, the past 40 years of SLA research findings" (p. 8). In Ellis's (2020) words, "the case for TBLT is stronger than for structure-based instruction" (p. 188).

Nevertheless, a key evaluative question remains – as Long (2015) put it: "Does TBLT work, and work better than alternative approaches?" (p. 351). As the cases of TBLT implementation that I have presented reveal, the situation is not necessarily clear-cut. It must also be acknowledged that, at a theoretical level, there are counterarguments to the effectiveness of constructivism. Kirschner et al.'s (2006) analysis of a range of studies led them to conclude that, despite strong advocacy, they could find no research that supported the approach. They maintained that, on the contrary, the evidence from controlled studies "almost uniformly supports direct, strong instructional guidance rather than constructivist-based minimal guidance" (p. 83). This appeared to be particularly so for beginner/intermediate learners. However, even with more advanced learners, they suggested, "strong guidance while learning is most often found to be equally [as] effective as unguided approaches" (p. 84).

The paper by Kirschner et al. (2006) began an interesting debate and, inevitably, rebuttal – see, for example, Hmelo-Silver et al. (2007) and Schmidt et al. (2007), who pointed out that the original authors did not distinguish between an *unguided* form of discovery learning (wholly learner-centred and experiential) and a *scaffolded* form (one that sees important roles for the teacher). Nevertheless, Coe et al. (2014), for example, built on the conclusions of Kirschner et al. (2006) with the assertion that a discovery learning approach "is not supported by research evidence, which broadly favours direct instruction" (p. 23).

Broader educational debates about the efficacy of learner-centred approaches to learning vis à vis teacher-led positioning also finds expression in the literature that considers effective approaches to *language* teaching and learning. Adamson (2004), for example, referred to language *teaching* as "a complex undertaking." This, he argued, is because such teaching is "shaped by views of the nature of language, of teaching and learning a language specifically, and of teaching and learning in general" (p. 604). Mitchell et al. (2019) asserted that language *learning* is "an immensely complex phenomenon" (p. 2). This, they went on to argue, is because it is "coloured by debates on fundamental issues in human learning more generally" (p. 11). On this basis they concluded that, when it comes to *teaching*, there can be "no 'one best method', however much research evidence supports it, which applies at all times and in all situations, with every type of learner" (p. 406). It should not surprise us, then, that the broader educational environment, and the debates within it, have led to sometimes strident critiques of TBLT.

Arguments Against TBLT

Arguably one of the most vehement critics of TBLT, and also of communicative approaches from which TBLT emerged, has been Michael Swan. Swan's early criticisms of Communicative Language Teaching (CLT) are found in two articles (1985a, 1985b). Although Swan (1985a) acknowledged that CLT is not "a coherent and monolithic body of doctrine" (p. 3), but, rather, that various stakeholders in the language teaching and learning endeavour demonstrate wide variety in their acceptance and interpretation of CLT's precepts, it is clear that Swan was particularly concerned with more exclusively learner-centred perspectives on the approach. Hence, his second paper (1985b) essentially argued that the meaning-based emphases that might be found in stronger forms of CLT neglected adequate attention to grammar due to their rejection of traditional structure-based syllabi. Swan did not appear to advocate for a return to a strongly teacher-led grammar-focused pedagogical approach to the exclusion of other (more communicative) elements. However, his perspective led Widdowson (1985), for example, to describe Swan's argument as "a reassertion of the traditional view that what learners need to be taught is grammar, lexis, and a collection of idiomatic phrases" (p. 159).

Some 20 years later, Swan (2005) turned his sights towards TBLT. In his introduction to a reprint, Swan (2011) argued that he wished to present "a full-scale criticism of hard-core task-based instruction, and of the hypotheses which are held to justify it" (p. 91). This was a criticism which he seems to have maintained over many years (see, e.g., Swan, 2018). Swan acknowledged the attractiveness of TBLT. In particular, in his view, its interactionist-informed stance to learning meant that TBLT was able to avoid the limitations of essentially behaviourist approaches (represented, for example, in grammar-translation) or essentially innatist approaches (such as the Natural Approach). He conceded, therefore, that TBLT appeared to offer the potential to combine "the best insights from communicative language teaching with an organized focus on language form" (Willis, 1996, p. 1).

The version of TBLT that Swan particularly critiqued was the strong form that sat at or towards the wholly learner-centred end of the interactionist continuum. In Swan's

(2005) words, TBLT at this point on the continuum "retains a powerful bias towards on-line learning at the expense of formal teaching," promoting an environment in which "potentially useful pedagogic procedures are discouraged or outlawed on doctrinaire grounds" (p. 283). Interpreting TBLT as a pedagogical approach in which traditional approaches are "ineffective and undesirable, especially where they involve proactive formal instruction and practice decoupled from communicative work" (p. 377), Swan's essential argument was that TBLT failed to fulfil its potential.

Of particular concern to Swan (2005) were so-called acquisition poor environments where, due to significant limitations on instructional time, learners may have very limited exposure to the target language. Swan suggested that, in such contexts, stronger forms of TBLT provided no guarantee either that L2 learners would be exposed to the most frequent or useful items of language, or that, having noticed a particular language feature, learners would have time to process the feature sufficiently and thereby acquire it. Swan continued that, when classroom time is lacking, the approach to language instruction needs to be carefully planned, with an emphasis on a limited and pre-selected range of priority linguistic items, sufficiently recycled to help establish "a core linguistic repertoire which can be deployed easily and confidently" (p. 394). This, he considered, may well need to involve direct and focused teaching of essential elements.

Swan was not alone in levelling criticism, particularly against stronger forms of TBLT in time-limited instructional contexts. Bruton (2005) expressed similar concern. Bruton *did* advocate for the need to develop students' communicative competence. He also *did not* advocate for a return to strongly grammar-focused approaches. Indeed, he recognised that a major contribution of TBLT was "to direct some attention away from over-itemised-input, over-form-focus, and over-control at the initial levels, where some student initiative should be encouraged" (p. 66). However, Bruton saw the teacher as having a more central role to play than might be the case in (at least) strong TBLT classrooms. He also appeared to reduce TBLT to a purely *spoken* communicative approach, leading him to critique this as TBLT's "most obvious limitation" (p. 56).

Criticism has not just been levelled at the stronger forms of TBLT. Klapper (2003) was more accommodating of the TBLT endeavour and regarded TBLT as being based on defensible theoretical principles and learner-centred pedagogical models that might promote SLA, even in time-limited contexts. As with Swan (2005), Klapper was critical of the stronger forms due to his perception of their apparent neglect of systematic exploration and practice of grammar. He was, however, also critical of what he saw as weaker forms that might incorporate form-focused instruction, at least in a form predicated on consciousness-raising (see Chapter 6). What he was arguing for was "a weaker version still," which acknowledges a strong focus on communication, but which "reinstates declarative knowledge and practice at the appropriate point in the task cycle" (p. 40).

In this regard, Klapper (2003) made the observation that many language learners in more traditional forms-dominated classrooms based exclusively on synthetic Type A syllabi appeared to have been highly successful with their language learning endeavours. Although this assertion mirrors the commentary put forward by Lightbown and Spada (2013) that I presented at the start of this chapter, it is nonetheless debatable (as I stated earlier). Klapper argued, however, that, on the basis of that assertion alone, it was evident that TBLT "has a lot more work to do before it can provide a convincing alternative pedagogical model, still more before it can claim superiority over other approaches" (p. 40).

Reflection Point

It seems that criticisms of TBLT largely focus on TBLT in its strongest forms, and, from this perspective, the apparent inadequacy of TBLT when it comes to direct instruction and practice. Nevertheless, the hallmark of TBLT is its essentially learner-centred and experiential approach.

1. To what extent do you think the criticisms of TBLT I have presented are valid or justified?
2. How would you respond to these criticisms, particularly with regard to direct instruction and practice?
3. In your view, how can TBLT remain essentially learner-centred and experiential if the teacher has interventionist roles to play?

Counter-arguments for TBLT

It should come as no surprise that advocates of TBLT within the academic community have engaged with the criticisms levelled against the TBLT endeavour. In what follows, I present counter-arguments mounted by Long (2016) and Ellis (2009, 2017).

Long's (2016) useful, detailed and systematic article challenged several aspects of Swan's (2005, 2011) criticisms of TBLT and also addressed aspects of Bruton's (2005) and Klapper's (2003) concerns. Long made the assertion that, when critics dismiss the claims of TBLT, the only viable replacement they offer seems to be to return to a traditional, teacher-led model as operationalised, for example, through PPP. Long went on to present a range of theoretical arguments and research studies that refuted the efficacy of pre-determined, hierarchical linguistic/structural approaches.

Long (2016) was unequivocal in his counter-stance. He maintained, "the task syllabus stands alone, not as one strand in a hybrid of some kind" (p. 6). In Long's view, a programme of learning can only be said to be genuinely task-*based* when the programme, including its syllabus and its assessment – Nunan's (2004) plan/process/outcome – is "task-based throughout" (p. 8).

Importantly, however, Long's (2016) perspective was not an argument for a wholly learner-centred approach in which there was no role for the teacher. For Long, the apparent absence of formal attention to grammar which had emerged as a central criticism against TBLT did not mean that grammar was not addressed. In Long's view, the distinguishing feature of TBLT was that the grammar focus was not undertaken as "a separate activity" or "an end in itself," as was the case with a focus on forms approach, but, rather "*during* (and if necessary after, but not before) task work" (p. 17). In this interactionist-informed pedagogical approach, grammatical problems that emerge as students engage in task completion are addressed reactively, typically by some kind of teacher intervention or feedback, but also through peer-to-peer interaction during task completion. I took up several of these important issues in Chapter 6.

Long (2016) further reinforced an interactionist stance by refuting Swan's claim that TBLT unhelpfully polarises meaning-based and form-based instruction. He asserted that, in fact, there is no such polarisation for TBLT, either in theory or in practice, and no exclusion of either component. Long argued, on the contrary, that TBLT represented a more *integrated* model than more traditional language teaching when it comes to attention given to form and meaning. This, he said, is because the form focus in TBLT takes place "in context, embedded in meaning-based activities, not in separate drill-and-kill sessions" (p. 24).

Ellis (2009) provided another useful article that sought to redress the criticisms levelled against TBLT. In responding, for example, to the criticism that in TBLT the teacher's role is purely supportive and never directive, Ellis argued, "the teacher is *much more than* a manager and facilitator of tasks" (p. 236, my emphasis). He went on to assert that during-task teacher intervention and feedback might not only be *reactive* (as Long had suggested), but also *proactive*, utilising both implicit and explicit feedback strategies and, on occasions, directly teaching about an aspect of language. Furthermore, in Ellis's view, opportunities arise in TBLT for the explicit teaching of language not only post-task, but also pre-task. He drew the conclusion that TBLT is well-suited to a learner-centred educational philosophy, although it also provides room for teacher input and direction.

As I pointed out in Chapter 6, it would seem that Ellis's conceptualisation of TBLT sits at a place on the interactionist continuum that allows for more specific inclusion of teacher-led grammatical elements than would be the case with Long, for whom (as I have previously stated) the syllabus in TBLT must be *solely* task-based and not hybridised to contain more structural elements. Indeed, in a quite recent paper that might be regarded as something of a response to Long, Ellis (2017) contrasted his own position with Long's – Ellis did not see TBLT as "a single, monolithic approach" (p. 522), but, rather, as something that "can be used alongside a more traditional approach" (Ellis, 2009, p. 242).

The perspectives of Long (2016) and Ellis (2009, 2017), albeit representing somewhat different takes on the components that make up TBLT, embody important counter-arguments to the essential critiques of TBLT as presented, for example, by Swan (2005, 2011), Bruton (2005) and Klapper (2003). They also illustrate, as Ellis (2009) put it, that "there is no single way of doing TBLT" (p. 224). It seems that even the experts disagree, with their perspectives placing them at different points on the interactionist continuum. It is clear, however, that both Long and Ellis reject the argument that a teacher-led, grammar-focused approach is a prerequisite for successful language learning to occur, and simultaneously support an argument for learner-centred experiential learning. Thus, a strong case is made for TBLT, with its clear focus on the learner's role in successful SLA. I turn now from theory and research to the role, place and influence of teachers in TBLT.

Practical Challenges for TBLT

As I stated at the start of this chapter, it is no exaggeration to say that the success (or otherwise) of TBLT at the classroom level ultimately rests on individual teachers in individual classrooms. A starting point in discussing the practical challenges for TBLT from the teacher's perspective is to acknowledge (as I did towards the start of Chapter 1) that most teachers want to be effective and, as a consequence, want to create the most powerful learning environments and opportunities for all their students (Burns, 2010; Van den Branden, 2009a). From this perspective, teachers will inevitably weigh up the pros and cons of ideas about pedagogy with which they are presented.

Borg (2015) made it clear that teachers do not function as "mechanical implementers of external prescriptions." He argued on the contrary that teachers influence what happens in the classroom as "active, thinking decision-makers" (p. 8). Thus, simply telling teachers that they are required to follow a task-based approach is unlikely to be effective (something I acknowledged in Chapter 8, and something that can be seen in several of the case evaluations I presented in that chapter). In Borg's view, what teachers do in classrooms is influenced by a range of "complex, practically-oriented, personalized, and context-sensitive networks of knowledge, thoughts, and beliefs" (p. 321). As Nunan (2004) argued, although it may not always be apparent or explicit, all of the actions teachers take in classrooms are "underpinned by beliefs about the nature of language, the nature of the learning process and the nature of the teaching act" (p. 6). In other words, what teachers *think* about teaching and learning, and what they *believe* to be pedagogical best practice, will have substantial influence on what they choose to *do* in their classrooms, and their choices will be influenced by what seems to work and what seems not to work in their own classroom contexts.

Several factors shape teachers' beliefs and subsequent actions. One powerful influence on teachers is their own early experiences as learners. As Van den Branden (2009a) put it, teachers "teach in the way they themselves were taught, and show strong resistance toward radically modifying the teaching behavior that they are so familiar with" (p. 666). In many contexts, a simple reality is that a good number of teachers contemplating TBLT or attempting to enact TBLT ideas will have experienced more traditional, teacher-led and grammar-focused models of language pedagogy in their early language learning years. Moreover, they may have perceived these models as satisfactory and successful. These early experiences of teaching and learning will have left a mark which is hard to erase.

It is not just a question of the influence of early learning experiences. As teachers face their classes on a day-to-day basis, a variety of contextual factors will play a part in shaping teachers' on-going thinking, beliefs and practices. These may include the ethos of the educational establishment that teachers are working in, or expectations imposed on them by those in leadership and/or other colleagues. Where these expectations are aligned with TBLT ideas (perhaps made apparent in a Type B syllabus and/or in a range of teaching resources), teachers will likely begin to wrestle with those ideas and start thinking through what they mean for practice. Alternatively, teachers who may wish to experiment with tasks in non-conducive environments will also think through the implications in and for their contexts.

Additionally, teachers respond on a moment-by-moment basis to events that happen in their classes and are required to deal with individual differences in students (which may include students who prefer a more deductive, rule-based approach). Also, as I noted in Chapter 7, in contexts where high-stakes examinations loom large in students' (and therefore teachers') lives, this will have a washback effect, which (in terms of TBLT implementation) may be negative. The cases of TBLT implementation that I outlined in Chapters 4 and 8 also illustrate that, as Ellis (2009) suggested, "there may [be] cultural barriers to the uptake of TBLT" (p. 243). Thus, openness to new ideas in theory may well be challenged by conflicting realities in practice, perhaps leading to "a hybrid and evolving set of accommodations to local cultures which ultimately may be assimilated by them" (Adamson & Davison, 2003, p. 36).

Even where there is openness to innovation and a willingness to experiment with something new, teachers' understandings about the innovation, alongside teachers' skills in implementing the innovation, will be variable. In Chapters 4 and 8, I presented the New Zealand case, a context where TBLT, although not mandated and not governed by any kind of prescriptive syllabus, was being encouraged as one means to fulfil the communicative language learning goals of a revised national curriculum for schools. In East (2012), I made the observation that, despite considerable Ministry of Education investment and initiatives to introduce teachers to TBLT ideas, teachers showed variable understanding of what might be involved. For illustrative purposes, I presented the response of one teacher who, when asked about her own understanding of TBLT, made the assertion, "don't we all do that?" (p. 194). By way of commentary, I noted that this teacher's response could be interpreted in two ways. It might perhaps be indicating that, as a consequence of various teacher education and professional development initiatives, all L2 teachers in New Zealand were already putting TBLT into practice. This was, however, clearly not the case. Alternatively, it might be indicating that teachers were labelling what they were doing in their classrooms "task-based," regardless of whether, and the extent to which, task-based principles were actually being enacted.

The research that has investigated TBLT from the teacher's perspective has made it very clear that teachers in a range of contexts hold a variety of interpretations and understandings of TBLT. In East (2017), I explored the extent to which important elements of TBLT theory and key findings from empirical TBLT research were having an influence on teachers' actual classroom practices. I argued that perhaps the most valuable positive classroom application of theory and research has been an increased emphasis on helping learners to engage in meaningful, authentic interactive tasks that promote fluency.

Brown (2014), for example, had spoken of a "turn-of-the century wave of interest," influenced by social constructivist perspectives, whereby teachers were "treating the language classroom as a locus of meaningful, authentic exchanges among users of language," with L2 learning seen as "the creation of meaning through interpersonal negotiation among learners" (p. 206). Several studies among practitioners in a range of contexts exemplify the positive potential of this emerging interest, for which learner-centred and experiential tasks have a clear role. It seems that teachers' engagement with TBLT ideas in several contexts has led in practice to increased emphasis on meaningful, authentic interactive tasks that students have found motivating and that have developed their fluency in the target language.

Leaver and Willis (2004) presented a range of accounts of tertiary-level task-based initiatives for a variety of international languages. These accounts reported improvements in students' language proficiency and enhanced student satisfaction and enthusiasm. Tasks were:

- seen to promote student engagement and risk-taking, with evaluations revealing "that students *like* tasks," and course results indicating "that students *learn* from tasks" (p. 65) (courses for Slavic languages)
- perceived as "a tool that helps [students] carry out specific real-life activities" (p. 77), contributing to a course that was seen by students as "engaging and informative," "really fun," and "very interesting" (p. 78) (courses for Spanish)
- regarded as "an excellent choice to motivate students and promote higher levels of proficiency," creating "a low-anxiety learning environment where students can try out their ideas and practice their language to develop confidence" (p. 140) (courses for Japanese).

Accounts of primary school classroom practices presented by Van den Branden et al. (2007) similarly highlighted motivational and proficiency advantages for learners. In three different primary school contexts, a task-based approach had:

- stimulated "higher levels of involvement and motivation" (p. 119) (Dutch as L2 in a Belgian Dutch-medium context)
- helped students to "lower their anxiety and boost their confidence and motivation," with language seen as being used "for real purposes" (p. 150) (Hungarian English as L2 context)

- led to "positive impact" for both teachers and learners in terms of "increasing their use of English" (p. 252) (Hong Kong English as L2 context).

Challenges in practice have also emerged. A critical challenge for TBLT in practice is teacher uncertainty about exactly what a task is for purposes of TBLT. Teachers often struggle both with understanding the theoretical construct of task and with differentiating a task from the kinds of more structured communicative activities that may have been commonplace in the weak CLT classroom and a PPP model. Even when teachers have developed a level of understanding of the task construct, this understanding may be filtered by their own prior experiences and beliefs, leading them to make a range of context-specific adaptations to task scenarios (Van den Branden, 2009b). I noted in East (2017) that flexibility with the notion of task gives teachers considerable freedom to make context-specific decisions about what they consider to be suitable tasks for their learners and how to implement them. This, I suggested, is a potential strength. Problems occur, however, when there is misunderstanding about even the basic concept of task and its place in teaching and learning sequences. In some cases, tasks may be modified to the extent that they lose critical features that originally made them tasks. They are therefore "detaskified" (Samuda, 2005).

Allied to teachers' misunderstandings about the task construct is a strong and persistent impression that TBLT is all about speaking (see the final section of Chapter 3). This impression persists, simply by virtue of the fact that many tasks are indeed designed to foster spoken interaction. It is therefore not surprising that a task in TBLT is often seen to be synonymous with a *speaking* task. It is also not surprising that, as a consequence of this perception, pair work and group work are regarded as central (perhaps even defining) features of the task-based classroom. Unfortunately, these perceptions downplay the importance and use of a variety of tasks that draw on a range of skills (listening and reading as well as speaking and writing) and different ways of working (individual and whole-class as well as pairs and groups), and serve to undermine teachers' understanding about what TBLT actually is.

A further challenge for TBLT is how teachers conceptualise and enact attention to grammar. Once more, teachers' prior beliefs and understandings likely play a role in this. As I noted in Chapter 6, grammar instruction is one arena that has been relatively uninfluenced by research findings, and a widespread scenario persists of the teacher at the front of the class carefully explaining grammatical rules in a top-down teacher-led way, with these rules subsequently practised through a range of grammar exercises (East, 2012, 2017; Larsen-Freeman, 2015). Savignon (2018) put it like this: teachers "remain adamant about explicit attention to form through practice drills, completion of textbook activities, and grammar practice worksheets." Mirroring Van den Branden's (2009a) argument, Savignon went on to assert, "[l]ong-held professional values and beliefs and specific instructional rituals often reflect how teachers themselves have been taught" (p. 7). The tendency for teachers to hold onto more traditional, teacher-fronted approaches to grammar represents a phenomenon where theory and research in the TBLT space have had inadequate influence on classroom practice.

My own more longitudinal research with beginning teachers (e.g., East, 2014, 2019, 2020) has revealed several other constraints for TBLT in practice. At the *resource* level, these include a lack of ready-made "go-to" resources and task-based ideas (which teachers would use if they could find them) alongside the amount of time it takes to create useful tasks (time which teachers often lament that they do not have). This problem is further compounded (and confused) by language textbooks that are marketed as "task-based," but can turn out to be not task-based at all (Long, 2016). At a *collegial* level, teachers may experience a persistent adherence to more tried-and-tested pathways for language learning among older and more established colleagues. For beginning teachers in particular this can set up potential for conflict that can be difficult to manage. Each of the above pressures mitigates against more wholesale adoption of TBLT in real classrooms.

Reflection Point

I have presented the argument that the teacher variable is the most important when it comes to the success or otherwise of the TBLT endeavour. To what extent do you think that the following assertions pose genuine risks for the implementation of TBLT, and how might they be addressed?

1. Teachers do not fully understand what a task is.
2. Teachers often assume that TBLT is all about paired or group speaking tasks.
3. Teachers teach grammar directly and practise the rules through a range of grammar exercises.

When Theory and Practice Collide

It seems that the TBLT project is subject to criticism by both theorists and practitioners, due essentially to its apparent neglect of more traditional and teacher-led elements, and, more broadly, misunderstandings about what TBLT actually is. Other practical challenges (lack of resources, lack of time, textbooks that may be task-based in name only, uncertainty among teaching colleagues) also have their impacts. Added to the complex scenario that task and TBLT "mean different things to different people" (Long, 2016, p. 5) are the broader educational debates about what constitutes effective pedagogical practice and the relative balances to be maintained between teacher-led and learner-centred (Adamson, 2004; Coe et al., 2014; Kirschner et al., 2006; Mitchell et al., 2019; Schweisfurth, 2013; Weimer, 2013). What does all of this mean for those of us who wish, as theorists, researchers and/or practitioners, to advance the cause of TBLT as a learner-centred and experiential pedagogical approach?

Advancing the Theory of TBLT

Bygate (2020) spoke of TBLT as an ambitious project, one that is "yet to fulfil its promise as a free-standing approach to second language education, endorsed not only by researchers but also by teachers and other stakeholders" (p. 276). Bygate went on to explain that the perspective of researchers in the TBLT endeavour has largely been to investigate how and in what ways communicative interaction impacts on and influences SLA. This perspective brings us back to Nunan's (2004) foundational claim that "learners learn to communicate by communicating" (p. 8), whereby a focus of TBLT research (and practice) is on "learning to communicate through interaction in the target language" (p. 1).

It is important, first, to acknowledge the wider (and ever-increasing) range of research into aspects of TBLT that is happening in different contexts across the world. The findings of studies into different facets of task implementation and task use enable us to take incremental steps that advance our knowledge and understanding of the field. Many of these studies demonstrate the efficacy of tasks to promote SLA. This empirical research is imperative and must continue.

A problem for empirical research, however, is that it does not necessarily impact on teachers' practices. Markee (1997) early suggested that, contrary to the belief (or hope) that the findings of SLA research "trickle down to practitioners, who then, ideally, adopt them" (p. 80), the common reality is that theory and research "do little to promote change in language education because they do not address the real-life concerns of teachers and policy-makers" (p. 81). Considerably more recently, Mitchell et al. (2019) spoke of the "continuing need for dialogue between the practical theories of classroom educators, and the more decontextualized and abstract ideas deriving from programmes of research," adding that it is incumbent on researchers to make their findings and interpretations as accessible and understandable as possible for "a wider professional audience with other preoccupations" (p. 407). Thus, in addition to on-going empirical research, it is important to acknowledge the vital interface that must exist between TBLT in theory and research and TBLT in practice.

Bygate (2020) argued for a broadening of the research endeavour whereby research needs to move beyond particular models of SLA to take on board what stakeholders in real classrooms think and do, and the pressures and demands they face. That is, a focus on communicative interaction (which may well be a dominant interest for theorists and researchers in the TBLT space) does not consider "the breadth of human language learning" (p. 277) and appears to ignore other possibly important pathways that might contribute to learning. For Bygate, if we are concerned to persuade teachers and administrators to engage with the TBLT endeavour, we need to start from where teachers are currently at in their practice. This bottom-up approach is likely to lead to greater success longer term than a top-down imposition of task-based ideas and principles emerging from a narrow research focus.

Engaging researchers and teachers as co-participants in classroom-based TBLT research is one way in which a reciprocal dialogue between researchers and teachers can occur. All being well, this dialogue will be mutually informative and beneficial (see, e.g., Sato & Loewen, 2019). In this partnership, researchers must be willing to broaden their scope and take on board what teachers are currently doing and why they are doing it. Bygate (2020) raised the concern that, unless researchers do this, their approach and findings may fail to convince teachers of what TBLT can genuinely offer as "a full-blown language teaching approach" (p. 281), or, alternatively, as an approach that can support the achievement of realistic goals in the time-limited contexts that face many teachers and learners.

Fundamentally, for theorists railing against the TBLT endeavour and for teachers wrestling with task-based ideas, the crux of the matter (beyond better under-standing of the task construct) comes down to when (and how) to instruct and when to step back, when (and how) to intervene and when to remain silent. Mitchell's (2000) early reflection on TBLT that "much remains to be done before the most 'effective' mixes and sequences of instruction and use can be identified" (p. 296) remains apposite. Research in the TBLT space could usefully broaden its horizons in this regard.

Advancing the Practice of TBLT

In light of the above considerations and debates, how can teachers, as crucial variables in the TBLT endeavour, best be supported to enact TBLT ideas in real classrooms? What mediating steps can be taken to enhance teachers' practices?

There is evidence to suggest that, where teachers' current beliefs are addressed through teacher education programmes, new understandings can be successfully established (Borg, 2011; Cabaroglu & Roberts, 2000). I have argued elsewhere that teacher education initiatives, whether these are for beginner (pre-service) teachers or for more experienced (in-service) teachers, are essential components for the successful implementation of TBLT in real classrooms. Depending on practitioners' needs and experience, teacher education and professional develop-ment initiatives will take a variety of forms. There are three principles that I believe are important components of effective teacher preparation:

1. Establish a baseline of beliefs. As I noted above, Bygate (2020) argued that exploration of TBLT as innovation should be built on what teachers cur-rently think and do, and the concerns they are currently facing in class-rooms. The first step for me as a teacher educator has been to *establish a baseline* by addressing with participants a key question – what do you cur-rently know, think and believe about effective language pedagogy? It is important here to recognise that beliefs are neither right nor wrong – they simply are what they are. Acknowledging this creates a safe environment in which teachers can think about and identify their own beliefs, how these beliefs differ between individuals, and possible reasons for that. Discussion between and among colleagues can help teachers to become more aware of

the beliefs they hold right at the start of a teacher education or professional development initiative.

2. Introduce key theoretical concepts. Bygate (2020) went on to argue that TBLT ideas, and the use of tasks, could be introduced in *response* to teachers' current beliefs, practices, apprehensions and aspirations, taking into account the processes and resources that teachers are already drawing on. Having established a baseline, it is important to address key *theoretical* concepts that underpin and inform TBLT. In this regard, there may be some use in presenting teachers with a whole range of theoretical arguments in favour of TBLT and empirical studies that demonstrate task efficacy. However, and depending on the context and the amount of time available, this might also be overwhelming and therefore counter-productive. Fundamentally (and minimally), teachers need to be introduced to, and have opportunities to explore, the task construct, both theoretically and practically. As Ellis (2009) put it, teachers require "a clear understanding of what a task is" and need also to be "involved in the development of the task materials" (p. 241). Beyond the task itself, other issues of concern will include the different components that make up both a single lesson and a series of lessons, among them: task sequencing; task complexity; focusing on form; types of feedback. It is here that the reality that there is no one "right" way of doing TBLT needs to be acknowledged. As Ellis (2017) made clear, both the task and the activities surrounding the task represent genuine matters of concern that require continued exploration.

3. Try out tasks in a real classroom. Teachers then need opportunities to try out tasks for themselves with real classes, ideally in contexts where they can receive both feedback and feedforward from a mentor who understands and is sympathetic to task-based ideas. Teachers need to observe carefully how the task implementation goes and (perhaps in dialogue with their mentors) draw conclusions from successes (and failures) that might inform future task design and implementation.

Underpinning the above approach to teacher education and development is the notion of critical reflective practice. The three components of the reflective cycle that I outlined in Chapter 8 (reflection for-in-on action) are important components supporting the three stages of baseline, theory and practice. In light of the challenges for TBLT, both theoretically and practically, that I have raised in this chapter, the TBLT endeavour will likely be most successful if teachers are given opportunities to engage *critically* with TBLT in theory, including room to *question* its assumptions. They also need support as they *test out and evaluate* for themselves the extent to which TBLT and tasks can be shown to work effectively.

Essentially, critical reflection, alongside sufficiently mentored or mediated practice, has the potential to nudge teachers along the interactionist/constructivist continuum towards the more learner-centred approaches on which TBLT is built.

Reflection Point

Teachers represent significant players in the teaching and learning process as "the major source of controllable variance" in education systems (Hattie, 2012, p. 169). Hattie's argument that the variance is *controllable* suggests that there are mediating steps that can be taken to enhance teachers' practices.
Now that we are reaching the end of this book:

1. To what extent do you think your own thinking and/or practices will be enhanced in the future as a consequence of reaching this point?
2. What barriers to TBLT in practice do you think will remain for you?
3. To what extent do you think the three mediating steps I have proposed above (baseline, theory and practice) will likely enhance TBLT in practice, for you or for others?

Conclusion

The purpose of this book has been to present several foundational principles that inform and underpin the approach to L2 pedagogy known as TBLT. As this book comes to a close, I pose a final question – what exactly is TBLT? As I highlighted towards the start of Chapter 1, and have acknowledged elsewhere in this book, it can be challenging to answer that question due to significant differences in conceptualisation among TBLT's advocates (Hall, 2018). There remain, in both theory and practice, "numerous interpretations and orientations to the concept" of TBLT (Nunan, 2004, p. 14). Sometimes, the boundaries of a task can be "somewhat fuzzy" (Richards, 2006, p. 31) and the complaint of teachers, "I'm still not sure what a task is" (Erlam, 2016), is widespread. These assertions are potentially unsettling for those contemplating TBLT. The problem in pinning down TBLT is exacerbated by the nomenclature that surrounds the TBLT phenomenon (task-based, task-supported, strong, weak).

It may be argued that distinctive nomenclature helps with distinguishing clearly between different emphases. Both Long and Ellis, for example, noted that the differentiation between task-*based* and task-*supported* comes down to the syllabus that underpins the two approaches and a recognition that the two approaches draw on different psycholinguistic rationales (Ellis, 2017, 2019; Long, 2015, 2016). Furthermore, Long and Ellis asserted that the argument for a stronger form of TBLT is compelling due to its alignment not only with SLA theory and research but also with sound educational practice. Ellis (2018) recognised nonetheless that strong TBLT "can conflict with teachers' and learners' beliefs about language, leading at best to doubts and at worst to rejection of TBLT." On this basis, Ellis suggested that there is "need for a curriculum that includes a structural component" (p. 274). This leads to several questions.

What distinguishes task-*based* language teaching (TBLT) and task-*supported* language teaching (TSLT) in practice? If the distinction is simply down to the syllabus, the curriculum as *plan* (i.e., the syllabus as prescribed) might end up looking quite different when it becomes the curriculum as *action* as teachers respond to the demands and needs of the students they have in their classrooms. In other words, teachers will often make their own choices about practice, regardless of the syllabus. Besides, the theoretical distinctions between TBLT and TSLT may well be unimportant for teachers in classrooms whose primary concern is with what seems to be effective for learning. As Thomas and Brereton (2019) cogently put it, teachers often just "prefer to *get on with it*" (p. 276) and "go with their own instincts regarding what works, what gets a good reaction, and what engages learners" (p. 278). Moreover, as Ellis (2017) expressed it, the two approaches represented in TBLT and TSLT are "mutually supporting" (p. 522).

Following on from the argument that TBLT and TSLT are reciprocally supportive, how much explicit teacher input actually makes TBLT no longer TBLT? From the interactionist/constructivist perspective that I have emphasised throughout this book, educational practice is "a continuum from less learner-centred to more learner-centred" (Schweisfurth, 2013, p. 11). Teachers will place themselves at different points on the continuum for a range of reasons. Additionally, teachers' positioning on the continuum is not static but fluid, and teachers may move to other points, in different contexts and at different times, and with different classes and different learners.

Seen from the perspective of a fluid continuum of practice, the distinctions within TBLT are more nuanced than specific labels might suggest. Thus, for a book whose purpose has been to explore the foundational principles of TBLT, perhaps the differentiating labels are unhelpful. Rather, the defining characteristic of TBLT, and the primary focal point for learner-centred and experiential classroom experiences – regardless of where on the interactionist continuum its proponents sit – is the task itself. The task is what makes TBLT task-based. Moving out from that focal point, the foundational goal for TBLT in practice must be for teachers (whether individually or collegially, or in co-partnership with researchers or teacher educators) to try things out at different points on the continuum, to collect evidence of outcomes in light of different interventions and to evaluate for themselves what seems to be working.

Suggested Further Reading

Ellis, R. (2017). Position paper: Moving task-based language teaching forward. *Language Teaching, 50*(4), 507–526.

Long, M. (2016). In defense of tasks and TBLT: Nonissues and real issues. *Annual Review of Applied Linguistics, 36*, 5–33.

Note

1 As I explained in Chapter 1, I use *interactionism* and *interactionist* as umbrella labels under which a range of stances and orientations necessarily sit – their unifying feature, however, is that they allow room and space for what the teacher does as well as what the learners do.

References

Adamson, B. (2004). Fashions in language teaching methodology. In A. Davies & C. Elder (Eds.), *The handbook of applied linguistics* (pp. 604–622). Wiley-Blackwell.

Adamson, B., & Davison, C. (2003). Innovation in English language teaching in Hong Kong primary schools: One step forward, two steps sideways? *Prospect*, 18(1), 27–41.

Borg, S. (2011). The impact of in-service teacher education on language teachers' beliefs. *System*, 39(3), 370–380.

Borg, S. (2015). *Teacher cognition and language education: Research and practice.* Bloomsbury Academic.

Brown, H. D. (2014). *Principles of language learning and teaching* (6th ed.). Pearson.

Bruton, A. (2005). Task-based language teaching: For the state secondary FL classroom? *The Language Learning Journal*, 31(1), 55–68.

Burns, A. (2010). *Doing action research in English language teaching: A guide for practitioners.* Routledge.

Bygate, M. (2020). Some directions for the possible survival of TBLT as a real world project. *Language Teaching*, 53(3), 275–288.

Cabaroglu, N., & Roberts, J. (2000). Development in student teachers' pre-existing beliefs during a 1-year PGCE programme. *System*, 28(3), 387–402.

Coe, R., Aloisi, C., Higgins, S., & Elliot Major, L. (2014). *What makes great teaching? Review of the underpinning research.* The Sutton Trust.

East, M. (2012). *Task-based language teaching from the teachers' perspective: Insights from New Zealand.* John Benjamins.

East, M. (2014). Encouraging innovation in a modern foreign language initial teacher education programme: What do beginning teachers make of task-based language teaching? *The Language Learning Journal*, 42(3), 261–274.

East, M. (2017). Research into practice: The task-based approach to instructed second language acquisition. *Language Teaching*, 50(3), 412–424.

East, M. (2019). Sustaining innovation in school modern foreign languages programmes: Teachers' reflections on task-based language teaching three years after initial teacher education. *The Language Learning Journal*, 47(1), 105–115.

East, M. (2020). Replication research: What do beginning teachers make of task-based language teaching? A comparative re-production of East (2014). *Language Teaching*. doi:10.1017/S026144481900048X.

Ellis, R. (2009). Task-based language teaching: Sorting out the misunderstandings. *International Journal of Applied Linguistics*, 19(3), 221–246.

Ellis, R. (2017). Position paper: Moving task-based language teaching forward. *Language Teaching*, 50(4), 507–526.

Ellis, R. (2018). *Reflections on task-based language teaching.* Multilingual Matters.

Ellis, R. (2019). Towards a modular language curriculum for using tasks. *Language Teaching Reseach*, 23(4), 454–475.

Ellis, R. (2020). In defence of a modular curriculum for tasks. *ELT Journal*, 74(2), 185–194.

Erlam, R. (2016). "I'm still not sure what a task is": Teachers designing language tasks. *Language Teaching Research*, 20(3), 279–299.

Fosnet, C. T. (Ed.). (1996). *Constructivism: Theory, perspectives, and practice*. Teachers College Press.

Hall, G. (2018). *Exploring English language teaching: Language in action* (2nd ed.). Routledge.

Hattie, J. (2012). *Visible learning for teachers*. Routledge.

Hmelo-Silver, C. E., Duncan, R. G., & Chinn, C. A. (2007). Scaffolding and achievement in problem-based and inquiry learning: A response to Kirschner, Sweller, and Clark (2006). *Educational Psychologist, 42*(2), 99–107.

Kirschner, P. A., Sweller, J., & Clark, R. E. (2006). Why minimal guidance during instruction does not work: An analysis of the failure of constructivist, discovery, problem-based, experiential, and inquiry-based teaching. *Educational Psychologist, 41*(2), 75–86.

Klapper, J. (2003). Taking communication to task? A critical review of recent trends in language teaching. *The Language Learning Journal, 27*, 33–42.

Krashen, S., & Terrell, T. D. (1983). *The Natural Approach: Language acquisition in the classroom*. Pergamon.

Larsen-Freeman, D. (2015). Research into practice: Grammar learning and teaching. *Language Teaching, 48*(2), 263–280.

Leaver, B. L., & Willis, J. (Eds.). (2004). *Task-based instruction in foreign language education: Practices and programs*. Georgetown University Press.

Lightbown, P., & Spada, N. (2013). *How languages are learned* (4th ed.). Oxford University Press.

Long, M. (2015). *Second language acquisition and task-based language teaching*. Wiley-Blackwell.

Long, M. (2016). In defense of tasks and TBLT: Nonissues and real issues. *Annual Review of Applied Linguistics, 36*, 5–33.

Markee, N. (1997). Second language acquisition research: A resource for changing teachers' professional cultures? *The Modern Language Journal, 81*(1), 80–93.

Mitchell, R. (2000). Applied linguistics and evidence-based classroom practice: The case of foreign language grammar pedagogy. *Applied Linguistics, 21*(3), 281–303.

Mitchell, R., Myles, F., & Marsden, E. (2019). *Second language learning theories* (4th ed.). Routledge.

Norris, J., Bygate, M., & Van den Branden, K. (2009). Introducing task-based language teaching. In K. Van den Branden, M. Bygate, & J. Norris (Eds.), *Task-based language teaching: A reader* (pp. 15–19). John Benjamins.

Nunan, D. (2004). *Task-based language teaching*. Cambridge University Press.

Richards, J. C. (2006). *Communicative language teaching today*. Cambridge University Press.

Samuda, V. (2005). *Leading from behind: A role for task design awareness*. Symposium: The role of the teacher in TBLT. 1st international conference on task-based language teaching, From Theory to Practice, 21–23 September, Leuven, Belgium.

Sato, M., & Loewen, S. (2019). Do teachers care about research? The research-pedagogy dialogue. *ELT Journal, 73*(1), 1–10.

Savignon, S. (2018). Communicative competence. In J. I. Liontas (Ed.), *The TESOL encyclopedia of English language teaching* (pp. 1–7). John Wiley & Sons.

Schmidt, H. G., Loyens, S. M. M., Van Gog, T., & Paas, F. (2007). Problem-Based Learning *is* compatible with human cognitive architecture: Commentary on Kirschner, Sweller, and Clark (2006). *Educational Psychologist, 42*(2), 91–97.

Schweisfurth, M. (2013). *Learner-centred education in international perspective: Whose pedagogy for whose development?* Routledge.

Swan, M. (1985a). A critical look at the Communicative Approach (1). *ELT Journal, 39*(1), 2–12.

Swan, M. (1985b). A critical look at the Communicative Approach (2). *ELT Journal*, 39(2), 76–87.

Swan, M. (2005). Legislation by hypothesis: The case of task-based instruction. *Applied Linguistics*, 26(3), 376–401.

Swan, M. (2011). Legislation by hypothesis: The case of task-based instruction. In *Thinking about language teaching: Selected articles 1982–2011* (pp. 90–113). Oxford University Press.

Swan, M. (2018). Applied linguistics: A consumer's view. *Language Teaching*, 51(2), 246–261.

Thomas, N., & Brereton, P. (2019). Practitioners respond to Michael Swan's "Applied Linguistics: A consumer's view". *Language Teaching*, 52(2), 275–278.

Van den Branden, K. (2009a). Diffusion and implementation of innovations. In M. Long & C. Doughty (Eds.), *The handbook of language teaching* (pp. 659–672). Wiley-Blackwell.

Van den Branden, K. (2009b). Mediating between predetermined order and chaos: The role of the teacher in task-based language education. *International Journal of Applied Linguistics*, 19(3), 264–285.

Van den Branden, K., Van Gorp, K., & Verhelst, M. (Eds.). (2007). *Tasks in action: Task-based language education from a classroom-based perspective*. Cambridge Scholars Publishing.

Weimer, M. (2013). *Learner-centered teaching: Five key changes to practice* (2nd ed.). Jossey Bass.

Widdowson, H. (1985). Against dogma: A reply to Michael Swan. *ELT Journal*, 39(3), 158–161.

Willis, J. (1996). *A framework for task-based learning*. Longman Pearson Education.

POSTFACE

This book started from the premise that, despite increasing global popularity, TBLT has remained in practice a contested endeavour. Challenges for TBLT arise from its learner-centred and experiential contrasts to more tried and tested or teacher-led pedagogical approaches, alongside misunderstandings about exactly what TBLT is or can be in instructed contexts.

In this book, I have aimed to give those who are interested in exploring TBLT ideas (such as postgraduate students, teacher educators, researchers and teachers) a foundation (or, better, several foundations) on which they might build their knowledge, both theoretically and practically. I have sought to demystify the phenomenon of TBLT by going back to some of the foundational principles that have informed its development and by explaining TBLT in theory and practice on the basis of those principles. My hope is that, by uncovering some of the foundational principles and by giving opportunities for readers to reflect on these principles at different points in light of their own experiences, I have provided greater clarity about what TBLT is (and what it is not), and the various ways in which it has been, and can be, enacted. As I pointed out in the Preface, there is a danger of over-simplification in this reductionist back-to-basics approach. However, throughout this book I have sign-posted further readings that those who are interested may follow up.

TBLT is in fact a broad and flexible phenomenon that allows for considerable variety in what both teachers and students do in language classrooms. I have argued in this book that, provided that the central task construct is understood and enacted as the focal point for student-centred experiential learning, there is considerable scope for experimentation around how tasks are enacted and sequenced, and how teachers scaffold the learning, both prior to and after the task (or series of tasks) is completed. However, this does not necessarily make TBLT easy. In the concluding chapter, I raised several key dilemmas for the TBLT endeavour which reveal that TBLT sits within far broader and more complex arguments about effective SLA and effective educational practice.

Lightbown and Spada (2013, pp. 120–121) provided a cogent perspective:

> Educators who are hoping that language acquisition theories will give them insight into language teaching practice are often frustrated by the lack of agreement among the "experts". The complexities of second language acquisition … represent puzzles that scientists will continue to work on for a long time … [and] agreement on a "complete" theory of language acquisition is probably, at best, a long way off. Even if such agreement were reached, there would still be questions about how the theory should be interpreted for language teaching practice.

Even where a level of agreement exists with regard to research findings, Mitchell et al. (2019) noted that instructed SLA research "is not identical with problem-solving and development in classroom language pedagogy, and does not ensure a shared agenda between teachers and researchers" (p. 407). The issues and debates I presented in the concluding chapter, all real and all important, can be disquieting, and might tempt teachers and others to shy away from promoting or introducing task-based ideas in real classrooms because it might just seem too hard. However, the "chalk-face" is ultimately the arena in which the battle for the longer-term survival of the TBLT endeavour will be fought.

In a published and updated version of the opening plenary of the very first TBLT conference (Leuven, Belgium, 2005), Long (2015) argued that two strengths of the TBLT endeavour are that it is aligned not only with theory and research into effective SLA but also with contemporary general educational theory and practice. On these two bases alone, TBLT has much to commend it. Long acknowledged nonetheless that TBLT is "no panacea." Rather, it is a "work in progress," and "[t]here are problems – some we know of … others yet to be discovered" (p. 20). This means that its implementation must be seen as a journey along "a road as yet unbuilt" (p. 21). As the journey through this book reaches its end, I commend the on-going TBLT journey to you so that you can be part of the continuing building of that road. If, at some stage in the future, our paths should cross at a junction in the road, I would be interested in learning from you how the journey and the road-building are going.

References

Lightbown, P., & Spada, N. (2013). *How languages are learned* (4th ed.). Oxford University Press.

Long, M. (2015). TBLT: Building the road as we travel. In M. Bygate (Ed.), *Domains and directions in the development of TBLT: A decade of plenaries from the international conference* (pp. 1–26). John Benjamins.

Mitchell, R., Myles, F., & Marsden, E. (2019). *Second language learning theories* (4th ed.). Routledge.

Postscript – Some Resources to Help on the Journey

The International Association for Task-Based Language Teaching (IATBLT) has implemented a resource bank to support the effective enactment of tasks in classrooms – the *TBLT Language Learning Task Bank*. The initiative is managed on behalf of the IATBLT by Laura Gurzynsky-Weiss, and builds on work that Laura and colleagues began at Indiana University (https://tblt.indiana.edu/). The Task Bank is a go-to resource site for teachers and researchers looking for language learning tasks, whether or not they have appeared in published research. Members of the IATBLT can upload tasks for inclusion and receive feedback from an advisory board. The site provides the facility for anyone, anywhere, to search and download/edit the tasks for use in language classrooms.

INDEX